Turbulent and Mighty Continent

Books by Anthony Giddens:

Capitalism and Modern Social Theory
Politics and Sociology in the Thought of Max Weber
The Class Structure of the Advanced Societies
New Rules of Sociological Method
Studies in Social and Political Theory
Emile Durkheim
Central Problems in Social Theory
A Contemporary Critique of Historical Materialism
Sociology: A Brief but Critical Introduction
Profiles and Critiques in Social Theory
The Constitution of Society
The Nation-State and Violence
Durkheim on Politics and the State
Social Theory and Modern Sociology
The Consequences of Modernity
Modernity and Self-Identity
The Transformation of Intimacy
Beyond Left and Right
Reflexive Modernization (with Ulrich Beck and Scott Lash)
Politics, Sociology and Social Theory
In Defence of Sociology
The Third Way
Runaway World
The Third Way and its Critics
Where Now for New Labour?
Europe in the Global Age
Over to You, Mr Brown
The Politics of Climate Change
Sociology, 7th edn (with Philip W. Sutton)

Edited Works:
Emile Durkheim: Selected Writings
Positivism and Sociology
Elites and Power in British Society (with Philip Stanworth)
Classes, Conflict and Power
Classes and the Division of Labour
Social Theory Today
Human Societies
On the Edge: Living with Global Capitalism (with Will Hutton)
The Global Third Way Debate
The Progressive Manifesto
The New Egalitarianism (with Patrick Diamond)
Global Europe, Social Europe (with Patrick Diamond and Roger Liddle)

ANTHONY GIDDENS

TURBULENT AND MIGHTY CONTINENT

WHAT FUTURE FOR EUROPE?

Revised and Updated Edition

polity

First published in 2014 by Polity Press

Polity Press
65 Bridge Street
Cambridge CB2 1UR, UK

Polity Press
350 Main Street
Malden, MA 02148, USA

ISBN-13: 978-0-7456-8096-5
ISBN-13: 978-0-7456-8097-2 (pb)

A catalogue record for this book is available from the British Library.

Typeset in 12 on 15pt Janson Text by
Servis Filmsetting Ltd, Stockport, Cheshire
Printed and bound in Great Britain by
TJ International Ltd, Padstow, Cornwall

The publisher has used its best endeavours to ensure that the URLs for external websites referred to in this book are correct and active at the time of going to press. However, the publisher has no responsibility for the websites and can make no guarantee that a site will remain live or that the content is or will remain appropriate.

Every effort has been made to trace all copyright holders, but if any have been inadvertently overlooked the publisher will be pleased to include any necessary credits in any subsequent reprint or edition.

For further information on Polity, visit our website: www.politybooks.com

Contents

Figures and Tables   vi

Acknowledgements   viii

Introduction   1

1   The EU as Community of Fate   18

2   Austerity and After   56

3   No More Social Model?   89

4   The Cosmopolitan Imperative   123

5   Climate Change and Energy   155

6   The Search for Relevance   186

Conclusion   213

Notes   225

Index   239

Figures and Tables

Figures

1   Churchill tips his hat to the crowd, Zurich,
    19 September 1946 (Diplomatic Documents of
    Switzerland, online database Dodis: dodis.ch/33386)   4
2   'The last battle: how Europe is wrecking its
    currency' (2010 *Der Spiegel*)   23
3   The cause of the instability of the euro is not debt
    as such   25
4   'My name is Bond. Euro Bond. Never say never'
    (taz.die tageszeitung, 16 August 2011)   28
5   Expressed support for the EU has plummeted   43
6   The effect of the euro on borrowing   62
7   EMU lacks the adjustment mechanisms necessary to
    compensate for the loss of exchange rate flexibility   67
8   GDP per capita in major geographical regions
    of the EU (USA = 100), 1950–2007   71
9   Wages in Europe are less differentiated than in
    other regions   97
10 Unemployment in the euro area and beyond
    (*The Economist*, 2013)   105

11   After the London bombings: Muslim women
     register their protest against violence
     (© AFP/Getty Images)   145
12   World energy-related carbon dioxide emissions by
     fuel, 1990–2035   164
13   World coal consumption by region, 1990–2005   171
14   World nuclear generating capacity, 2008 and 2035 174
15   US Military spending vs. the world in 2008   196
16   A restaurant in Pristina sporting the EU flag
     alongside the Albanian national flag on the day
     before the Kosovar declaration of independence,
     February 2008 (Chris Hondros/Getty Images)   204
17   'Saving the euro' (Klaus Stuttman, 2013)   217

Tables

1   Percentage of population aged 65 and over,
    selected European countries   116
2   Top ten citizenships of immigrants to EU-27
    member states, 2008 (© European Union,
    1995–2013)   126
3   Numbers travelling each year: a hyper-mobile
    world – but unevenly so   131
4   Reasons mentioned why accession talks with
    Turkey should not proceed (Reprinted by permission
    of SAGE)   209

Acknowledgements

Many people have helped me in the preparation of this book. As always I should like to thank everyone at Polity Press for their efficiency and responsiveness. I owe especial thanks to John Thompson, Gill Motley, Neil de Cort, Elliott Karstadt, Breffni O'Connor and Ginny Graham. Caroline Richmond did an outstanding job in copy-editing the text. Anne de Sayrah transcribed an early version of the work and provided numerous other forms of assistance. I owe a large debt to Andreas Sowa for the research contributions he made as well as for his work checking its factual accuracy. I am very grateful to him for his penetrating insights and criticisms. My daughters, Michele and Katy, read several of the chapters and made important critical comments. David Held read the manuscript more than once and made many valuable observations, to which I have tried to respond, and Gerry Bernbaum did the same; I am very grateful to them both. I would also like to thank Kevin Featherstone for his extremely useful feedback. Alena and Maria Ledeneva helped sort through what was originally a rather disorganised first version. For valuable conversations and observations I have to thank Olaf Cramme, Martin Albrow, Roger Liddle,

Enrico Franceschini, John Ashton, Alistair Dillon, John Urry, Mark Leonard, Montserrat Guibernau, Monica Mandelli, Giles Radice, Mary Kaldor and Susie Astbury. I was inspired to write the book by my membership of the Council for the Future of Europe, set up by Nicolas Berggruen and Nathan Gardels. Members of that group hold a variety of views on Europe, and those expressed here are my own take on how things stand. I have gained enormously from interaction with my colleagues on Sub-Committee 'D' of the House of Lords, concerned with European Union policy in the areas of Agriculture, Fisheries, Environment and Energy, and would like to pay tribute to them.

Anthony Giddens

Introduction

Excerpts from an address by Winston Churchill, delivered at the University of Zurich, Switzerland, on 19 September 1946:

I wish to speak to you today about the tragedy of Europe. This noble continent, comprising on the whole the fairest and most cultivated regions of the earth, enjoying a temperate and equitable climate, is the home of all the great parent races of the Western world ... And what is the plight to which Europe has been reduced? ... Over wide areas a vast quivering mass of tormented, hungry, care-worn and bewildered human beings gape at the ruins of their cities and their homes, and scan the dark horizons for the approach of some new peril, tyranny or terror. Among the victors there is a babble of voices: among the vanquished the sullen silence of despair ...

Yet all the while there is a remedy which, if it were generally and spontaneously adopted by the great majority of people in many lands, would as if by a miracle transform the whole scene ... What is this sovereign remedy? It is to re-create the European Family, or as much of it as we can, and to provide it with a structure under which it can dwell in peace, in safety and in freedom. We must build a kind of United States of Europe . . .

We British have our Commonwealth of Nations . . . why should there not be a European group which could give a sense of enlarged patriotism and common citizenship to the distracted peoples of this turbulent and mighty continent? And why should it not take its rightful place with other great groupings and help shape the onward destinies of men? . . . Therefore I say to you: let Europe arise!

It is 2006, the 60th anniversary of Churchill's speech. There is no United States of Europe, but what has become the European Union is riding high. The Cold War is over. The USSR has long since dissolved, remarkably almost without the firing of a single shot. A divided Germany has become one again. West and East Europe have been reunited too, with the EU playing a key role in the process. The euro has been launched, its apparent success confounding its critics. In its report in September of that year, the IMF pronounces the global economy to be in robust shape even if it notes a few causes for concern. Not much more than twelve months later the world lurches into what turns out to be its biggest economic crisis since the 1930s. European leaders originally see the problem as an American one, brought about by the free-wheeling nature of its version of capitalism. That is in some part true, but its effects in Europe* then start to become profound and disturbing. The hubris of the EU leaders rapidly turns to something close to despair as they struggle to cope. The existence of the euro – a fully fledged currency but without the backing of a sovereign power – compounds the wider problems. The eurozone countries become engaged in an almighty struggle to keep the euro alive.

---

* In this book I follow convention in using the terms 'Europe' and the 'European Union' interchangeably except where the context needs them to be clearly differentiated. A precise line is difficult to draw, because national policies can have a major impact at the European level – for example, in the areas of welfare and energy policies.

Move forward to the present day. The travails of the euro have been contained but by no means fully overcome. The EU's problems remain serious and dangerous: serious, because the whole project of building a united continent could founder; dangerous, because if things should go badly wrong the consequences could be cataclysmic. Some say that the same antagonisms that produced wars in the past are still around. 'The demons are not gone – they're only sleeping, as the wars in Bosnia and Kosovo have shown.'[1]

When the single currency was introduced, the EU was in effect taking a huge gamble, and consciously so. From the beginning the euro was a political project as well as an economic one. Those who founded the euro were aware that the full conditions needed for a currency to be stable and successful were not there. The idea was that they could be developed as the euro helped foster a more cohesive European economy. The extent of the gamble may not have been realised by those who initiated the project, because economic conditions were fairly propitious at the time and remained so for some while.

Europe is no longer mighty but has again become turbulent as conflicts and divisions spring up across the continent, as well as alongside its borders. Unemployment has risen to a new high and is especially pronounced among younger people. Countries that before the financial crisis balanced their books have now run up spectacular levels of debt. Among those that were more profligate, some are in a depressed state economically and lack the means to devalue their currency. They have had to accept huge bailouts. The fortunes of the northern and southern eurozone members have diverged quite radically. Under the impact of the crisis, support for the Union began to corrode, above all in the countries of the South. The findings of Eurobarometer, the survey carried out by the European Commission every six months, showed increasing disillusionment with the EU almost everywhere.[2] In Spain, for example, in 2007, 65 per cent of respondents expressed trust in the EU, compared with 23 per

Figure 1 Churchill tips his hat to the crowd, Zurich, 19 September 1946

cent who did not. By early 2013, those figures were more than reversed: 20 per cent still endorsed the EU, compared with 72 per cent who took the opposite view. Similar figures applied in countries such as Greece, Portugal and Ireland, as well as in some of the former communist nations such as Hungary and Romania. In the UK, long the country with the lowest level of public support for the Union, views of the EU turned even more sour than before. Over the past few years, there have been anti-EU protests and demonstrations in many different countries.

Few if any groups have been seen on the streets demonstrating in favour of the European Union. It would be fair to say that, in spite of its many successes, the Union has not put down emotional roots anywhere among its citizens. As academics are fond of saying, it is a 'functionalist' enterprise, driven by results rather than affection, let alone passion. Thus it is hardly surprising that, when the results are no longer forthcoming, people's support plummets. The 'sense of enlarged patriotism and common citizenship' of which Churchill spoke has simply not arrived. I argue in what follows that the EU must move closer to its citizens over the next few years – and vice versa – or it will not survive in recognisable form at all. I have written this book to explore how such a process might happen. I introduce new concepts to help understand the limits of the Union as it stands and its potential for the future. If I am quite often critical, it is with the aim of helping to propel the European project onwards. The fate of the Union *matters*, it matters a great deal. Over 500 million people live in the EU states. What happens in Europe is world-historical in terms of its importance. The stakes are high indeed.

The structural make-up of the EU explains a lot about why it is so remote from its citizenry. To put things baldly, the Union suffers from a simultaneous lack of democracy and effective leadership. The three main institutions in the EU are the Commission, the Council and the Parliament. The Commission is formally responsible for initiating plans, projects and policies for the Union as a whole. Decisions on the Commission's proposals are made by Council and the Parliament, often a long-winded process and one with no guarantee of ultimate success. Moreover, citizens are nowhere directly involved. Until recently at least, the European elections have been fought largely on national issues. The Parliament tends to operate on the sidelines, its procedures obscure to the wider public. National leaders, especially of the larger countries, often want to have their cake and eat it. They proclaim their European credentials, but in practice what is perceived as the national interest comes first. So far as its citizens are concerned, the EU has only a shallow pool of legitimacy to draw upon, since it has no deep roots in their everyday lives.

Normal EU governance is incremental and the Commission plays the most prominent part in it. It even has a name, the 'Monnet method'. Jean Monnet, one of the great European figures, held that a European architecture could be built most fruitfully brick by brick. Dialogue and discussion to initiate such steps took place mainly in small circles of people; national parliaments and citizens were left out. The EU was thus created in some substantial part 'out of sight'. When rapid or especially consequential decisions have to be taken, there is a big, big problem. Effectively, they cannot be handled within the formal institutions themselves. In such circumstances a handful of individuals, usually from the big member states, take over, shape what has to be done and push it through. This is what took place, for example, with the reunification of Germany and with the initiation of the euro. The lack of effective leadership in the EU is thus temporarily resolved. France and Germany have normally been the key players, along with a finite and shifting number of other states, plus sometimes the heads of international organisations.

The governance of the Union hence takes place through two intersecting structures, which for want of better names I shall call *EU1* and *EU2*. EU1 is the Europe of the Monnet method, with the Commission and the Council, plus more latterly the Parliament, in the driving seat. EU2 is where a lot of the real power lies, exercised on a selective and informal basis. The EU1/EU2 distinction is quite different from that between the Commission and the Council. It focuses upon the differences between how things are supposed to be done and how they really are done, especially in crisis situations. However, a more nebulous version of EU2 operates behind the scenes in a more chronic way, and indeed could be seen as intrinsic to the Monnet method. It is a point of recourse for the Commission and the other EU bodies, which consult specific national leaders informally before pursuing policy initiatives.

The EU2 which is *de facto* running Europe at the moment consists of the German chancellor, currently Angela Merkel, the French president (François Hollande) and one or two other national leaders, plus the heads of the European Central Bank

(ECB) and the International Monetary Fund (IMF). The presidents of the European Council and of the Commission quite often get a look in. The term *Troika* has become widely used to refer to the heads of the ECB, the IMF and the Commission in their role as overseers for the failing economies. The label carries an overlay of heavy irony. It originally designated the leaders of the Soviet Union – the heads of the Communist Party, the government and the state. Yet the notion is misleading in the current context. Chancellor Merkel is in fact the most important figure in Europe today. Whatever the Troika may agree has to be ratified by her.

The concepts of EU1, EU2 and what I shall call *paper Europe* are crucial to this book. I argue that the evolution of the Union can be interpreted in terms of them, as can its current struggles. Because of the absence of democratic leadership, the Union occupies a space where these three intersect. The EU's aims in a variety of fields, from economic success through to global peacekeeping, are often very ambitious. As ends rather than means, they stand in contrast to the caution of the Monnet method. Paper Europe consists of a host of future plans, roadmaps, regional strategies, and so forth, drawn up by the Commission and other EU agencies. Many, however, remain just that – aspirations that cannot be fleshed out and made real because there are no effective means for their implementation. Paper Europe isn't the same as bureaucracy, although it overlaps with it. The point is not its procedural nature but the fact that ambitious schemes and proposals are drawn up which remain largely empty. The existence of paper Europe is obvious inside and outside the EU and hence affects its credibility. One wouldn't take an individual too seriously who was full of grandiose but undelivered promises, and the same is true of an institution.

Almost all observers writing about Europe at the current time focus upon the schisms that have opened up across the continent. I want to diverge rather radically from this conventional perspective. I suggest that there are in fact two processes going on, intertwined with one another – division and conflict, yes of course, but also *de facto* integration. Driven precisely by the depth of the current crisis, the EU has become experienced as a *community of fate* in a way in which it never was before. What I mean by this is that citizens and political leaders across Europe have become aware of their interdependence. There is for the first time a European political space. In spite, or because of, all the tensions and the protest movements, Europe has risen way up the political agenda, both for the member nations and, more crucially, for citizens. National elections reflect European issues more directly than has ever previously been the case. One can hardly open a daily newspaper without seeing a feature about the EU (even in the UK). This transition is momentous because it is almost certainly irreversible.

For those like myself who want to see the European Union survive and prosper, there is a simple question to ask and try to answer. Can the changes happening under a negative sign be converted into a positive one? EU2 under a positive sign would be not an *ad hoc* cadre of individuals with no legitimacy, but an institutionalised system of leadership with a democratic mandate. Turning the Union into a community of fate in a positive sense means building solidarity and feelings of belonging to the EU as a whole rather than only to its constituent nations or regions. I believe these developments are not only possible but necessary if Europe is to emerge from its malaise.

My argument is as follows. The euro has performed the task its founders intended. It has made the eurozone, and by extension the EU as a whole, far more interdependent than ever before. However, it has done so in an oblique, explosive and in some respects irresponsible way, bringing much suffering in its wake. The economic discipline and fiscal mechanisms that should have been there from the beginning are being created because of fear of further disasters. EU2 has moved fairly quickly, at least by the usual standards of the Union, to make needed innovations, although all need German acquiescence. A great deal more remains to be done. On the face of things, Germany seems to have achieved by pacific means what it was unable to bring about through military conquest – the domination of Europe. As a permanent condition, however, 'German Europe' is a non-starter.[3] Its existence is at the origin of the resentments that divide the continent. In essence, Europe must choose a new future, and this time the citizens must be directly involved. The eurozone countries have to set the pace, but the states outside the euro will be affected just as much by the innovations that are made.

The path ahead is in principle quite clear, although the practical and political problems standing in the way are formidable. The chain of reasoning goes as follows. The euro must be saved – even winding it back progressively would be extremely difficult and possibly disastrous. Moreover, the EU would be finished as a credible influence in world affairs. Structural reform is needed on a wide scale, not just in the weaker economies but to some degree across the board. In more concrete terms, defending the single currency means setting up a banking union and transferring some fiscal powers from the eurozone states to economic governing bodies. In turn, such a move implies acceptance of *mutuality* – shared responsibilities between richer and poorer economies alike. If this step is not taken at some point, all bets for a stable future for Europe are off. Intensified coordination, the EU's usual path, cannot substitute for that key move. The EU has, one might say, a detailed, indeed overly complex, anatomy but a poorly developed physiology.

Economic interdependence on this scale in turn at some point presumes further political integration. To put it bluntly, a federal solution of some sort, even if minimalist in character, is not just back on the agenda but an exigency – and in the relatively near future. Nothing provokes the wrath of the Eurosceptics more. Eurosceptics come in different hues, but they almost all fret about 'rule from Brussels'. Yet they don't seem to worry at all about rule by the bond markets, or by the giant corporations, which are far more distant and impersonal. They don't seem to worry that immigration into Europe would be far harder to regulate than is the case now. They don't seem to worry about the possibility that national conflicts of a serious nature could reawaken. They don't seem to worry about the fact that, if the EU disappears or becomes shrivelled, what could be left is a G2 world, dominated by the US and China. Most concerns about federalism are about loss of national sovereignty. However, to have any meaning, sovereignty must refer to real control over the affairs of the nation. You cannot surrender something you have largely lost anyway. The power of individual nations in the global arena is slight. The rationale for the further pooling of sovereignty in the EU is what I shall call *sovereignty+*. Through their collaboration, the member states of the EU acquire more real influence in the world than they could as individual actors. Each, in other words, experiences a net gain. This effect is not confined to communal decisions. Because of the implicit back-up provided by EU membership, individual nations have more influence than they otherwise would have even when acting alone.

I write this book as a committed pro-European. I am a pro-European because the evidence as to why sovereignty+ confers large-scale benefits is so strong. The EU and its forerunners have helped bring together a war-torn continent. Many say that this phase of the Union's development is now over, as the prospect of war in Europe has disappeared. Yet a lot of work remains to be done. There has been a bitter and bloody conflict in recent times, consequent upon the break-up of Yugoslavia. The war has left its trail behind it, including some extremely challenging problems. Croatia is the latest member state of the Union. It is of the first importance that adjacent states, especially Serbia, at some point follow suit. It would be a massive achievement if the Balkan countries as a whole at some point could be incorporated as full EU members. The EU can play a role in global politics well beyond that open to any of its component nations. In other words, it can and should become a significant world influence at a time when the orthodox international institutions have reached gridlock.[4] For better or worse, the international arena is dominated by a handful of the larger states. A fragmented Europe has little chance of making its voice heard.

Common action is needed in many areas in Europe and around its borders – most of which would apply were the EU to exist or not. A whole diversity of concerns can be included in this category, among them frontier management, customs controls, combating crime, applying international law, coordination of monetary systems (were there not to be a single currency), environmental cooperation, disease prevention and control, and a multitude of others. The EU can perform most of these functions more effectively and cheaply than would be possible with a multiplicity of *ad hoc* arrangements. New areas of instability now exist along the EU's periphery, especially in the Middle East and Ukraine. They will demand a collective response should their consequences spill over further into Europe. The EU can help promote values which, if not unique to European civilisation, are deeply embedded in it – alongside, one must say, its violent and colonial past. These include ideals such as the promotion of peace, the rule of law, rights of democratic participation, the equality of the sexes and other moral imperatives. If the Union should fade in importance, or worse, Europe would become a backwater, a jumble of small and medium-sized states. Yet it could not withdraw from a world of massive change and would at the same time be geopolitically vulnerable.

Implausible although it may appear in current circumstances, the EU is there to promote common economic prosperity. Before the financial crisis hit, the single market in 2006 was calculated to add 2.2 per cent a year to EU overall GDP. The EU economic arena is larger than the American economy. In many domains, businesses operate with a single set of rules rather than the multiplicity that would otherwise exist. The EU can negotiate trade deals externally that single nations could not match. In the short term, economic reconstruction is likely to be the key to almost everything else in Europe. Should the eurozone, under the aegis of greater economic integration, return to prosperity, the attitudes of Europe's citizens would probably be transformed. The Union would be seen as the solution rather than the problem.

On the face of it, the situation looks problematic indeed. There is only a feeble and partial return to growth. Unemployment on average remains dauntingly high. All the EU states, indeed all the industrial countries, have accumulated huge debts. Amazingly, some analysts seem to be acting as though the current economic troubles were simply a temporary hiatus. It cannot be so. There is abundant evidence that deeper factors are involved. We may be at the point of a major transition in world economic history and one that remains imperfectly understood. No one has lived before in such an interconnected world. The dominant theory of the global economy over the past three or so decades has been confounded without a replacement in sight. In the established orthodoxy, the way to run an economy effectively was through keeping inflation low, while maintaining a fiscal balance and allowing large-scale deregulation. The real world has turned out to be quite different. In this world, system shocks may be impossible to predict, low interest rates do not stimulate economic activity, capital flows destabilise rather than enhance economic stability, and financial bubbles may become identifiable only when it is too late. It is not at all clear that Keynesian economics has an alternative to offer, deriving as it does from a time very different from that in which we now live. There may be further shocks stored up, given the complexity of the world financial system, where reforms made so far have still been relatively marginal.

At this point we have to think radically and in an innovative way. The recession is not simply one in which a resurgence of demand and consumer spending will put everything right again. It is deeply structural. Remedies have to be commen-

INTRODUCTION

surately wide-ranging. Where will new jobs come from in the
industrial countries and in the volume required? It is a huge
issue, especially acute in Europe because of its overlap with the
problems of the euro; and it goes well beyond the question of
the relationship between austerity and proactive investment.
Deindustrialisation has done much damage in Europe, as elsewhere. We should not be content just to accept it as a given,
but see if and how the trend can at least to some extent be put
into reverse. Profound changes are affecting not only industrial
production but the service industries, driven in some large part
by the extraordinary global transformation that is the internet.
Digital production looks to be a revolutionary force in the
making. I believe that I was one of the first, years ago, to deploy
the notion of globalisation; yet I had no inkling at the time how
intensive and ubiquitous that process would be. Even so, it is
perhaps only in its early stages, with much more to come.

I shall argue that, largely because of the acceleration of globalisation and the rise of the internet, we (human beings as a
whole) are living in a different kind of social and technological
system from that even in the quite recent past. I call this the *high
opportunity, high risk society*. Partly because of our new-found
global interdependence and partly because of an accelerating
overall level of scientific and technological innovation, opportunities and risk intertwine for us in a way that has no precedent
in prior history. We have no easy way in advance of telling
how the balance of opportunities and risks will pan out. There
are fundamental system risks in a much more interdependent
world, as we see from the financial crisis. We simply don't know
how far we can contain the risks from climate change, the possible proliferation of nuclear weapons, pandemics and other
fundamental threats. On the other hand, the level of innovation
in some areas, such as genetics or nanotechnology, is stunning.
Opportunity and risk combine in very complicated ways, difficult or impossible to predict in advance. I fold these ideas
into every chapter of the book. Rethinking will be needed in

many areas, from the economy through to coping with climate change.

No matter how far-reaching they may be, policies internal to the EU or its constituent nations are not likely to restore significant, let alone stable and sustainable, growth without a reshaping of the world economic order. The Union absolutely must seek to play a central part in such a process, which may stretch over years: it will be far easier to do so if the euro is stabilised as a global currency. One should be cautious, I think, about all the talk that this will be the Asian century or that the industrial countries are condemned to relative decline. It may be so, but history tends to progress dialectically. Existing trends often call into play their opposites. In any case, the situation that has existed over the past several decades cannot continue. This was one in which the Asian countries, especially China, produced goods for Western consumers that essentially those consumers could not afford. They then borrowed extensively to do so, accumulating debt that was bought up ... by the Chinese, in the shape of sovereign bonds and other assets. In the meantime, the propensity of Chinese citizens to save rather than spend (rational in the absence of a welfare system of any note) dampened Chinese internal demand, which was needed to develop the country further. An extensive adjustment is in order. Adventurous thinking and policy-making will be necessary here too if a major impact is to be made upon these difficulties.

At the time of such profound problems for the EU and for the industrialised world more generally, it makes sense to look again at all of its major areas of activity, opening them up to scrutiny. There are serious concerns about whether Europe's cherished 'social model' can survive in a period of severe economic retrenchment. The social model – in other words, a comprehensive and effective welfare system, coupled to goals of equality and inclusion – was always part reality, part aspiration. Major reforms will be needed in most countries if the first is not going to be wholly displaced by the second. Yet, if transformed into what I call a *social investment state*, it can both survive and flourish. The social model has to be integrated with the achievement of economic prosperity, not just treated as dependent upon it. A connected question, hugely controversial, is the impact of immigration. Some see immigration as almost as great an issue as the continent's political and economic problems. Multiculturalism, they say, has been a disaster. I don't agree at all and try to show why. However, the issue has to be reframed in the context of the age of 'super-diversity' in which, as a result of the internet, we now live. The world has moved on from the early days in which the notion of multiculturalism was originally framed. A better concept for grasping this is that of *interculturalism*.

One of the EU's special emphases has been its focus on environmental questions, especially its aspiration to be in the vanguard of the rest of the world in combating climate change – a worthwhile and urgent endeavour if ever there was one. Yet the United Nations meeting in Copenhagen in 2009, which was supposed to be the crowning effort of Europe's leadership, famously became a wholesale fiasco. As a result of its usual problem – who speaks for the EU? – the Union's leaders played no direct part in the meeting at which the agreements that were reached were drawn up. A big rethink is needed, starting with the concepts of 'conservation', 'sustainability' and the 'precautionary principle'. The difficulty with these notions as widely understood is that they developed within the green movement, with its characteristic emphases upon protecting the natural environment and upon the limits to growth. Hence they emerged as essentially conservative and defensive ideas, with the aim of preserving nature. Yet nature today has become thoroughly humanised. When examined closely, the precautionary principle turns out to be incoherent. Innovation is the wild card in the pack so far as sustainability is concerned. In the energy field, for example, no one anticipated even only a few years ago that shale gas would be so transformative in its implications. The US has reduced its CO_2 emissions by a larger percentage than the EU over the past few years, in some part because of having turned towards gas and away from coal. Its energy prices have become cheaper, thus helping in its industrial renaissance.

It is a great mistake to think of energy policy as peripheral to the prime concerns of the EU – not only because of its connections to the imperative of limiting climate change, but because of the issue of energy security. The EU states import a very high proportion of the energy they consume. The significance of this dependency has been brought home in the confrontation with Russia in Ukraine. Some of the smaller EU states are 100 per cent dependent on Russia for their supplies of natural gas, while several of the larger ones, including Germany, are large importers. Paper Europe plans that could serve to lessen this dependency have been around for years. Now there is an altogether new urgency to bring them closer to reality.

In the sphere of international relations, I argue, the EU should *drop its flight from power*, including military power, understandable though the origins of that attitude are. The new narrative for the EU in fact has to be about power – the power to do good in a world which is not a Kantian sphere of eternal peace or a Hobbesian war of all against all. Nor is the international order a balance of power in the sense which that term had in the past. Rather, it is a world of multipolar collaboration between the major states and groups of states, albeit regularly punctuated by tensions and divisions. The European ideal of replacing its own destructive past with the promotion of peace through negotiation and the rule of law is surely wholly justified. Yet in practice it has involved a good deal of hypocrisy too. The EU will turn to the US to bail it out when necessary, as happened in the conflict in ex-Yugoslavia; and it is content to shelter under the protection of NATO, which is funded mainly by American money and whose operations demand the use of American technology. The Union should seek to be more of an equal partner with the US in these respects, at least in the context of operations in and around Europe.

After the end of the Cold War, there was a period when the eastern and southern borders of the EU seemed relatively stable, notwithstanding the regular episodes of war that punctuated the recent history of the Middle East. The Union's failure to develop an effective security framework did not seem especially worrying. Today, however, the EU is surrounded by instabilities stretching from its eastern flanks through much of the Middle East to North Africa. Greater integration in foreign policy, coupled to rethinking the role of NATO in relation to Russia, has become a matter of urgency.

Following a path of greater political integration will mean giving up some of the EU's conceits. The Union will not be the experiment in international relations that so many have seen it to be. It could have far more impact on the wider world than hitherto, but it will not be a contribution to global governance in its actual form. A *mea culpa* is needed here. Along with many others, I used to think that the EU could pioneer government without any of the trappings of a state. I have had to revise my views.

In a restructured Europe, with the eurozone as its driving force, there might not be much space any longer for 'variable geometry'. That is to say, member states with opt-outs from the euro and a range of other EU provisions are not likely to stay that way indefinitely. The direction of movement of the EU, if it is to overcome its current woes, must of necessity be more or less along a single trajectory. There are worrying problems in wait here for the UK. The country might find itself seriously isolated within the EU and perhaps opt to leave. It would be in the position Churchill foresaw, but without the mantle of empire that still existed in his day – for better or worse, on its own in a very large and perturbing world.

Chapter 1

The EU as Community of Fate

The malaise of the euro does not stand on its own. It reflects issues that stretch a long way beyond Europe itself, including a series of deep economic problems shared across the industrial countries. Within the European context, the problems surrounding the euro have brought to the fore weaknesses in the Union that are of much longer standing but now demand resolution.

Europe at the moment is dominated by a specific version of EU2, called into existence by the euro crisis. It features an informal 'president' of Europe, Angela Merkel. If Barack Obama wants to influence what is happening in Europe, he talks in the first instance to Mrs Merkel. The 'president' has an 'inner cabinet', of varying composition, with whom she takes the key decisions – especially in periods of particular difficulty – and seeks to push them through. The 'cabinet' consists of a small number of the leaders of influential states, the president of the ECB, plus one or two IMF officials. Of course, there is also a range of connections with EU1 and its several presidents, still labouring away in the background. The German leader calls the tune because of the size of the country's economy and its relative success in comparison with the other larger European states. That situation has to be a transitional one. It is dangerous because of noxious divisions that have opened up between member states as well as its more general ramifications in politics. Countries in the south that depend on German acquiescence to release needed funds are as resentful of that fact as are the 'donors'. The German public is put off by the image of the 'feckless' Greeks that has taken root in the wake of the turmoil in the country. Meanwhile, some Greek politicians have been raking over the coals of the Second World War, demanding that Germany pay reparations for its historic brutalities. Populist parties have appeared almost everywhere, although the most prominent antedate the crisis itself. Most are nationalist and Eurosceptic in one sense or another. Some, such as that led by Geert Wilders in the Netherlands, have participated in government. Democratic processes have sometimes been put in suspension. In November 2011 the prime minister of Italy, Silvio Berlusconi, resigned from his position and was replaced by a 'technocrat', Mario Monti. Monti initiated a reform programme in Italy, approved of by Chancellor Merkel, the then president of France, Nicolas Sarkozy, the ECB and the IMF – EU2, in other words.

Monti then stood for office in the general election of February 2013, at the head of a new coalition group. His coalition, however, finished bottom of the four main contenders. The big surprise was the success of the 'Five Star Movement', led by the comedian and actor Beppe Grillo. As a consequence of the division of the vote, no coherent government could initially be formed. Grillo described Mr Monti as an agent of the banks and repeatedly called for a referendum on Italy's membership of the euro. He is not, he said, a Eurosceptic or anti-European, but a critic of how the EU has evolved. 'Why is only Germany getting richer?' he asked.[1] Monti was replaced by a new Prime Minister, Enrico Letta. He in turn gave way to another unelected leader, Matteo Renzi. Grillo was scathing about the manner in which Renzi came to power, calling it a coup.

The euro could in principle be wound back, one or two

members could either be ejected or leave, or even the whole thing could be abandoned. I defer detailed discussion of these possibilities to the end of the book. Even the more limited options could prove far more difficult than many who have proposed such courses of action seem to imagine. Following the path of further integration is the only way the Union can effectively deal with the problems it faces today. The basic theorem is simple. Saving the euro means moving towards greater economic cohesion within the eurozone. Because EU2 leadership is inherently too unstable and divisive, this in turn presumes a transformation of the EU's political institutions. The deep, and connected, flaws that have haunted the European project since its inception must be dealt with – its lack of both democratic legitimacy and effective leadership. The politics of getting from here to there, however, are testing indeed, since they reflect the very limitations of the system that needs to be replaced.

Progress so far has been substantial, if erratically so. Since reform is crisis-driven, decisions are quite often taken, and interventions made, at the last minute. Once things appear a bit more placid, the impetus to push through major change can be lost. The personalities involved count for a lot, as does how well they get on with one another at any particular point, since their association is informal – that is, not based upon an established institutional system. Moreover, EU2 is unstable because of the vagaries of national election processes which, being timed differently, act against continuity of leadership. Thus for some while commentators used to speak of Europe being led by 'Merkozy' – the duo of Angela Merkel and Nicolas Sarkozy. Some newspapers even published photos in which the traits of the two were combined to form a single face. The German tabloid *Bild* carried a headline: 'Merkozy – sieht so das neue Europa aus?' ('Merkozy – is this how the new Europe looks?')[2] Although in the early days there were many tensions between them, Merkel and Sarkozy became 'Europe's indispensable couple'. Sarkozy explained in private the dynamics of the 'marriage' and

he put it very appropriately: 'Germany without France frightens everyone. France without Germany frightens no one.'[3] By
acting together they could mute each of these qualities and
could also underpin the wider activities of EU2.

Germany has become Europe's indispensable nation.
Merkozy, however, proved more transitory than many imagined. Suddenly, Sarkozy was gone. In his place came François
Hollande, a different personality from his predecessor and one
holding different political views. The newspapers tried, but they
could not come up with a catchy merging of the names of the
German chancellor with that of the new French president. The
abortive attempt matched up to reality. Hollande became part
of EU2, but its inner dynamics changed. No one would think of
making a composite face for the two of them. Nonetheless they
are obliged to work together.

The dialectic of EU1 and EU2 has always been Europe's
way of doing things. However, since the crisis, a new player,
the IMF, has become involved and is a key member of the
Troika. The involvement of the IMF is humiliating for the
Union, but has proved absolutely essential. Its current head,
Christine Lagarde, is a former finance minister of France and
thus intimately familiar with European politics. She is the first
ever female head of the IMF. Apart from Mario Draghi, the
president of the ECB, she and Merkel are the most prominent
leaders in EU2 at the moment, a unique moment in the history
of the EU, which has long been a resolutely male affair. The
EU claims many founding fathers, but so far as I know there
are no founding mothers at all. Lagarde and Merkel appear to
have a good relationship, although they have had their public
disagreements. Lagarde has said that Merkel is the 'unchallenged leader' on the European scene. The two exchange
presents and sometimes dine alone with each other. Lagarde
thinks, however, that the progress of reform in the EU has
been too slow. She has advised Europe's leaders to 'get on with
the union. Make sure you have a banking union, down the road

fiscal union, and that you keep that currency zone together and solid.'[4]

There have been other tensions within the Troika. An IMF report published in June 2013 criticised the EU's handling of the first bailout given to Greece in 2010, which amounted to about €110 billion.[5] It was a mistake, the IMF said, not to oblige investors in Greek bonds to accept losses at that point, rather than waiting until late in 2011. If this had been done, the government would not have had to make such swingeing cuts in expenditure. Olli Rehn, the European commissioner for economic affairs, rejected the criticisms. 'I don't think it's fair just for the IMF to wash its hands and throw the dirty water on the Europeans', he said. He pointed out that Lagarde had resisted any debt restructuring when she was a member of Sarkozy's government. The Greek government at the time also came in for forthright criticism, for moving too slowly to begin with in making the reforms that were part of the bargain.[6]

HOW MUCH PROGRESS HAS BEEN MADE?

'It is imperative to break the vicious circle between banks and sovereigns' – the declaration was first made in an EU communiqué in June 2012 and repeated following a European Council meeting a year later.[7] To achieve such an end, as is very widely recognised, a banking union must be set up, accompanied at some point by a version of fiscal union. The one will not be water-tight without the other. Most banking unions have three elements: powers of supervision, powers of resolution of debts and a deposit guarantee. So far as the first of these is concerned, an important threshold was crossed in March 2013 with the endorsement of legislation to set up a Single Supervisory Mechanism. It places a range of supervisory powers in the hands of the European Central Bank, which will directly monitor the larger banks and those that have received direct assistance from the EU. States not in the euro can sign up should they choose

Figure 2 'The last battle: how Europe is wrecking its currency'
A view from the influential magazine Der Spiegel *in 2010*

to accept the conditions imposed. A European resolution mechanism, equally important, is still in the making. Here the EU lags well behind the United States. Banks still in trouble – and there still seem to be plenty of them – have been called by critics 'the living dead', 'zombie institutions' stuffed with toxic assets. They cannot be closed down, and their assets written off, until further progress with banking union has been made. An American banker observed in May 2013: 'The ECB and politicians spin a nice story. But behind the scenes the market is concerned that Europe may just go into a slow decline that cannot be reversed.'[8]

The issue is a serious one because, until the banking system is further consolidated, even the healthy banks are likely to limit investments that could help promote growth. There is some considerable way to go to reach an acceptable framework. Ecofin meetings in June 2013 agreed upon how the European Stability Mechanism could be deployed for direct bank recapitalisations and the 'bail-in' rules for ailing banks.[9] Since the Cyprus crisis, it has become accepted that bail-ins should replace bailouts, placing responsibility in the hands of banks and their investors to accept losses. What seemed like a perverse and dangerous strategy at the time has now become accepted as the norm. It has also been agreed that the Single Supervisory Mechanism demands a Single Resolution Mechanism, but that is still at the design stage. The EU is in danger of slipping into a leisurely EU1 way of proceeding when the problems to be resolved are still urgent. Angela Merkel has rejected unified European deposit insurance 'at least for the foreseeable future'.[10]

Fiscal integration is happening, but so far is based on an extension of the traditional EU1 practice of coordinating policies across the eurozone. The measures taken include the 'six pack', the 'two pack', and the Treaty on Stability, Coordination and Governance, all grounded in the 'European Semester', the EU's policy-making calendar. The treaty is often referred to for short as the Fiscal Compact. It was endorsed by twenty-five of the twenty-seven EU states – Britain and the Czech Republic did not sign up. The UK in fact blocked the proposal in the original form in which it was presented. The complex series of measures is aimed at supplying the discipline lacking in the original Stability and Growth Pact, introduced when the euro was established. The aim is also to try to identify future crises before they develop and nip them in the bud. This is all very well, but what is missing in the steps taken so far is the acceptance of mutuality – material recognition by the eurozone members of shared financial obligations to one another. The most important intervention that stabilised the financial situation in Europe was none of the above but was a strictly EU2 move. It was when

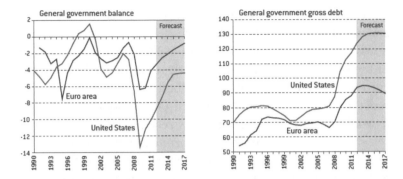

Figure 3 The cause of the instability of the euro is not debt as such

Source: Zsolt Darvas: *The Euro Crisis: Ten Roots, but Fewer Solutions.*
Bruegel Policy Contribution, October 2012.

Mario Draghi announced that the ECB 'is ready to do whatever it takes to preserve the euro'. To which he added: 'And, believe me, it will be enough.' He was signalling very firmly that the eurozone would stand collectively behind its currency. Yet so far the pledge has not been backed up institutionally. The euro remains vulnerable.[11]

It is precisely the 'whatever it takes' that is at issue. The flaws present in the construction of the single currency at its point of origin must be corrected. There has never been an enduring monetary union without mutuality and the means to back it up. Germany has stated its commitment to a banking union. Angela Merkel has verbally endorsed the need for fiscal integration too. So far, however, the German government has resisted demands for anything more far-reaching. Some other northern states are dubious, to say the least. The prime reason given is the moral hazard that would thereby be introduced – the impetus to reform in the weaker countries would be lost while the richer countries, most notably Germany, would foot the bill.[12] Here is a crunch issue: will Germany, its leaders and its people, at some point accept mutuality in some guise or another or not? If the answer is no, then the status of the euro will remain uncertain, and with it Europe's future. In April 2013, the financier George Soros went to give a public lecture in Frankfurt on the subject of the crisis. He argued, quite rightly, that the fatal flaw in the euro is that member states have 'become indebted in a currency they do not control'.[13] When Greece looked as though it would default, 'financial markets reacted with a vengeance, relegating all heavily indebted eurozone members to the status of a Third World country over-extended in a foreign currency. Subsequently, the heavily indebted member countries were treated as if they were solely responsible for their misfortunes, and the structural defects of the euro remained uncorrected.'

The solution, Soros said, is plain to see: the introduction of eurobonds. 'It would be like waking from a nightmare.' The Fiscal Compact could be adjusted to become a tighter form of discipline. Taken together, the two would ensure that any risk of default would become minimal, if clear limits to debt obligations also were put in place. Germany, he recognised, remains strongly opposed to eurobonds. If such remains the case, he declared, the country should leave the euro and the remaining eurozone states should go ahead with eurobonds on their own, as all would benefit. I presume he was being deliberately provocative. Although an anti-euro party has emerged in Germany, the chances of the country unilaterally abandoning the currency are vanishingly small. Soros's arguments were derided by critics. Otmar Issing, former chief economist and board member at the ECB, was the discussant at the speech. The introduction of eurobonds would mean that the German taxpayer would indirectly finance other countries' debts. It would mean redistribution would happen without democratic mandate. He invoked the principle 'No taxation without representation'. Others were even more dismissive. Fellow economist Hans-Werner Sinn accused Soros of 'playing with fire'.[14] The real cause of the crisis of the euro is the lack of competitiveness of the Southern countries. To regain it, the price of their goods must come down, while the northern states will have to stimulate internal demand. The weaker economies must undergo painful reforms.

The unpopular message that Soros brought to Germany, however, was entirely apt. It is as much in Germany's interest to accept some form of mutuality as it is that of other euro-zone countries. Reform cannot forever be driven by externally imposed austerity measures but has to be based in some part upon incentives, coupled with ambitious pro-active investment. Germany has nothing to gain from a further deepening of the slow-down and structural unemployment in the weaker econo-mies. Europe has everything to lose because of the bitterness thus created. Behind closed doors, Angela Merkel apparently made the remark that eurobonds wouldn't be introduced in her lifetime; it was leaked and named 'Quote of the Year' by the *Frankfurter Allgemeine Zeitung*.[15] The Social Democratic Party has backed away from them too. Yet an EU2 leadership with Germany in pole position is inherently fragile and cannot survive indefinitely. In a now famous speech given in Berlin in 2011, Poland's then foreign minister, Radosław Sikorski, declared that he feared Germany's power less than her inac-tivity. 'We ask Berlin', he said, 'to admit that it is the biggest beneficiary of current arrangements and that it therefore has the biggest obligation to make them sustainable. As Germany knows best, she is not an innocent victim of others' profligacy.'[16]

Sikorski was right and remains so today. The advantages that Germany gets from being in the eurozone are substantial, and it is an obligation of the country's leadership to help citizens understand this. Enhanced protection from future economic fluctuations is in the interest of all. I believe that at some point eurozone members will accept some form of conditional pool-ing of debt, if only because the alternatives are too unpalat-able. It would be far, far better, however, to introduce it as a positive step forward for Europe rather than as an obligation grudgingly conceded. If the euro is to be fully stabilised and able to withstand shocks, the only questions at issue are at

Figure 4 'My name is Bond. Euro Bond. Never say never.'
Sometimes jokes capture reality more effectively than
any amount of serious prose.

what point mutuality will be formally acknowledged and what form it will take. Among other consequences it will bolster the euro's position as an international reserve currency. There are several proposed versions of eurobonds to consider, including one endorsed by the Commission, that would limit liability and contain other forms of protection for the more affluent states.

Joseph Stiglitz is another author who has stressed the crucial importance of some form of mutualisation of debt in the eurozone.[17] In current circumstances, he points out, this would make it possible for the eurozone to borrow at negative real interest rates, as is the case for the US. Such a capability could in fact be a crucial element in helping deflect the risk of deflation, still looming large. An important further contribution has come from the work of the Glienicker group, composed of eleven German economists, political science and jurists. They quite rightly point to the inadequacy of the reforms made within the eurozone so far. In 2013, van Rompuy claimed at the UN General Assembly in New York that 'the existential crisis of the euro is over'. The members of the group say they believe this view to be 'fundamentally wrong' and they are right to do so. The euro has been temporarily stabilised but more extensive reform is required if prosperity is to return.

'We speak as German', they say, 'but also as EU citizens who are connected with other EU citizens in a community.' It is in the German self-interest to overcome anxieties about the implications of a transfer union 'and to stop dismissing any constructive proposal as an attempt to pull the money out of German pockets'. Austerity policies can only work up to a certain point, after which they become self-undermining. There are clear limits to the degree to which either creditors or debtors will believe that states can take direct responsibility for themselves within the framework of a common currency. 'The monetary union', they continue, 'cannot be permanently stable without a controlled transfer mechanism.' Such an innovation in turn, they hold (as I do), cannot be managed in the longer term without the democratisation of the political structure of the EU.[18]

A few authors seem to think that the EU can muddle through indefinitely once banking and fiscal integration have been pushed through to some sort of reasonable degree, or even if

neither is realised. In his otherwise outstanding history of the
EU, Luuk van Middelaar says a 'federal leap' on the part of the
Union is not needed to avoid a relapse into potential chaos:
'Neither fate awaits us: not a revolution, since Europe is patient;
nor a break-up, since Europe is tough. The adventure of turning a continent into a Union, although spurred on by crises and
dramas, is a slow affair . . .'[19]

I profoundly disagree. The EU indeed has to move forward
at this point, but it cannot follow its traditional incremental
approach. The Union must develop an EU3 – a system confer-
ring more dynamic leadership and political legitimacy as well as
greater macro-economic stability than exists at present. To put
it simply, economic federalism, now inevitable if the euro is to
be saved, has to be accompanied by political federalism in some
guise or another. As the outgoing president of the Commission,
José Manuel Barroso put it in a speech in 2013, there will have
to be an 'intensified political union' in the EU, stretching across
all member states. The mainstream forces in European politics
must seize the initiative, should leave their comfort zone to
welcome and embrace this debate, rather than relinquish the
momentum to Eurosceptic or Europhobic forces.'[20]

As a result of the efforts of the Eurosceptics, the term 'federalism' has managed to acquire a sinister ring – and even more
so the spectre of a European 'federal super-state'. In fact, the
terms 'federal' and 'super-state' do not really belong together.
A federal system is classically defined as one in which there
is substantial devolution of power, not where a central state
is dominant. Political scientists have spoken of a 'new age of
federalism' as countries struggle with the morass of influences
they confront. Federalism, it has aptly been said, allows for
'shared rule and self-rule, co-ordinated national government
and diversity, creative experiment and liberty'.[19] Save for China,
all the large countries in the world are federations. Those
unitary states that remain, such as the UK, France, Spain, Sri
Lanka and Indonesia, have mostly faced secessionist move-

ments. Federalism is not an ideology but a pragmatic form of government, at its best flexible and adaptable. Of course, in federal nations there are many squabbles between the states or regions and the political centre, and it is always difficult to get the balance right. Yet because they are essentially decentred they make possible forms of local experimentation, often in fact because of the frictions that have to be overcome.

A federal system in Europe would have to deal simultaneously with the leadership problem and the long-standing democratic deficit. Leadership and legitimacy go together. The EU's problem of lack of effective leadership is directly connected with its narrow veneer of democracy. As in other areas, the EU should not simply play 'catch-up' but aim to be ahead of the game so far as other available models are concerned. Political integration in Europe must look above all to correct some of the core deficiencies of the EU, not to multiply them. The approach to leadership and democracy should not just be formal – in other words, concerned only with electoral mechanisms. A fundamental aim should be to reduce bureaucracy.

As they currently exist, there are structural difficulties with each of the major EU governing institutions, as well as the relation between them. The European Council and the Council of the European Union are where much of the real decision-making occurs in EU1 circumstances. However, they have a low level of visibility to the public, while their proceedings are not widely disclosed. Many citizens have never even heard of them and, if they have, might mix up the two. They are easily confused not only with each other but also with the Council of Europe, which is not an EU body. So far as citizens are concerned, therefore, the EU tends to be identified with the Commission. It is more visible mainly because it proposes policies and publishes its proposals in the form of consultation documents. The Commission is not like an orthodox civil service, because there is no elected government formed in conjunction with the parliament as there is in a conventional state. Its role is not limited to enacting policies initiated elsewhere. It is in large part the policy-maker, but with little power actually to enact the policy programmes it comes up with. The peculiar position of the Commission is one of the main reasons for the existence of paper Europe. It cannot be blamed for this, which comes from its structural situation. The plans it sets out are not integrated with an effective political process.

The European Parliament has acquired more influence over the past two decades, but as yet it has not succeeded in generating public legitimacy for the EU. The reasons are well known. Whatever valuable work it may do, it is disconnected from the concerns of the European electorates. So far as most citizens are concerned it is marginal and relatively invisible. Levels of voting are low and elections have been concentrated mostly upon national problems and dilemmas. Some say the best way to cope with this difficulty would be to set up closer connections between the European Parliament and national parliaments.[22] The powers of the EU concern mainly the single market, monetary policy, competition and regulation – not the main preoccupations of voters. If national parliaments were more directly involved in EU legislation, some of the legitimacy they possess could become transferred to the European level. For example, the level of scrutiny maintained by such parliaments over EU affairs could be stepped up. Alternatively national parliaments and the European Parliament could work more closely in tandem. I do not think this route is the way to go. The last thing needed in a restructured Union is another layer of bureaucracy, multiplied across all the member states. EU1-style governance is not compatible with a world that is speeding up all the time.

THE KISSINGER QUESTION THAT WASN'T

Federalism has travelled all the way from being the remote dream of Churchill and the founding fathers of the EU to a demand of the moment today. The past three or four years have seen innumerable publications,' among academics and in the media, discussing what form on a European level it might take. It is one example among many others of the emergence of a genuine trans-European political space. I have no intention of trying to summarise these discussions here. I limit myself to a few observations. Two main questions have to be answered: what type of political order should it be and, equally important, how could it be created given the EU's current low level of popularity?

A new system would have to be a form of 'lean federalism', since a more intrusive political system is neither politically feasible nor needed. The aim would be simultaneously to enhance the EU's leadership capacity and to create greater democratic participation on the part of Europe's citizens. No specific country should be taken as an exemplar. Churchill spoke of constructing a United States of Europe, and many others across the years have done the same. Whether that term is employed or not, the American example should not figure as a direct model – nor should any single existing country. There is not much point comparing the situation of the EU today to the United States in the eighteenth century, even if there has been a great deal of talk recently of Europe's 'Philadelphia moment'. It is not just a question of reframing the institutions. Reforms must be consistent with, and respond to, the wider problems and possibilities of democracy brought about by new technology. Flexibility and adaptability should be core concerns. A restructured system of governance must be grounded in, and responsive to, groups in civil society.

Leadership is a good place to begin. To me that means, as many others have argued recently, the direct election of a European president. It is the best strategy to combine leadership with popular legitimacy. Direct election is the only way of fully answering Henry Kissinger's famous question: 'Who do I call if I want to call Europe?' An amusing sequence of events happened after the Lisbon Treaty was signed. José Manuel Barroso said there was no longer a question of to whom the call should be made. It would be to Cathy Ashton, the 'foreign minister' for Europe, since Kissinger at the time was secretary of state. 'The so-called Kissinger issue', he said, 'is now solved.'[23] Yet he went on to say that the EU was also represented by the head of the European Commission and the government of the country holding the EU's six-month presidency. Herman Van Rompuy, the head of the European Council at that time, made it clear that a US president should in the first instance call him.

In his spare time, Van Rompuy wrote charming *haikus* – a verse style from Japan, which traditionally had a rigid five-, seven-, five-syllable structure, difficult to reproduce exactly in a European language. An example:

> Brussels:
> different colours
> tongues, towers and gods
> I search my way

His efforts have spawned numerous imitators.[24] Here is one that has no poetic qualities, but which hits the nail on the head:

> Kissinger calling
> Van Rompuy answers the phone
> Henry: 'Wrong number'

To pile irony on irony, Kissinger admitted in a debate in 2012 that he wasn't sure he ever actually said what was for so long attributed to him.[25] In any case, the time when the EU's leadership could be largely anonymous and unknown to most citizens has surely gone. Europe must have a 'face', as it does temporarily at the moment – that of Mrs Merkel. Such a person must hold real power (as she does now) and 'speak for the EU'.

The other pieces of the jigsaw fall into place relatively easily, although in practice the devil is bound to be in the detail.[26] In a restructured Union, a greater range of powers would have to be given to the European Parliament. The European Council over time could be transformed into a senate, representing the nations and regions. The Commission would become more of an orthodox civil service, concerned less with proposing policies and more with actualising them.

Since the advent of the euro crisis, the notion that there should be a eurozone parliament has been widely canvassed. It would consist of a modest-sized chamber, whose members would be elected via the national parliaments of the eurozone countries, with size of representation being more or less proportional to the population of each member-state. The idea is that it could eventually displace the Council, which would in any case be increasingly sidelined. According to some commentators, momentous though it may be, since it would initially be confined to the eurozone, such an innovation would not necessarily involve treaty change, at least at the outset. Certainly more open and transparent means of steering the direction of development of the eurozone will have to be found and this will spill over into other EU institutions.

The Eurosceptics are right to criticise the bureaucratic and remote nature of the EU as currently constituted. For them, a move towards federalism would make these features even more oppressive. Yet such a system would in fact help transcend some of those traits. The EU would be both more fast-moving and brought much closer to its citizens. The ponderous nature of EU1 decision-making comes largely from the specific traits of the existing system, where detailed coordination between twenty-eight member states stands in the place of political integration. The dense thicket of committees surrounding the EU's three main institutions could be greatly hacked back.

To my mind it is essential that some powers be returned to nations, regions and localities as part of the deal (although not as *ad hoc* opt-outs). It is not right and proper that, once swallowed up, devolved powers should never be returned or substantially modified. Some existing political systems embody such mechanisms. They are important because they help provide flexibility and adaptability in the face of change, as well as offering a means to introduce innovations. Subsidiarity should be real, not the largely empty term it has become across the years. The existing EU competencies do embody a 'flexibility clause', but it relates only to the top. It allows the EU on occasion to act beyond its legally defined limits if circumstances are deemed to warrant it. What level and forms of integration should there be in the various domains of activity the EU covers? There would have to be a variegated structure, with greater integration in some areas than others. Fiscal union presumes the development of a budget within the eurozone, whose relationship to the existing European budget would have to be clarified. That in turn means that there should be some funding for trans-European welfare, health and education projects although, in spite of its title, the 'European social model' will remain largely in national hands. There could and should be more pooling in the area of the military, where there is enormous waste and duplication of resources. Were it not for the American presence in NATO, Europe would have very little military capability relevant to its current security needs (see chapter 6).

There remains an enormous amount of work to be done on all of these issues. For example, if there is to be an elected European president, how will candidates be chosen? There will presumably have to be Europe-wide hustings of some sort: how will such a complex process be organised? How will the multilingual nature of Europe be coped with? Would nations vote in blocs, as they tend to do in that rather less consequential event the Eurovision Song Contest? Given the will and the resources, I don't see any of these problems as insuperable, but they will have to be thought through and a working consensus on procedure reached.

Even if things moved smoothly – a big if – we are looking at a period of years from initiation to resolution. Can the whole enterprise even get off the ground? The EU seems caught in a trap of its own making. The euro was introduced in some part to create political integration within the EU. Yet it has helped produce the very crisis that is turning citizens away from the

European project as a whole. A federal Europe manifestly should not and cannot be imposed upon citizens against their wishes.

How to resolve these dilemmas? There are both short- and longer-term problems that must be confronted. One must have some sympathy with those who declare that Europe has simply got itself into an impossible position as a result of the introduction of the euro.[27] It can't go backwards, they say, but transformational change is not possible because of the political and organisational hazards that have to be overcome. The paradox, at least in my view, is that the impossible position they describe is itself impossible. The EU might be between the devil and the deep blue sea, but that itself is a position of great danger. The Union simply cannot use its time-honoured strategy of cautious change punctuated by the occasional grand referendum. The structural obstacles can be listed briefly. An entire book, much longer than this one, could be written specifically about them, and I'm sure many are already in the works. I certainly hope so.

Any proposed solutions must deal with the division between the eurozone and the rest of the EU states. The eurozone has to be a sort of *avant garde* and, as has been mentioned, can in fact introduce quite a range of changes on its own; but they have to be reconciled with the interests of the non-eurozone states, since some necessary policies will at some point have to apply not only to the eurozone countries but to all EU states. There are obvious difficulties here. The continuing problems involved in creating a more rational system in place of the Common Agricultural Policy give an indication of the resistances that would have to be overcome.

The nations at the core of the European project in the past have had discrepant views from one another, as well as different internal political constraints to surmount. In the case of Germany, the main question, as I have stressed several times, is whether the country will accept the logic of interdependence in the eurozone. France sustains the *hauteur* of a post-imperial country still reluctant to recognise the reality of its relative insignificance in the contemporary world. Memories of past imperial grandeur are strong in the UK too and form one of the reasons for its aloof attitude towards the rest of Europe. At the same time, the smaller states quite rightly object to the dominance of the larger ones in EU2 decision-making.

'Federal Europe' is a fairly vacuous term until flesh is put on the bones. There are a lot of different possible models around. Those who want greater political integration might not be able to agree about what form concretely it should assume. Some see the term as implying a version of their own preferred national model writ large – for instance, a form of social market economy with strong elements of corporatism. Others see the EU as a force against economic globalisation and place an emphasis upon protectionism, closed borders, and so forth. Yet others (including myself) see globalisation as a new condition of life rather than some sort of external force to be succumbed to or defended against. They want an open but also flexible and dynamic Europe.

As I stress throughout this book, one should beware of treating such issues in too 'internalist' and institutional a fashion. Some of the core political dilemmas and difficulties that have to be grappled with in Europe are found more or less across the world. Falling rates of voting, mistrust of political leaders, coupled with the rise of diverse forms of populism, are visible in many countries. No doubt the origins of these trends are complex, but one reason for their emergence lies in the limitations of the nation-state in an era of accelerating interdependence. Politicians are prone to make claims that they are simply not able to realise, given the weight of the transnational forces they confront.

THE POPULIST SURGE

Populism in Europe shares traits with its counterparts elsewhere. Most populist parties across the world have an anti-establishment, anti-elitist theme. Orthodox political institutions are seen as out of touch with the hopes, fears and anxieties of ordinary citizens. Populists deploy the language of democracy and often play a part in the political process. Yet the aim of at least some versions of populism is to subvert democratic processes – to amend or suspend liberal values in the interests of the greater good. Anti-establishment parties can come from either the left or the right, as is the case in Europe today. Very few populist parties have policies that span the whole spectrum of political concerns. Instead, they tend to centre their appeal upon one or two key issues that represent wider feelings of antagonism or resentment.

The successes of the populist parties in the 2014 European elections should be judged against this wider backdrop, as well as in relation to circumstances specific to Europe itself. Quite legitimate criticisms of the EU's limitations mingle with wider sources of discontent or feelings of alienation, whose origins have nothing directly to do with the EU. In other words, the EU is to some extent a scapegoat for anxieties whose real sources lie elsewhere. There is a perversity here, since the collective power of the EU, if appropriately shaped and coordinated, offers the chance to achieve a measure of control over transnational forces that otherwise might reign unchecked.

In terms of overall patterns of voting, the impact made by the populist and Eurosceptic parties was small – a 2 per cent swing overall. However such parties made large gains in some key countries. Two particular cases in point were the UK and France. In the former country, the United Kingdom Independence Party topped the polls, as did the Front National in France. Populist parties performed well also in some of the smaller states, such as the Netherlands and Finland. The low overall swing is explained by the fact that in some member-states, such as Italy, the populist groups lost votes to the mainstream parties. Election turnout, at 43 per cent, was slightly higher than in the preceding elections, although much lower than the 62 per cent figure in the original European elections

of 1979. The 43 per cent average masks big variations in per-
centages. The level of voting was very low in some countries,
most notably Slovakia and the Czech Republic. Turnout was
relatively high in Germany, Greece and Sweden.

Some have argued that the fact that overall turnout did not
sharply increase means that the 2014 elections unfolded more or
less like their predecessors – it was business as usual. Analysed
in more detail, this was not at all the case. In most member-
states, it was the first time that the elections had been fought
substantially around European issues rather than national or
local ones. The very presence of the populist parties more or
less guaranteed such would be the case. Perversely, these parties
are in some part the agents of the very Europeanisation they are
concerned to rebut. They have a diversity of grievances and aims
and it remains to be seen what their collective impact will be in
the Parliament, where the mainstream party groups still hold
sway. Whether their popularity endures on a national level will
of course depend upon how events and trends unfold in Europe
and indeed the world as a whole, over the next few years, given
the interconnected global system in which we now live.

The advent of what is likely to be a vociferous minority in the
Parliament coincided with a significant alteration in the way in
which the incoming president of the Commission was chosen. A
clause in the Lisbon Treaty states that, when a new Commission
head is appointed, the results of the European elections should
be 'taken into account' by the Council, which makes the ultimate decision. On that basis, candidates from the main political
groups in the Parliament campaigned across most of the EU
states prior to the election (although not in the UK). A good
deal of controversy surrounded the whole process. The eventual
outcome was that Jean-Claude Juncker, the candidate of the
largest group in the Parliament as a result of the elections – the
centre-right – was appointed as the Commission president.

How significant was the innovation? In my view, very significant – which is why hostile critics, including British Prime

Minister, David Cameron, opposed it so vociferously. It was only the beginning, to be sure, but marked a new departure. It is true that the campaigns of the candidates did not brook large in the consciousness of the electorate. That will only come if, at some point, there is agreement to introduce a directly elected European presidency (which ideally would combine the two posts of president of the Commission and the Council). If the candidates in the run-up to the 2014 elections did not exactly become household names across Europe, their visibility was certainly heightened. They developed active political programmes, open to public assessment and reaction. The very fact that Juncker and the process whereby he was appointed were attacked so much, once he had emerged as the candidate of choice, ironically helped bring him at that point to far wider public attention than would otherwise have been the case.

Survey results taken just after the 2014 elections did, in fact, show some positive developments. Following the elections, the proportion of EU citizens who felt that their voice counted in the EU went up from 29 per cent in November 2013 to 42 per cent. 65 per cent stated they felt like European citizens, a rise from 59 per cent on the previous date.[28] A range of other measures showed similar results.

In the case of the appointments to other key posts, including those of President of the Council and High Representative for Foreign Affairs, it was back to business as usual – and the contrast was stark. Tortuous negotiations between the heads of state, held behind closed doors, dragged on for weeks. As much research has shown, the public are not exactly enamoured of such opaque ways of reaching key decisions. Following this unseemly process, to the new Parliament, Commission and Council, falls the task of steering the Union through shoals that still look murky and threatening. They will have to develop a renewed vision of the path that the EU should follow over the next period and show more concretely how that could be pursued in practical terms.

To my mind, it is essential that such a vision does not become just another set of paper European aspirations, with no real substance to back them up. No country in the world, including the United States, has made a safe and assured exit from the financial crisis and indeed there is at least the possibility that there are further major troubles to come. Reform of the euro, as I have stressed, is not more than halfway through. Short of major new policies, with real bite, the divisions between north and south will still loom large. The recovery, such as it is, in the European economies is weak and unevenly spread. The events in Ukraine could have enduring economic as well as political effects upon the EU states. More assured and effective leadership is as crucial in foreign policy as elsewhere.

Declines in popular support for the EU as shown in surveys since 2008 should be treated with some caution. Since attachment to the Union is relatively shallow, it is not surprising that support can fall when economic progress has stalled and the agreements the EU needs are not yet finalised. Probably a better measure is the level of public endorsement of the euro. A recent survey of eight key EU countries by the US-based organisation the Pew Research Centre is helpful here.[29] The countries in question were Germany, Britain, France, Italy, Spain, Greece, Poland and the Czech Republic. Expressed support for deeper European integration has fallen dramatically, standing at 32 per cent. Yet 65 per cent of citizens within the eurozone countries endorse the continuation of euro membership. There is no country in which the figure is below 60 per cent. The Pew survey turns up some telling findings about Germany. In the words of its authors, it 'contradicts oft-repeated narratives' about the attitudes of the German population. Germans are not paranoid about inflation. On the contrary, they are the least inclined among the populations of the countries surveyed to see it as a significant problem. Among the richer states, they are the most likely to be in favour of providing financial help to other EU states which are in economic difficulty.

Current official EU strategy appears to assume that national

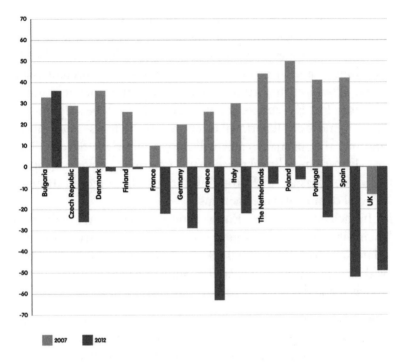

Figure 5 Expressed support for the EU has plummeted

Source: Jose Ignacio Torreblanca and Mark Leonard: *The Continent-Wide Rise of Euroscepticism*, ECFR Policy Memo, 2013.

elections will follow their usual form and not be focused on European questions. Apart from the European elections, the idea seems to be to postpone democratic involvement in political reforms until there is a finished product, which will then be decided upon in the form of referendums held across the member states. As Jürgen Habermas has put it, 'the ultimate democratisation is presented as a promise like the light at the end of the tunnel.'[30] It is not the approach to follow. The danger inherent in such a strategy is clear from the fate of the Constitution the first time around. Democratic support and involvement must be built up along the way rather than postponed until the big bang.

Europe has become a community of fate. Short of collapse, I don't see this changing over the next few years. New dynamics will develop, even in the short term – indeed, have already developed, since Europe is a more or less ever present issue today. Division may triumph over integration, but it is all to play for. The EU and its potential evolution will be a significant topic in most or all national elections for the foreseeable future and one that in many cases will have a left–right flavour. The pan-European political space that is emerging provides a forum in which ideas about Europe's future can be explored through normal democratic mechanisms.

In such circumstances Eurosceptic parties will have to develop their views in a more cogent way than has been true hitherto. Many are driven almost wholly by what they are against. They will have to say what they are *for*. Someone who is critical of the EU as it stands could want:

- a looser type of Union than the one that exists at present – that might mean, for example, abandoning the euro and returning to an EU centred upon the single market;
- a Union that is reshaped in a specific way, for example, to make it more democratic or decentralised – there are many possibilities in this category, depending in part on national context;
- a free trade area and nothing more, along the lines of NAFTA or ASEAN;
- one or more specific nations to exit the EU – for example, Britain – on the grounds that the country in question wishes to go its own way, whatever happens in the rest of Europe; or
- the complete dissolution of the EU and a reversion to a Europe of nation-states in their pre-existing form.

One should note that all of these options involve complexities, not only in the specific form they might assume but also in how they might be achieved. Eurosceptics will have to show not only how these would be dealt with but what would be a practical way to achieve them. Unwinding existing institutions, for example, would in many cases be an extremely difficult and contested process, with many legal hurdles to be overcome. Those who wish to see the break-up, or a radical scaling-back, of the EU must spell out what would follow for the array of separate states that would be left. Some forms of cooperation and even common governance would certainly be required, since so many problems today reflect shared concerns. Regional connections will continue to count for a great deal. No Eurosceptic can be taken seriously on a policy-making level who does not spell out a practical scenario of a positive sort. If the arguments of the Eurosceptics should be brought out into the open, so also, of course, should those of pro-Europeans. It is what I am seeking to help achieve in writing this book.

Even in today's fraught atmosphere, the possibility of forging ahead with greater economic and political integration is real. There is a platform for potential endorsement of such a process, and with a democratic component, especially if pro-Europeans henceforth become as politically active as their opponents. Much will depend in the medium term upon such developments being associated with a return to greater economic health, especially in the context of the weaker states. Germany may be the most significant influence, but other countries have to come on board. Will France, a country with a great deal of national pride, accept the logic of sovereignty+? François Hollande has said he endorses the idea of an elected European president, although there are many groups in the country which are opposed to ceding further powers to Europe. Member states will be required to shed the have-their-cake-and-eat-it attitude that has persisted for so long. In other words, their leaders want to behave like independent actors when they feel like it, yet want the advantages of the Union at the same time. It will take a shift in mentality to achieve, but the time to begin to do so is now.

FROM THE BOTTOM UP

Citizens must at this point become more deeply involved in processes of European reform – the bottom-up element must be strong and persuasive, not confined to occasional consultations or even to elections.[31] There should be a renewed attempt at identity-building. It won't do to repeat truisms such as 'Europe gets its strength from its diversity'. Pro-Europeans can take comfort from the fact that, amid this diversity, the nationalisms and the regional divisions, there has emerged a Europeanised younger generation. Active programmes, such as the Erasmus scheme, have helped create it. Such is the case even in the UK, where there is a big division between the over fifties and the under thirties.[32]

As with all other areas, there are shorter- and longer-term initiatives that could be introduced to help produce what would be in effect a European-wide civil society. Many Commission-driven projects already exist. There is the European Voluntary Service scheme, which makes it possible for people aged eighteen to thirty to do volunteer work in a member state or accession country for a period up to a year. 2011 was designated as the European Year of Volunteering (EYV). The EYV was developed as a concept by a group of volunteer networks in different countries and supported by the Commission. About 100 million people in Europe engage in some kind of regular volunteer activity; the point is to get them to connect up more and to draw others in. There are serious difficulties here, however. One is that of Brussels patronage itself. It has been said that EU funding can have a 'toxic effect' upon the state of NGOs. A large number of civil society organisations are represented in Brussels. Most of the money emanating from the Commission finds its way to them. Hence there are strong pressures to conform to whatever lines of thinking the Commission puts forward, while the NGO leaders themselves become detached from their grassroots – and grassroots movements are what civil society is supposed to be all about.[33]

The Commission has recently initiated a series of public debates all over Europe. The aim, it says in a slightly patronising tone, is to give 'ordinary people an opportunity to speak directly to EU politicians' about the future of the continent. The debates originated as part of the 2013 European Year of the Citizens – a peculiar designation in itself. Shouldn't every year be the year of the citizens? No doubt it is a worthwhile endeavour in any case. The debates were signalled in President Barroso's State of the Union Address of 2012. His speech stood little comparison with the similar address given in the United States by the president each year. Who, among European citizens, even knew that it had happened? If some listened to (or watched) the speech directly, in which language would they have listened to it? Which foreign leaders from other parts of the world tuned in or took any notice? How many European citizens could even name the president of the Commission?

It is a deeply contentious issue, but serious attention should be given to making English the official language of the EU, alongside national languages, and taught as such in all schools. 'English' is no longer itself only a national language but by far the dominant global one in terms of overall communication. The idea has been endorsed by German President Joachim Gauck among others.[34] Most of the younger generation are growing up speaking reasonable English in any case. It would certainly help de-bureaucratise. Some 1.8 million pages of translation are produced by the EU each year. Much more important, it would facilitate the development of trans-European media organisations and sources, thereby reinforcing the public domain that has been created by recent events.

Reconciling leadership and democracy at this point in the EU must go beyond proposals for formal institutional arrangements. We have to consider how the deeper currents of change referred to earlier should be integrated with the proposals just discussed. The internet is global in the most elemental sense of that term. There are two 'worlds' interacting with and clashing with each other. One is representative government, territorial and quite slow-moving. The other is a much more lateral world of interaction, carried on billions of times every day and instantaneous in nature.

The logical consequence in a political context would seem to be that the EU should embrace electronic forms of direct democracy. As elsewhere in the world, there is a lively dialogue about the possibility going on both in the Commission and in academic circles. One prominent example is the European Citizens' Initiative, introduced through the Treaty of Lisbon and launched in 2012. So long as they include people from at least one-quarter of the EU states, 1 million EU citizens can put a legislative proposal to the Commission. The signatures are mostly collected online. The first to be successful was a petition to halt the sales of water utilities to private companies. Useful though it might be, the Citizens' Initiative is not a contribution to everyday participation in politics. It has nothing of the immediacy of communication in the constantly evolving digital sphere with its myriads of services – Twitter, Facebook, YouTube, Tumblr, Pinterest and the rest. No one in fact thus far has found a way of systematically integrating these with established democratic procedures. The social media have made a massive impact across the world in terms of stimulating an appetite for democratic involvement. Yet harnessing this desire to the mechanisms of day-to-day governance has proved elusive. It is hard not to believe that at a certain point it will happen, and probably with profound consequences, but that point is not yet.

Representative democracy, therefore, will continue to be fundamentally important. How might the coming of the internet improve its functioning? The main way, I suggest, is through what I call the *rule of transparency*. For better or worse, the coming of the digital world signals the end of privacy – every electronic trace can be unearthed. When Marshall McLuhan spoke of the coming of the global village, he was more prescient than even he can have imagined. Just as in a village, everybody knows what everyone else is doing and few secrets can be kept for long. The consequences are by no means all benign. Yet they have basic implications for the operations of power. Closet deals, behind the scenes manipulation, direct corruption, and even inefficiencies more generally have become much more difficult to conceal from the public gaze.

We in Europe live today not just in representative democracies but in what has been called 'monitory' ones.[35] Monitory democracy means the more or less continuous scrutiny of decision-makers, within the political sphere but also in other areas too, including business and industry. It is carried on by a diversity of groups, among them the media, civil society agencies, internet groups and bloggers, and many more. All these groups themselves are subject to monitory democracy as well as facilitating it. Because the internet is global, it is not limited to territory in the way that representative democracy is, and it interacts with representative institutions in complex and even contradictory ways. Thus many people become disenchanted with political leaders in some part because they become 'all too human' – their fads and foibles are known to everyone and the mystique of power is readily punctured. Personal and political attacks of all kinds, including abuse, become a daily part of their experience.

There is a very strongly positive side, however. Political leaders will have to adhere to higher standards than before in their personal as well as their public lives, in some countries implying a wrenching adjustment to normal practice. Consider what has occurred over the past few years in the UK. One by one, the major British institutions have become open to scrutiny in a way that has never taken place before. It is as if a can-opener has peeled off the lid – and what is revealed is not exactly salubrious. It has happened in the case of politicians, particularly as concerns their expenses claims; in banking, where banks have been revealed as conniving in distorting the market through fixing Libor rates, turning a blind eye to money-laundering on the large-scale, and other dubious practices; in the police, where widespread malpractice has been revealed; in the news media, where phone tapping and other illegal practices have been shown to be widespread; in the health service, where a range of scandals have been disclosed in hospitals; in the BBC, where cases of sexual abuse, dating back several decades, have been brought to light; and in the churches, where in some cases sexual indiscretion seems to have been a way of life.

There are parallels everywhere in other EU countries, showing how deep-lying the new processes at work are. It is not accidental that there has been a spate of corruption cases across Europe over the past few years. All the major European states have been involved, from north to south. A report from Transparency International published in 2012 was damning in its conclusions. It reaffirmed what is obvious – that, in Greece, Portugal, Spain and Italy, low levels of public accountability, malpractice and corruption are not only embedded but deeply embroiled in the crisis itself. The chair of TI Greece observed that 'Corruption created all the elements of the financial problems in Greece . . . [It] has imbued the mentality of the people and the institutions of the country.'[36] (See below, Chapter 2.) The difference now is that there will have to be structural change, not just in these states but elsewhere in Europe too. For the first time there is intense pressure for reform, from above – in the shape of the obligations of states seeking to reduce their levels of debt – and from below – in the shape of movements such as the *indignados* in Spain.

The EU has led a number of campaigns to promote transparency, but it has defined the notion much too narrowly. Moreover, it has not applied them sufficiently to itself. The Union is non-transparent on the grand level precisely because of the existence of EU2 – key decisions essentially taken behind the scenes by key states' leaders. When Bernard Connolly wrote *The Rotten Heart of Europe*, which is about the origins of European monetary union, this is what he meant, even if he used unnecessarily bellicose rhetoric to make his point.[37] The connection between democracy and transparency in the internet age is not simply informational, as many think. It is structural. In other words, transparency is not only about the inevitable step-change in the visibility of what leaders do; it is about how the mechanisms of government should best be reordered and reformed.

THE UK AND EUROPE

In his Zurich speech Churchill made it clear that Britain would not be part of the federation he envisaged for the rest of Europe. As he said in another context: 'We are with Europe but not of it . . . If Britain must choose between Europe and the open sea, she must always choose the open sea.'[38] From the earliest days of the emergence of the European project, many have joined Churchill in seeing Britain as a nation apart. A Labour government turned down the opportunity to take part in the meetings that led to the setting up of the Coal and Steel Community. It was mainly the economic success of what was to become the European Union that persuaded the British government, under the Conservative Edward Heath, to join up in 1973.

Economic motivation is what was stressed in a speech by Prime Minister David Cameron on British membership of the EU, delivered four decades later almost to the day. He affirmed that the British 'have the character of an island nation' jealous of any threats to its sovereignty. Yet at the same time Britain is a country 'that reaches out. That turns its face to the world . . .' The prime foundation of the EU in British eyes 'is the single market rather than the single currency'. Member states of the EU have a commitment to 'lay the foundations of an ever closer union among the peoples of Europe'. The UK, he said, respects the wish of others to pursue this goal, but for Britain – 'and perhaps for others' – it is not the objective. Cameron acknowledged that the eurozone at this point must go its own way, involving 'much closer economic and political integration'. Yet Britain 'would never embrace that goal' or

join the euro. The country will seek to negotiate a new settle-
ment with the rest of the EU, allowing it to pursue a different
path from most, or even all, other member states. There will be
a referendum within a specified time-period to give the people
the chance to decide.

As the response from across Europe to his speech showed,
Cameron's conception of the future of the EU, with the single
market as its defining feature, is not shared by other EU members. Even the leaders of states ordinarily thought to be close to
the UK, such as Denmark or Sweden, gave the prime minister's
speech only a muted response. There is probably no other
member state that sees the EU, in Cameron's words, as 'a means
to an end' and 'not an end in itself'. A large part of the motivation for the speech was an attempt to neutralise, or placate, the
Eurosceptics within the Tory Party. It had little success in this
respect.

The current situation leaves everyone with difficult dilemmas. Should the UK decide to try to veto changes needed to
push through necessary eurozone reforms, it will meet with a
furious response from other member states. Yet the EU itself
would be diminished were one of its largest member states
simply to up sticks and leave. Of course, the issue might be
fudged. Some kind of patchwork deal might be made. The
British could claim they got much of what they wanted; the
rest of the EU could maintain that the line was held against
the UK's demands. However, such a situation would not seem
to be in anyone's best interests. Britain would remain the awk-
ward, carping partner – part of the EU, while distancing itself
from the direction of development the Union is compelled to
follow for its survival.

It looked at one time as though the UK might be able to be
a leader among the substantial group of 'outs' – the member
states outside the eurozone. Such a situation has not material-
ised. The outs are in fact a less unified group than the eurozone
'ins'. There are three different categories of outs. The majority

are 'pre-ins'. In other words, they are obliged in due course to adopt the euro, and most intend to live up to that obligation. It is in their interests to track developments within the eurozone, modify their policies accordingly and participate fully in relevant meetings and agreements wherever they can. Two other states have a more ambiguous position – the above-mentioned states, Denmark and Sweden. Like the UK, Denmark has an opt-out from the euro. Yet its currency is pegged to it. Denmark is therefore 'a de-facto euro country with national coins'.[39] The country has signed up to the Fiscal Compact. Sweden is in a different position again. It has come through the financial crisis in good shape and is in no mood at the moment to contemplate eurozone membership; yet it has no opt-out. The British government stands alone in its declaration that the country will never join the euro, that a new deal has to be fashioned specifically tailored to British interests, and that there will be a referendum on EU membership within a specified period.

So what to do? I accept that the UK should at some point hold an in/out referendum. The decision will be the most momentous the country will have taken for the past half a century. It has to be preceded by an open and informed public debate, in which both sides spell out in an extensive and grounded way the implications of their views. Putting a specific time-limit on when it should take place, as Mr Cameron has done, is surely a mistake so far as the interests of the country are concerned. The worst thing that could happen is that a government – any government – should be rushed into a referendum for internal party reasons. I shall not try to detail here the arguments on both sides.[40] Much will depend in any case upon the fate of the euro and how the EU evolves from this point on. Supposing a new Europe can be built, I believe that the UK would be better off politically, economically and culturally inside looking out rather than outside looking in. Yet, if it is comprehensive, a debate on the issue could be of value in and of itself. It should then become clear to Britons that what is at stake is not only EU membership as such, but what kind of nation Britain should be. In other words, should the country leave, a new and forward-looking identity would have to be forged.

I see no reason why whatever entity remains should not survive in good shape outside the Union, although in world terms it will be much diminished. Comparisons with Norway and Switzerland are vacuous. If any such comparisons are to be made at all, a better analogy might be Canada. Canada is a prosperous nation living in the shadow of a vastly more powerful neighbour. So far it has managed to contain its own internal divisions. Its economy is heavily dependent upon that of the US and its average standard of living only somewhat lower. Canada has a significant diplomatic presence on the international stage and has a positive image in many parts of the world. It is a member of NATO. It is also a member of the Commonwealth, for some the main organisation to which Britain would turn on leaving the European Union. The country would hope to have a larger influence than Canada because it is bigger in terms of population and because of the residues of its historic role in the world, such as its permanent membership of the UN Security Council. Yet a substantial part of rebuilding the nation after leaving the Union would have to be looking beyond those residues. Withdrawal would undoubtedly place the country under extreme pressure as regards its seat on the Security Council and would deprive Britain of allies willing to support its continuation. Scotland would almost certainly seek another vote on leaving the UK; and this time would very likely opt to do so.

The transatlantic relationship would become diminished, although it would not disappear. The United States would necessarily negotiate directly with the European Union on almost all significant matters. If a free trade agreement is set up between the United States and the EU, leading to a broader partnership, an independent Britain would have to negotiate special terms for itself, a process that could pose serious difficulties. The City of London could not expect to retain its level of influence if Britain leaves Europe, but in terms of the balance of the economy that might not be a bad thing.

Britain would have to do what most of the Eurosceptics propose, although usually in only a vague way – develop its trading connections with the emerging economies. To do so, however, it would have to up its level of competitiveness and become less insular and addicted to tradition than is true at the moment. A more cosmopolitan and outward-looking attitude would be an imperative. Immigration would become more rather than less important, both statistically and in terms of its economic value to the country. It is not an unattractive vision and one grounded in contemporary realities. At least some of those who advocate withdrawal from the EU have this sort of future for Britain in mind. Most Eurosceptics, however, are thinking of something very different. They have an image of the future in which Britain somehow retains most of its current influence – or, indeed, achieves more. Their outlook is driven by nostalgia for a lost past rather than by the realities of the present. It is up to them to show how a country that has severed its direct involvement in the EU, and whose closeness to the US will thereby suffer, can still act like some sort of great power.

What sort of EU will emerge from the crisis will be unclear for some while. It is only sensible for Britain to wait until some sort of reasonably permanent solution is reached. After all, EU-wide referendums will have to be held at some point anyway. The country will confront a more integrated Union and should decide on that basis where its future lies. One way or another, at the appropriate point the uneasy relationship of Britain with the rest of the EU must be clarified.

Chapter 2
Austerity and After

Europe's economic woes have to be understood against a wide backdrop. The economic downturn, already in existence for more than five years, is plainly not just cyclical but the result of much deeper trends. Remedies have to be of equivalent scope. Virtually all of the industrial countries are being forced to make substantial adjustments to their economies. Conventional economic thinking seems to be floundering, having been complicit in creating the very crisis that is proving so obdurate. The debate about austerity versus stimulus investment is important and consequential but seems, in some large part, a replay of controversies from many years ago. The world economy is massively different now. To a large extent we are in don't know territory. No one knows whether the industrialised world will return to steady growth, take another leap forward or lapse into stagnation. The same applies to the global economy, which at a minimum needs substantial rebalancing.

How can the EU states, especially those that are most beleaguered at the moment, best chart a path back to growth and prosperity? Plans and proposals abound. Some authors, for example, have suggested a reworked version of the Marshall

Plan, so crucial to Europe's development after the Second World War. The Marshall Plan, however, was largely funded by the United States government. No source of such largesse exists today. Moreover no single programme, no matter how big, is going to make much dent on the deeply embedded problems faced in the EU. Action will have to happen on a variety of fronts, from the local to the transnational. A good deal of innovative thinking will be needed. What form should such thinking take?

The questions discussed in the previous chapter are highly relevant to this one. Progress with banking and fiscal union is of vital importance. If the banks are not properly recapitalised and sovereign risk curbed, credit for investment will continue to be stifled. German acceptance of mutuality is essential for renewing economic progress within the eurozone. Germany moved within a few years from being the sick man of Europe to becoming its star performer in part because of wage restraints and labour market reforms enacted under Gerhard Schröder. Yet it has also been helped by its membership of the euro, from which it gains disproportionately. The southern countries must reform, and most are doing so under EU2 pressure. Some are at real risk now of sinking into oblivion, however, if austerity is not complemented by investment. A return to growth is obligatory, given the levels of debt that the EU states have. Yet growth is not an end in itself: its quality and distribution are crucial. Empty homilies about sustainable growth will not do. A return to growth must be reconciled with reductions in carbon emissions, a testing issue given the limited progress that has been made so far within the EU. Moreover, the price of energy at the moment risks damaging the competitiveness of the EU states. Somehow that circle needs to be squared. Lopsided growth is no good either. Growth limited to a fraction of the population is of no social or economic value. Correcting the inequalities that have emerged at the very top is now directly related to regenerating economic prosperity – or so I shall argue.

Given the very high levels of unemployment, a prerequisite in the EU is the creation of net new jobs. In other words, far more jobs must be created than disappear at any one point in time. Since the current economic difficulties are structural, it follows that such jobs cannot be created in sufficient volume only by a renewal of demand and a strengthening of purchasing power. Interventionism, led by EU2, is required to further necessary reforms and help promote investment. Spending on infrastructure at a European level can play a part in stimulating growth and can have both short- and longer-term multiplier effects. The EU should work at setting up policies to generate such investment, the large bulk of which will have to come from private sources. The same applies at the other end of the scale – to the small and medium-sized enterprises which make up most of Europe's productive capacity. Trade with the emerging economies offers great opportunities for the EU states and can at the same time help promote development in poorer countries. After all, most of the growth in the world economy over the past two or three decades came from the non-industrialised world. Yet there are many more problems here than might appear at first sight. We cannot assume that the trends will be the same over the next few years as they were in the past. Moreover, unless the poorer-performing EU states improve their productivity and overall competitiveness, the eurozone will not retain even its current market share. 'The world does not owe us a living!' It is a reminder that might well be posted in offices and workshops across Europe.

The debate about reindustrialisation that has sprung up in the United States has to be taken seriously in Europe too, even if its outcome is as yet uncertain. Like the US, Europe has some major strengths in manufacturing, with the German economy in the forefront. Yet a return to making things more generally is a goal to be striven for. Deindustrialisation should not be regarded as an inevitable and irreversible phenomenon. Most growth will still come from the service industries. However, there are some remarkable trends in process. The distinction between manufacturing and service industries is breaking down, potentially a change of momentous proportions. Reform of institutions outside of the economy will be integral to any foreseeable growth scenario. Obvious examples are education, research and development, welfare, pensions, and improving the efficiency and responsiveness of public institutions. Immigration policy is not marginal to Europe's future prosperity but central to it. The reason is that it overlaps with so many other areas of importance. The difficulties the EU states are having in absorbing large-scale immigration could pose a threat to the stability of welfare and educational systems, as well as to wider feelings of solidarity. The arrival of Muslims in large numbers has been a source of major tension. Hostility to immigration has been especially pronounced since the coming of the crisis. Yet, without a continuing flow of immigration, some of Europe's most difficult problems, such as how to cope with an ageing population, will become worse.

To help secure most of these objectives, advances in international cooperation will be needed. Some of these need to be far-reaching. It is a scandalous indictment of the current world order that at any one time about half the world's liquid capital rests in tax havens, where it escapes taxation and hence translation into social good. Other forms of tax evasion are seriously on the agenda too. Changes in these areas that not long ago seemed impossible to achieve are now becoming well advanced. The proposed free trade agreement between the EU and the United States could be a major source of job and wealth creation. So also, in a less far-reaching way, could such an agreement with Japan, currently in the works.

In this chapter I focus only on some of the issues listed above. The remainder are covered in other parts of the book. I begin with the austerity debate and consider EU1 strategies for growth. There is quite a bit of paper Europe around here. In the real world there is a puzzling tangle of influences to deal

with, including the likely effects of the extraordinary pace of
technological change today. I shall then look at attempts in the
United States to rebalance the economy and examine whether
they could apply in Europe. I call this 'bringing back the jobs'.
But we have to 'bring back the money' too – that is, recover
resources that are urgently needed for domestic spending
and investment, as well as to begin to redress the problem of
extreme inequality.

THE IMPACT OF AUSTERITY

The debate about austerity is unfolding not only in Europe
but across the industrialised world. In the light of the factors
mentioned above, however, we have to go a long way beyond
it if a return to prosperity is to be achieved. It has become the
new conventional wisdom to conclude that austerity measures
in Europe have failed. Some have spoken of 'the austerity delu-
sion'.[1] The picture is more mixed than that. Austerity is not just
economic but political. It should not be embraced as a permanent
condition, but as a short-term strategy it was probably unavoid-
able. A country cannot go on borrowing if its creditors refuse
to lend any more. The point of austerity, in the context of the
EU countries today, was not just to bring the books into closer
balance but to help enforce change and reform, partly through
its very shock value. Austerity is like a bitter medicine, unpleas-
ant to the taste and with disagreeable side-effects.[2] Taking the
medicine is vital to counteract the disease but will not produce
a healthy patient unless combined with a range of other cura-
tive measures, including a large amount of self-discipline and
changes in habits for the future. It is crucial to get the dosage
right, as too large an amount could kill the patient it is supposed
to save. Once a corner has been turned, the nature of the treatment should change and focus upon active rehabilitation.

Does the metaphor hold in present-day Europe? The *Euro
Plus Monitor*, produced annually by the think-tank the Lisbon

Council and the Berenberg Bank, helps make a judgement. It offers a detailed analysis of how the European economies are faring. The research covers the seventeen members of the euro-zone plus the UK, Sweden and Poland. Two scales are used. The first assesses how far structural reforms are advancing under the pressure of austerity programmes. The second set of measures assesses the overall economic health of the countries concerned.

The findings are important and revealing. The changes going on are 'uneven and subject to serious risks'. Yet significant progress is being made more or less across the board. The countries that most needed reforms are pursuing them, in some cases at impressive speed. The eurozone states which received large-scale external financial support – Greece, Ireland, Portugal and Spain – all show accelerated change over the course of the year. Greece is at the top in terms of progress in structural adjustment, Ireland is in second place, Spain at number four, with Portugal in fifth position (Estonia is ranked third). In the words of the report, 'the countries that need to shape up fast are doing so'. There is one exception among the eurozone countries and it is a significant one: France, which lags behind and whose competitive position is worsening.[3] Hence what the Lisbon Agenda (see below) failed to achieve – economic convergence – is taking place. The recession, which has seriously reduced demand, has obscured the underlying progress made. Wage costs are converging most rapidly of all. Real wage costs have dropped substantially in Greece, Ireland, Portugal and Spain. They have risen in countries where previously they were constrained – most notably, Germany. These results show that 'serious structural adjustments can happen – and are happening – within the confines of monetary union.'

The ranking of member states in terms of overall economic health looks very different from that measuring the dynamics of change. Two tiny countries, Estonia and Luxembourg, rank at the top, followed by Germany, Sweden and the Netherlands. Greece comes out bottom, with Portugal just above and Spain

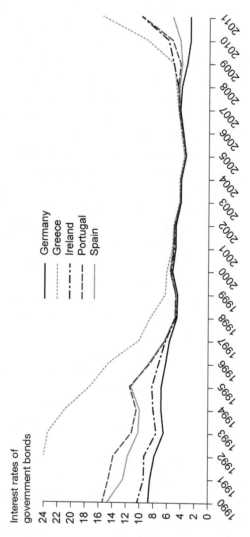

Figure 6 The effect of the euro on borrowing

Source: OECD; Armin Schäfer and Wolfgang Streeck (eds): *Politics in the Age of Austerity.* Cambridge: Polity, 2013.

and Ireland somewhat higher. Italy and also France rank low down. The UK is an undistinguished performer on both of the measures used, even if its growth rate has now picked up. Very serious problems remain. Greece in particular risks going into a 'death spiral' because harsh austerity programmes have hit a country very ill-prepared to endure them. The substantial progress made in highly adverse circumstances has not stopped an increase in Greece's debt-to-GDP ratio. In GDP terms, the Greek economy has contracted by a quarter over the past five years. Greece needs to be treated by the EU as a special case. (The Country Report on Greece published by the IMF in January 2013 speaks in similar terms.)[4] It is time to turn towards renewed investment, the study concludes, for which the austerity has painfully prepared the ground.

THE FINGER IN THE DYKE

The conclusion is surely correct, although the report does not expand upon it or suggest what strategy Greece might follow. Greece produces less than 2 per cent of the EU's GDP. I concentrate here on that country, rather than the larger economies in trouble such as Spain or Italy, for good reason. A return to growth in Greece is of far more than merely emblematic importance. It is the finger in the dyke so far as the eurozone, and therefore the rest of Europe, is concerned. A Greek exit from the euro could possibly be managed without disastrous consequences (see the Conclusion), but no one can be sure. If Greece returns even to a semblance of prosperity within short order, and manages to maintain reasonable political stability, it will be a turning point of major importance for Europe as a whole. Before 2008, Greece was a high-growth society, or appeared to be one. Over the first six years after the country joined the euro in 2002, its growth rates were well above the EU average, and in fact higher than that of the United States. Yet virtually all of that economic expansion was the result of increased spending by government and consumers, consequent upon low interest rates. Private consumption in Greece was fully 20 per cent higher than the EU average, while demand remained very largely domestic. Even industries which could have been mainly export driven, notably tourism, were oriented primarily towards domestic consumption.[5] Spending by the state sector was based upon ever increasing levels of public debt.

When George Papandreou became prime minister in 2009, he asked one of his advisers, 'How many public servants do we have?' No one knew the answer. He commissioned a census to discover the number, which turned out to be not far short of 1 million – out of a total population of fewer than 12 million.[6] (The number has been reduced by some 200,000 to date, with further cuts to come.) Greek productivity was very low – 29 per cent below the EU-15 average in 2009 and 40 per cent below that of the US. The country also had one of the lowest rates of people in work in Europe. Youth unemployment was high even before the current period. Until very recently, civil servants in Greece were constitutionally guaranteed jobs for life, the result of an archaic law designed to stop them being dismissed for political reasons. Greece had one of the most regulated economies in the EU, its rigid labour market restrictions being one of the main reasons for the high level of young people out of work. The country was dogged by clientelism and by tax evasion which stretched from top to bottom of the society.

Against this unpromising background, progress over the past five years has been quite dramatic. The IMF concurs with the Lisbon Council's findings in this respect. According to the IMF, fiscal adjustment has proceeded very rapidly compared to parallel historical examples elsewhere. Greece is on track to reach a primary balance.[7] In other words, before interest payments are included, spending will be equivalent to revenue. Imports have been reduced very substantially. Competitiveness still lags well behind the best-performing EU states but has greatly improved from its low base.

Taxation revenues remain a major sticking point. Improvements have been made in tax collection from workers whose salaries are reported by their employers. Yet levels of taxation from the self-employed remain small as compared with the EU-15 average – and the self-employed sector is large. Tax evasion remains rampant. Some 30 per cent of overall economic activity in Greece is in the secondary economy. That activity provides for some flexibility in an otherwise constrained labour market, but it creates a huge hole in tax revenues. Estimates suggest that some €15 to 20 billion of tax revenue is lost every year, amounting to about 9 per cent of GDP. That sum comprises fully 80 per cent of the fiscal deficit, perhaps even more.

The extensive changes that have been made should help provide a springboard for a return of private investment. On their own, however, they are clearly not enough, and many people are without a job or even the prospect of getting one. There should be an EU2-driven investment plan for Greece, accompanied by strict conditionality, as is the case with the bailouts. Like the bailouts, it is in the wider European interest and would do a lot to dampen the antagonism that has developed between Greece and Germany at the level of citizens. The question of Germany paying reparations for its deeds in Greece during the Second World War has been raised in Greece in a serious way. According to media reports, the Greek government has put together a secret document concerned with the question.[8] It sets out a claim to €108 billion for damage caused during the occupation, plus €54 billion for an enforced 'loan' that Greece was obliged to make to Germany during the war. The affair has raised strong feelings on both sides, although it has been discussed openly in Germany as well as in Greece.[9]

It is very unlikely indeed that such an idea would receive official German endorsement. Instead, further German assistance to Greece should be based upon public acceptance by German leaders of shared concerns. It is in the German interest, and in the interest of the EU as a whole, that a tangible measure of hope returns to Greece. Greece needs further external help not just in terms of investment, but in the form of guidance and back-up in the further promotion of reforms. Reform should not, and beyond a certain point cannot, be driven by cost-cutting measures, even if these must continue. Further cutbacks in the public sector, for example, are imperative; but they should be coupled to best-practice reform too, in order to professionalise and update the system. It makes sense to fund such interventions, as well as others that complement structural reforms. If the 'death spiral' of which the report of the Lisbon Council speaks becomes real, the consequences will be felt right across the continent.

Greece at this point has to become a more outward-looking nation. It must attract foreign capital as well as radically raise its level of productivity. There are encouraging developments in each of these areas. Thus, after years of procrastination, Greece has got its privatisation programme under way. That programme has struck a variety of problems but is in fact attracting foreign investors to bring money into the country. 'We have to transmit the message that this is a different Greece', the development minister Kostis Hatzidakis said, and quite rightly so. The aim, he continued, is to start to internationalise Greece and turn it into an outward-looking country rather than one turned in on itself.[10] As we know from the experience of many countries, privatisation is far from being a universal panacea. All privatisations should be judged in terms of longer-term strategic implications as well as immediate economic returns. It is yet another concern that could be covered by a strategic plan worked out jointly between Greece and the EU.

Greece must outperform the EU average by a significant margin over the next decade if the country is to be brought back to prosperity, since it starts from such a low base. At this point 'fiscal shock' needs to be complemented by activism, encouraged and supported from the outside. Alongside the despair and resentment, there are signs that such activism is springing up in

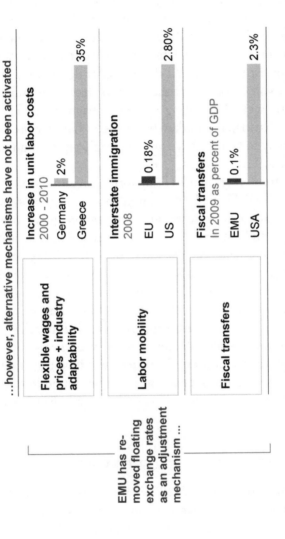

Figure 7 EMU lacks the adjustment mechanisms necessary to compensate for the loss of exchange rate flexibility

Source: European Commission; Eurostat; OECD; US Census Bureau; Tax Foundation; Bureau of Economic Analysis.

Greece, and it is just the sort of transformation that should be further promoted by outside help. Changes in mind-set do seem to be occurring. They are visible, for instance, in the key area of tourism. The number of tourists who visited Greece in 2014 was the highest ever recorded – an estimated 18 million people, one and a half times the population of the country. Many working in the tourist trade say that the events of the past few years have made them conscious of the need to change and upgrade their performance. The lifting of visa restrictions on visitors from China, Russia and Turkey has helped. Summer bookings from Germany to Greece have grown steeply after slumping in previous years.[11]

What, in brief, might an EU-supported investment plan for Greece look like? It would be geared to upping performance in the public and private sectors through target-linked professional advice and help – a more extensive version of what is happening at the moment. An absolutely basic area is tax evasion. Action on tax havens, discussed later in the chapter, would be a major contribution to this question, given the large number of Greek citizens who hold offshore accounts. The EU could seek to ensure that these are properly traced. Financial help, coupled to reform, for small and medium-sized firms could be a major stimulus to recovery. Infrastructure investment, especially in energy and transportation, could be slotted into wider schemes concerned with promoting growth across Europe more generally.[12]

STRATEGIES FOR GROWTH

The Commission's *Europe 2020* initiative sets out goals to be achieved in Europe by that year and includes a diversity of reforms designed to increase the competitiveness of the EU states. It replaces the Lisbon Strategy, more often called the Lisbon Agenda, drawn up in the city of that name in 2000. The Lisbon Agenda was supposed to make the EU 'the most

competitive and dynamic knowledge-based economy in the
world by 2010' – an aspiration that, to put it mildly, fell somewhat short of reality. *Europe 2020* sets out five 'headline targets'
for the EU as a whole to be achieved by 2020, plus seven 'flagship initiatives'. The targets are:

Employment – 75 per cent of 20- to 64-year-olds to be in work
Research and Development – a minimum of 3 per cent of EU
  GDP invested
Climate Change/Energy – greenhouse gas emissions reduced
  by 20 per cent over 1990 levels, going to 30 per cent if the
  conditions are right
Education – early rates of school leaving reduced to below 10
  per cent; at least 30 per cent of 30- to 34-year-olds having
  completed higher education
Poverty and Social Exclusion – at least 20 million fewer people
  in or at risk of poverty than in 2010.

The seven flagship initiatives are all about growth. They are
ordered in terms of achieving 'smart', 'sustainable' and 'inclusive' growth. *Europe 2020* is concerned to remedy long-term
structural weaknesses, but also to integrate these with manag-
ing the impact of the crisis. To complement them and promote
fiscal discipline, they are linked to national targets coordinated
through the European Semester.

The term 'smart growth' is an odd one. It turns out that it isn't
the growth as such that's smart. The Commission means that
growth needs smart people and smart strategies, as indicated in
the headline goals. 'Smart growth' means upgrading education
and innovation, R&D, and information and communications
technologies. Not much to quibble about there. 'Sustainability'
is a notoriously elusive term, and I shall have more to say about
it below (chapter 5). The main point I would make here is that
'smartness' and 'sustainability' should not be thought of sepa-
rately. How smart we are – our ability to innovate – will greatly

affect what sustainability, both economic and environmental, actually means. 'Inclusive growth' is defined by the Commission in wide terms. It means generating high levels of employment; getting more women into the labour force; doing the same for older people, but also for the young, whose levels of unemployment since 2008 have climbed steeply; reducing levels of poverty; and spreading growth more evenly across the nations and regions of the Union. Wide though the definition might be, it is still not wide enough. We must also include the issue of reducing inequalities at the top. Inclusiveness at the bottom is not sufficient – more about that later.

The single market, the Commission says, must essentially be relaunched. It can make a vital contribution to further job creation and growth. 'Current trends show signs of integration fatigue and disenchantment', partly prompted by the crisis.[13] There are still residual blockages to cross-border activity. In some cases companies have to deal with twenty-eight different legal systems for one set of transactions. The single market was designed before the arrival of the internet. New digital services offer a great deal of potential, but the current situation is one of fragmentation. The Services Directive is far from having been fully implemented.

In formal terms *Europe 2020* is admirably detailed and wide-ranging. Yet like the Lisbon Agenda, although it is called a 'strategy', it isn't one. Almost all the lengthy document in which it is outlined is about the what, not the how. Reflecting as it does the limitations of EU1, it looks eerily like the lapsed Lisbon process – high ambition with little means of realising its goals. This situation is disturbing, because its failure wasn't just a paper Europe matter. It was one of the root causes of the current crisis. In a detailed analysis of the Lisbon Agenda the commission has had to admit that it didn't meet any of its main targets. Of the positive changes that did occur, up to 2008 at least, it is more or less impossible to say whether or not they would have happened anyway, since they were concentrated

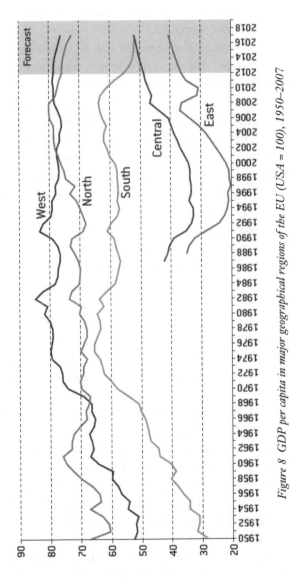

Figure 8 GDP per capita in major geographical regions of the EU (USA = 100), 1950–2007

Source: Zsolt Darvas: *The Euro Crisis: Ten Roots, but Fewer Solutions.* Bruegel Policy Contribution, October 2012.

mostly in the *avant-garde* states rather than among the poorer performers. The Commission says there is evidence that the Agenda played a significant role in promoting reforms, but no such evidence is actually supplied.[14]

More precise coordination between the EU member states in the Semester is helpful pending greater fiscal integration, but the core problem so far as growth is concerned is the same as in the case of the Lisbon Strategy. There are no effective sanctions to ensure movement in the right direction among laggard states. The only one is a clause saying that countries which don't meet the stated criteria can be fined. Yet the fine starts gradually and is set at a maximum of 0.5 per cent of GDP. It is unlikely to have much of a deterrent effect because there is some doubt as to whether it would ever be used, given political sensitivities among member states. It would increase the debt of bailout states. Moreover, it is an open question whether any country subject to it would actually pay up. It is EU2 that will determine progress, certainly so far as the struggling states are concerned.

As the Commission emphasises, there is still a great deal of potential for growth in services. The Western economies will certainly remain service-dominated. I shall argue that special prominence must be given to a resurgence of manufacture. To leave that statement as it stands, however, is to miss some of the most significant changes now occurring. Under the influence of the internet, and of digitalisation more generally, as mentioned earlier, the boundaries between manufacturing and service industries are breaking down. Digital technologies and other innovations are transforming what 'manufacture' and 'services' actually mean. The term most often used to refer to the digital world – information and communication technology – no longer really works. I prefer that of digital technologies (DT), since digitalisation underlies not only information and communications systems but our capability to intervene into the natural world. It is what makes possible, for example, the convergence of nanotechnology, biotechnology and information science now happening, and which is likely to have far-reaching consequences for our lives.[15]

THE COMING TRANSFORMATION OF MANUFACTURE AND SERVICES

Ann Mettler and Anthony Williams have written one of the best accounts of the opportunities these extraordinary innovations will have – are already having – for small and medium-sized enterprises (SMEs).[16] 99 per cent of EU businesses, in fact, are classified as SMEs. 90 per cent are micro-enterprises employing ten or fewer people. The coming of DT has the potential to revolutionise such businesses in Europe and indeed across the world. Smaller firms can make use of online business platforms to tap into pools of global talent, source new services and at the same time create them – all on a level of sophistication once available only to much larger firms. SMEs are in many ways the key to Europe's recovery. Up to now, however, as measured in global terms they have been relatively poor performers. Europe's familiar labour market troubles crop up again here. Thus a study of Portugal concluded that labour market restrictions were in large part responsible for the poor performance of the country's SMEs. SMEs necessarily live in a more volatile economic environment than larger companies. Labour market restrictions in Portugal both inhibit small business start-ups and mean that SMEs can't react quickly enough to changes in economic conditions. For this reason, even many successful ones decide to stay small when they could expand further and internationalise.[17]

Digital technology can't stand in for reforms that need to be made, but it can and does foster an altogether different level of dynamism. Studies show that the start-up cost of an average internet company fell tenfold between 1997 and 2008. The main reason is the availability of cloud computing and open source materials. Some of these make possible functions that once had to be performed by entire departments in traditional larger companies. And, of course, on the internet a company is connected from its first initiation to a global network of companies and potential customers. R&D capabilities can be licensed at a tiny fraction of the cost it would take for a company to set them up. DT has been shown to increase productivity more than any other single type of investment a firm can make.

Mettler and Williams suggest that the creation of a digital single market could make a decisive contribution to sustained economic recovery. The adoption of DT is not a niche issue but one that affects the whole of the economy. Even where DT is not central to their business model, companies small and large depend upon high-quality digital services to be competitive. Getting a single digital market under way could help the wider single market become more successful. Thus some 50 per cent of retailers in the EU offer online service for the purchase of their goods. Yet only just over 20 per cent of them sell their products in another EU state or states. Vital for the EU economy at this point is the creation of high-speed broadband, using super-fast fibre networks rather than the existing copper ones. Targets are given in the *Europe 2020* programme. One is that, by 2020, at least half of all connections should be super-fast ones. Once again the ambition is there, but there is a long way to go. At present only 2 per cent of connections are made using fibre, a much lower proportion than in the US and some of the Asian countries.

The amount of public money available for such projects is strictly limited, especially at a European level. Moreover, lending by banks is also at something of a historic low. Private investment more generally has been undermined by the string of reverses suffered by the European economies. The decline in such investment since 2007 has been twenty times greater than that in private consumption.[18] In the EU-27 countries over

the period from 2007 to 2011, private investment dropped by
€354 billion, a very much larger sum than in the state sector,
where the decline amounted to €12 billion. The phenomenon
is not confined to Europe but is visible across the industrialised
world since 2007. The drop in Europe has roughly matched
that in the US and Japan. From 2007 to 2011, investment in
the EU-27 states decreased by 15 per cent. These changes were
unevenly spread across the EU countries. A substantial proportion of the total is accounted for by Spain, Portugal, Greece and
Ireland, since those countries experienced property booms that
turned to bust. In Spain, investment fell by 27 per cent over the
period in question. In Portugal the figure was 34 per cent, for
Greece it was 47 per cent and for Ireland 64 per cent. However,
both the UK and France also suffered large declines in private
investment.

A study of a range of prior episodes where GDP fell in real
terms, and where private investment decreased by 10 per cent
or more, confirms that the current situation is quite unprecedented.[19] Private investment normally has played a major role
in economic recovery in the past but this time is not doing so.
In some countries, such as Spain, households ran up substantial
levels of debt even before 2007 and still are spending only very
cautiously. There is no way that governments can step into the
gap, given that in many cases they are obligated to reduce their
deficits. Nor are exports likely to be able to make the needed
impact, at least in the short term. The analysis of earlier episodes of economic decline indicates that, in the past, private
investment has driven about a third of growth when recovery
began. Following that period it returns to the 'normal' level of
about a quarter. The average recovery time in the past was five
years. The situation looks different this time, suggesting again
that we are confronting a structural transition, not just another
re-run of the past.

Converging with the analysis offered by Mettler and
Williams, the authors of *Europe 2020* conclude that, alongside

wider investments, what is needed is targeted activism on the micro-economic level. In the past, attempts at intervention have been ineffective because they were not grounded in local detail and in systematic research. Some of the barriers to private investment are regulatory. Others, however, are more intrinsic to the sector or context in question. Policy measures must be developed based upon a solid and clear factual base. In-depth understanding is needed of areas in which investment can be productive. Government departments or agencies should col-laborate actively with the private sector to specify best options, with clear accountability for delivery. Examples of best practice from around the world should be deployed. Where will the money to invest come from? Well, as of 2011, listed European companies were sitting on €750 billion of excess cash holdings. Most are looking to invest when they deem the conditions right. Macro-economic reform plainly must continue, since continued instability creates such an adverse investment cli-mate. However, unlocking opportunities at local level to attract capital investment is massively important.

DIGITAL PRODUCTION

The division between the digital universe – the universe of the computer – and the real world is becoming dissolved, an historic moment in the evolution of technology. The role of the com-puter used to be to design goods and production processes. Now computers can be used to fabricate them directly. 3D printers can already print a diversity of objects, including organic ones. Digital production can be expected to move far beyond the printers that exist at the moment, extraordinary as they are, and is converging with developments in nanotechnology and biotechnology.

There is a direct connection with SMEs. Some observers and practitioners speak of a return to artisanal production – small workshops rising again, perhaps in immense numbers across the world, to rival the large factories or even supplant most of them. The possibility has been likened to the shift from mainframe to personal computers. 3D printers at the moment can't even approach the economies of scale offered by mass manufacturing techniques. However the future might also lie with a merging of the older and newer techniques of production. It has been said that concentrating on 3D printers is like those in the 1950s who argued that microwave ovens were the future of cooking. The real revolution is the ability to 'turn data into things and things into data'.[20] Chris Anderson quotes the case of the Tesla car factory in Fremont, California.[21] The shopfloor is heavily robotised. High-tech electric cars are produced there, but the factory can be reconfigured to make almost anything. It has come as close as anywhere so far to realising the possibility of 'mass customisation' – every detail of the car can be modified at will to form the finished product. Since the vehicle is made within the factory, the long inventory chains needed by orthodox manufacturers do not exist. As Anderson puts it, the factory 'fabricates what it needs, when it needs it'.[22]

There is a large net gain in terms of carbon reduction because of a dramatic fall in transportation costs. The Tesla factory replaced a GM/Toyota unit which had to close down because of lack of orders. It is a robotised factory but created a thousand new jobs in ancillary services. The robots, incidentally, are made in Germany. Elon Musk, the CEO, has set the company the ambition of producing electric cars on a mass scale. The firm has now expanded to 3,000 employees, has a branch in the UK, and has begun to sell to international markets. It has also begun collaborations with Mercedes to work on electric versions of some of the latter's range of small cars, including the two-seater Smart car. Digital manufacturing companies already exist in numbers in Europe but are poised to make a very much larger impact in the future, even the near future. The sophistication of the technology available already makes small business start-ups easy. The companies are built up through the web and use its resources to speed development and cheapen the cost of marketing. They are in an important sense already competing on the global stage, so it is more difficult for imports to undermine them than is the case with traditional companies. Digital manufacture also converges with the wider processes promoting reshoring (see below) – not having to deal with complicated supply chains and the interruptions to which they can be subject, closeness to the customer, ease of checking on product quality, and so forth.

As in so many of the transformations discussed in this book, these developments are surrounded by uncertainties – key issues that won't be fully resolved until the changes still in their infancy become generalised and radicalised. If the example of mobile phones is an analogue, this process could unfold very rapidly, so it is essential for the EU states to ride the wave of change rather than stand aside from it. What will the impact of advances in robotics be upon unemployment? The evidence from economic history shows that technological innovation tends overall to create more jobs than it destroys. Will the impact of robotics be different? Some argue so.[23] Machines now can perform tasks once thought purely the province of human beings – for instance, the understanding of everyday language. They could become capable of taking over not just mundane tasks, or specialised treatments as in medicine, but also some of the work that professionals do. So far, however, the evidence indicates that, because of spin-offs and changes in lifestyle patterns that have been produced, robotics has created net new jobs.[24]

BRINGING BACK THE JOBS?

Reshoring is the opposite of offshoring. There are two senses in which such a process is particularly relevant to this chapter. Can jobs that have migrated overseas be brought back? The second, equally important, is can the huge amounts of free-floating capital that now escape taxation be brought under democratic control? I call these two processes bringing back the jobs and bringing back the money, but of course neither phrase should be taken too literally.

The debate about the reshoring of manufacture has one of its main points of origin in the US, in the work of the Boston Consulting Group (BCG). In 2011, the BCG published the first of a series of reports, entitled *Made in America, Again*.[25] It carried the subtitle 'Why Manufacturing Will Return to the U.S.'. Its authors, led by Harold Sirkin, argue that a variety of economic forces are reducing, or eliminating, the advantages of China over the US as a location for manufacture. Wages have increased quite steeply for Chinese workers, while for their counterparts in the US they have remained largely stagnant. The costs for transporting goods across the world are significant and may increase further if oil prices stay high. Long and complex delivery chains are vulnerable to disruption. Firms operating in the emerging economies find it hard to protect patents. They have to hire staff in the country of origin to supervise production and ensure that standards are maintained.

The increasing use of automation in China won't preserve its cost advantage but may in fact further undermine it, because such techniques can be reproduced or bettered in the US. Chinese demand is likely to rise, creating a large domestic market and reducing the need to export. It is indeed highly important for China's future prosperity that it does. Manufacturing is unlikely to shift from China to other areas such as Vietnam, Indonesia or Mexico because they lack adequate infrastructure and a skilled workforce. Moreover, they present even greater dangers for intellectual property rights than China ordinarily does. Chinese manufacture will continue to grow, they say, precisely because it will be devoted to serving a rapidly expanding internal market. In a subsequent study the BCG identifies seven sectors in which production is likely to shift back to the US in the near future.[26] Interestingly, the authors include several relatively low-tech as well as high-tech areas. They include the transportation of goods; computers and electronics; fabricated metal products; machinery; plastics and rubber; electrical appliances and equipment; and furniture.

The chief executive of General Electric, Jeff Immelt, has called offshoring and outsourcing 'yesterday's model'. GE is moving much of its IT work, as well as its production of kitchen goods and heaters, back to the US.[27] The same is happening in some service industries – for example, with call centres. There are other factors involved besides strictly economic ones. Political pressure has played a part, together with a new sense of responsibility to the customer. Many have complained that those answering lack the local knowledge needed for a properly personal service. The BCG anticipates that 2 to 3 million net new jobs could be added to the US economy in a relatively short period, representing $100 billion in annual output. The jobs will not come mainly from the actual manufacturing processes themselves but from supporting services. The trend will be not only for American manufacturers to relocate, but for foreign companies to move to the US. High productivity is an important factor. If wages are adjusted in terms of productivity, the average worker in the US is about 35 per cent cheaper than a corresponding worker in the EU – a real issue for Europe. According to the BCG, if current trends were to continue, production costs in the US within five years will be 15 per cent below those in Germany, 21 per cent lower than those in Japan and fully 23 per cent lower than those in Italy.

A further key factor in Europe is the price of energy, now well above that of the US, largely because of the shale gas revolution (see chapter 5). Shale gas and oil have not only radically reduced the US's dependency on external sources of energy, they have created jobs too. The steel products used in drilling, recovery and transport of the resources are almost all made in the US. The American steel industry is still struggling, but many now speak of a revival. New investments are being made by overseas companies. The indigenous oil and gas industries are expected to account for about a third of a projected 20 per cent growth in the American steel market over the next five years.[28]

The BCG's work has not gone uncriticised. Loss of manufacturing jobs in the US, critics say, is only partly explained by the movement of companies to lower cost areas. Many manufacturing jobs have disappeared because of the advance of automation. Some deny that reshoring will take place at all. Contrary to what the BCG says, they argue, if production leaves China it might in fact move to other low-cost producers instead of back to the industrial countries. Tim Leunig points out in addition that productivity in China is low compared to that in the US.[29] Three million people are employed in the electronics industry in China. If one-tenth of that output were returned to the United States, China would lose 300,000 jobs, but the net gain to the US would be fewer than 40,000. Because of increasing automation, the proportion of the labour force in manufacturing will continue to fall in all the industrial countries.

What should one make of such arguments? The situation is complex. Automated production destroys jobs within the factory but may create others elsewhere in the economy. One study carried out in the US showed that every job created in manufacturing results on average in the creation of 2.91 additional jobs. In contrast, jobs in business services generated 1.54 other jobs. The figure in the retail trade was only 0.88 extra jobs.[30] Smartphones, for example, are at the centre of an extraordinary range of knock-on products and services. At least part of the industry has moved back to the US already. Moreover, there is good reason to question the idea that manufacture will never again take place in the industrial countries at any level of volume. The pattern of European industry is different from that of the US and the level of interdependency with China less pronounced. Yet reshoring should be seen as a possible contribution to a wider process of reindustrialisation in Europe. A group of civil society organisations recently published a manifesto entitled 'Let's

Reindustrialise Europe'.[31] Antonio Tajani, commissioner for industry and entrepreneurship, has said: 'We cannot continue to let our industry leave Europe', and he is right.[32] In the US, the language of reshoring has already entered into local as well as national policy-making. A series of ads, for example, have appeared in different media sources extolling the virtues of local areas and towns for companies contemplating reshoring. They have mostly come from poorer states in the US – analogous, if you like, to some of the Southern countries in Europe. In the EU, none of this type of activism seems to exist at the moment.

A recent analysis confirmed that the US is well in the lead.[33] The researchers looked at a range of criteria relevant to reindustrialisation in a number of EU countries and the US. Those criteria included industrial production capacity, employment trends in manufacturing, productive investment, market shares in global trade, and the price of gas. Only in the US did the research show clear evidence of reindustrialisation. Some possibilities seemed to be emerging in the UK, notably in employment and investment. In Spain and Portugal, there was a small increase of market shares in global exports but no other indications. In France, Italy and Greece, the study concluded, there were no signs of reindustrialisation at all.

Would reindustrialisation in Europe compromise the carbon reductions targets that the EU has set itself? It might mean readjusting them. At the moment those targets do not include greenhouse gas emissions 'exported' abroad because of the transfer of manufacture away from Europe to other areas of the world. Any manufacturing processes directly drawn back to Europe would therefore be neutral in their implications for world emissions – perhaps a net reduction if the factor of trans-portation were therefore taken out. However, it is also entirely possible that manufacture and investment could be mostly of a low-carbon nature, especially where they are cutting-edge in character. It makes sense, as the Commission proposes, to make energy investment the centrepiece of a direct EU investment strategy. Current EU energy and climate policy, however, needs a radical rethink, as I shall try to show later.

One of the most significant moves relevant to job creation is the resolution of the EU and the US to move to create a transatlantic free trade agreement. It is a form of reshoring, since a substantial proportion of jobs that might otherwise be lost elsewhere can be maintained. The proposals to initiate such an agreement were formally endorsed by the EU and the US in June 2013. An even more ambitious proposal has been mooted on both sides of the Atlantic – that, if a free trade area is successfully established, it should lead to a transatlantic single market, based on the principles already in play in Europe of the free movement of goods, services, capital and people. The most systematic study of the impact of a free trade zone has been carried out by the Bertelsmann Foundation.[34] The results show that a far-reaching trade agreement would have a major impact upon GDP and job creation in both the EU and the US. It would contribute significantly to raising levels of employment in the struggling Southern economies as well as in other parts of Europe. (For further discussion, see Chapter 6.)

BRINGING BACK THE MONEY

Taking action on tax havens, and tax avoidance more generally, is today far more feasible than some years ago. One reason is that, in current economic circumstances, there is greater political will to do so. Another is that it is heavily backed by public opinion. A third, perhaps the most important, is what I have called the rule of transparency. In the era of the internet, secrecy is far harder to maintain in the face of organised scrutiny from political authorities. 'Tax haven' isn't as easy to define as might appear at first sight. Tax havens aren't by any means all small islands or principalities – although some are, and they proliferate within Europe as well as in many other regions. The best definition of a tax haven is a secrecy jurisdiction – a

setting which, by shielding transactions from financial regulation, allows those who take advantage of them to evade taxes or
reduce them to an absolute minimum. Tax havens exist or have
networks in the heart of the EU nations – for example, in the
City of London, which has been termed 'the centre of the most
important part of the global offshore system'.[35]

Research into some seventy secrecy jurisdictions around the
world indicated that they held $21 trillion in assets in 2010.
The Tax Justice Network provides a ranking of the countries
with the largest of such jurisdictions. In 2011, Switzerland (now
coming under increasing international pressure) was number 1,
the US number 5 and Germany number 9. Smaller tax havens in
Europe include the Isle of Man, Guernsey, Jersey, Luxembourg,
Lichtenstein, Monaco, Andorra, Gibraltar, Malta and Cyprus.
The problems encountered in Cyprus in 2013 were close to
damaging the whole eurozone; the country had bank liabilities
many times the national income. Although wealthy individuals
brook large, some of the most complex systems of tax avoidance
are operated by large corporations, which run worldwide networks. 60 per cent of transactions within secrecy jurisdictions
consist of internal accounting within multinational companies.
The consequences for the developing world are even more
noxious than for the developed one. In tax havens, 'legal'
transactions intersect with money deriving from drug dealing,
insider trading, the laundering of cash and many other directly
criminal activities. At a time when austerity is affecting some of
the poorest groups in society, the contrast becomes more than
just offensive, but utterly contradictory given that some of the
most cash-strapped countries are themselves home to secrecy
jurisdictions. It is corruption on a global scale, and it must end.

In April 2013, six major EU states met to develop new initiatives to open up secrecy jurisdictions. They agreed to exchange
data on a regular basis that would allow for more effective tax
collection. The agreement will apply to companies as well as
to individuals. The US passed legislation in 2010 that helped

establish bilateral agreements with other countries to the same effect. Why is taking action against tax havens so important in the context of a return to growth? One is that much of that money should be in the hands of governments or the taxpayer and used for productive purposes. Another is to help reduce the yawning inequalities that now threaten the social fabric. Yet another is to bring local forms of corruption out into the open, some of which affect the highest levels of politics or business. Finally, the salting away of money illegitimately is one of the very sources of the struggles of some countries. Research by the International Consortium of Investigative Journalists uncovered the offshore assets of thousands of individuals and corporations. Only four of 107 companies investigated doing business in Greece were registered with the tax authorities. The owners of the companies included many middle-class individuals and families, not just the rich.[36]

And so we come back to the big themes I touched upon at the beginning of the chapter. The EU should collaborate closely with the United States and the other G8 and G20 states, as well as the international agencies, to promote change in the global economy. Obviously there are many divergent interests, including those separating the emerging economies from the developed ones. Yet in respect of reform there is also much that is shared in common. At a G8 meeting held in June 2013, a ten-point plan to counter tax avoidance and evasion was agreed. The declaration stated that national tax authorities should share information on a global basis and should take steps to change the rules that allow corporations to shift their profits overseas to avoid taxes. The agreement was attacked for its absence of concrete policy proposals, but it added to what might and should become an unstoppable momentum of change. Global companies such as Microsoft, Apple, Google and Starbucks have come under the spotlight as never before. They pay minimal taxes in the countries in which they operate by channelling their profits through low- or zero-tax jurisdictions. They do not break the law, but they are able to escape huge amounts of taxation in such a way. The G8 agreement seeks to set up a new mechanism whereby multinational companies will have to disclose what tax they pay and in which countries they pay it, as well as accounts held in tax havens.

The G20 has subsequently backed such reforms and indeed extended them. A 'once-in-a-century' programme to introduce a new international regime to counter tax avoidance and evasion was endorsed in July 2013, building upon the G8 agreement. The OECD has supplied research and policy guidance. Parts of the agreement are due to be initiated within a year. The proposals include a measure whereby transnational companies with warehouses for the distribution of their goods will be taxed in the countries where their distribution centres are located. Thus at present Amazon has a £4.2 billion turnover in the United Kingdom but pays very little tax, since its enterprises are registered in Luxembourg. Corporations will be required to open their books to tax authorities in all countries, disclosing their profits, how much tax they pay and to whom. A series of new policies will be introduced to counter the complicated financial instruments deployed by companies to obscure their true earnings. These will be combined with stronger measures to force disclosure in secrecy jurisdictions. For example, new rules are scheduled to be introduced that would prevent the transfer of high-value intellectual property rights to tax havens. Of course, some or all of the proposals could be derailed by perceived divisions of interest between the participating nations. However, they do have the support of the leaders of China, India and Brazil as well as those of the developed economies. The point is not only to bring back revenue that can be invested in countries that desperately need it but also to help stimulate trade.

Germany, France and nine other EU countries have developed plans for a financial transaction tax in the face of fierce opposition from the banking industry and from the City of

London in particular. There are some real concerns to be dealt with, for instance the effect such a tax could have upon sovereign bond markets, pension funds and personal savings. Yet the potential benefits far outweigh the difficulties. The levy proposed by the Commission is 0.1 per cent on stocks and bonds and 0.01 per cent on derivatives. If instituted, it may help to achieve what was wanted many years ago by the originator of the idea, the American economist James Tobin: to discourage excessive risk-taking by traders. It would also generate significant revenue – possibly of the order of €35 billion a year, according to the Commission. The tax was supposed to be initiated in January 2014 but now has been put back some months, partly because of the issues mentioned above. 'Inclusive growth', to use the Commission's favoured term, will have to mean what it says. Those at the bottom cannot be cast adrift (see chapter 3). Just as important is what happens at higher echelons. Of what social use is growth if the fruits go almost wholly to the top 1 per cent of income earners? Yet in almost all the industrial countries over recent years that is what has been happening. And it is still going on through the crisis. In the United States during 2009–10 incomes overall grew by 2.3 per cent. Those in the top 1 per cent saw their incomes grow by 11 per cent over that time. For the remaining 99 per cent, incomes increased by only 0.2 per cent, a minuscule figure.

The top 1 per cent has outpaced all the rest in Germany, the UK, Italy, Spain and most of the smaller member nations. As with their counterparts in the US, they have managed to increase their total share of income even through the recession. How have they done so? They have managed it because they are a group apart, able to profit from their worldwide economic connections. They have been called a 'new virtual nation of mammon', separated economically and physically from the 'multitudinous many'.[37] Most work in the financial sector or derive their money from investments, but others are leaders of the large transnational corporations. They are able to exploit the opportunities offered by a deregulated world marketplace. The amounts of income they, and the organisations they head, keep offshore are colossal. A large proportion of that money belongs within nations, placed either in the service of social welfare or invested in promoting growth. Welfare, in the shape of the European social model, is what I turn to in the next chapter. That chapter meshes closely with this one. The key question is not so much whether the social model is affordable at a time of failing growth. It is how the social model can be adapted and reformed so as to contribute to its resurgence.

Chapter 3
No More Social Model?

In April 2013 a woman entered her bank in Almassora in eastern Spain, doused her body with petrol and set fire to herself.[1] She was in debt to the bank and had been issued with an eviction order from her home. Before carrying out the act, she shouted: 'You have taken everything from me!' She later died of her injuries. Her action became front-page news in many countries across Europe and elsewhere. Several unemployed people have set fire to themselves in Greece, making the media headlines too. Unemployment and homelessness, especially among younger people, has again become the scourge of Europe. It is a far cry from the stability and protection from economic fluctuations that European welfare systems were supposed to provide. The much lauded European social model seems in serious jeopardy.

Its importance to pro-Europeans is long-standing. Thus in 2003 two prominent public intellectuals wrote an open letter concerning the future of Europe in the aftermath of the Iraq War. One, Jürgen Habermas, came from Germany, the other, Jacques Derrida, from France. Thinking of contrasts with the US, the two proclaimed that the welfare state's 'guarantees of social security', 'trust in the civilising power of the state' and the state's capacity to 'correct market failures' were key parts of Europe's distinctiveness.[2] What the European social model (ESM) actually is, however, is more elusive than may appear from such descriptions. It has been aptly said that the ESM is not wholly European, not wholly social and not a model. If it refers to state-based institutions that provide for mass education and health insurance, and which offer programmes to protect the unemployed and the vulnerable, then such institutions are found in all industrial countries, including the United States. The ESM is not wholly 'social' because it depends in a fundamental way upon economic prosperity and economic redistribution from the affluent to the poor. It is not a single model, because there are large divergences between different EU countries in terms of the nature of their welfare systems, their levels of inequality and many other traits.

A North–South division reappears here, since welfare states have been more fully developed in countries such as the Scandinavian nations, Germany and France than they have, for instance, in Spain, Italy or Portugal. The European social model is in fact a mixture of values, accomplishments and aspirations, pinned together in varying ways, and with varying degrees of success, in different countries. The values include sharing risk through social insurance, limiting economic and social inequality, promoting workers' rights, and cultivating a sense of mutual responsibility or solidarity across the society.

A GOLDEN AGE . . . OR NOT?

In most member states of the EU today the ESM is under attack as austerity policies take hold. Yet its basic problems go a long way further back. It is sometimes said that the 1960s and early 1970s were the 'golden age' of the welfare state in Europe. There was good economic growth, low unemployment, relatively low inequality and developed health-care protection. Since that time, it is argued, the welfare state has become diminished or eroded by the advance of economic liberalism. The reality is more complicated. For some current EU member states there never was a golden age, since welfare provisions were weak and inadequate. Yet, even in countries with more advanced welfare systems, everything was far from golden in the golden age. Women's social and economic rights were restricted. Only a small proportion of people – again, mostly men – entered higher education in the majority of countries. The range of treatments offered in the health system was far more limited than is the case today. Once they reached the fixed age of retirement, older people by and large couldn't stay in work even though they might have wanted to do so.

Those working in heavy industry under primitive conditions often suffered from major health problems that forced them to give up work earlier still. The state generally treated people who depended upon the welfare system as passive subjects rather than as active citizens. An old joke, as jokes tend to do, captures this situation rather well. A doctor doing his rounds says to a nurse standing by a hospital bed: 'Nurse, this patient is dead.' 'No I'm not', says the patient. The nurse responds: 'You be quiet. Doctor knows best.'

Although 'social Europe' dates back further, the term 'European social model' came into wide currency only in the early 1980s. It was introduced precisely as an attempt to defend the 'European approach' at the time when free-market thinking was coming into the ascendancy and becoming the new orthodoxy. However, at the very same time, the ESM in its various incarnations was obliged to adapt to other changes. Some of these were encouraging developments – for example, the increasing emancipation of women or growing levels of life expectancy. Others were less welcome. Birth rates declined in most European countries, sometimes to well below reproduction levels. There was an increase in the numbers of one-parent families and of people living on their own, in the proportion of women and children living in poverty, and in unemployment in some key sectors. Heightened levels of immigration generally brought clear economic advantages but caused problems for countries not used to waves of new arrivals, often from very different ethnic backgrounds to those dominant in Europe.

Levels of public expenditure rose, while GDP growth rates declined year on year in the majority of EU states. A prominent observer of the European scene wrote in 2003 that 'the sustainability of the "European model" has become more and more questionable'.[3] At that time some analysts of the welfare state were already speaking of the need for a period of what they labelled 'permanent austerity'.[4] With a few exceptions, given the low levels of growth, the ESM had become unaffordable without serious reform. The best performers were the Nordic states, including those outside the EU, Norway and Iceland (although Iceland was to experience total bankruptcy less than ten years later because of over-lending on the part of its banks). What set the Nordic countries apart was that, following periods of economic downturn and readjustment, they managed to keep their welfare systems in robust condition while generating economic success, at least relative to most of the larger EU economies. They also comfortably outranked the majority of the other EU countries (and the US) in terms of quality of life indicators. All are small in terms of population, which probably makes adaptability easier than in the case of the bigger states. Yet being small doesn't guarantee innovation, as can be seen from the cases of Portugal or Greece.

The Nordic countries managed to combine continuing economic success with effective welfare systems. The level of female participation in the workforce was (and is) very high. Pension reform there proceeded further than almost anywhere else in the EU. Sweden, for example, introduced a contributory system, geared to growing life expectancy.[5] The Nordics invested heavily in human capital but at the same time took reform of the state seriously. Finland quite often tops the world league in terms of measures of educational attainment. Sweden and Denmark have introduced radical – and very controversial – changes in their education and health systems, allowing public and private providers to compete in a direct way. They have also sought to reform the administration of public services in such a manner as to render them client-friendly.

Many of the proposals enshrined in the Lisbon Agenda were well on the way to fruition in the Nordic countries when it was unveiled – reform of benefits systems, pensions, medical care, education and labour markets. Although they still had plenty of problems, these countries were closest to having achieved 'the elusive combination of social equality and economic efficiency' that the Agenda was set up to promote.[6] Some of the other major states in the EU, such as France, Italy and Spain among the larger countries, were unwilling or unable to push through comparable innovations. For instance, they persisted with their rigid labour markets, divided between insiders – with protected jobs – and outsiders – condemned to insecure and part-time work or without work at all.

In an era of accelerating and unpredictable technological change, 'employability' – being willing and able to move between occupations – becomes of prime importance. 'Moving on' also very often happens within the same job, as technology improves or knowledge expands. Flexibility should not be equated with a hire-and-fire mentality, which arguably even in its own terms is counterproductive, since the members of workforce can become demoralised even if they themselves keep their jobs at a given point in time.

Co-determination, for example, as it exists in Germany can provide a means of increasing flexibility rather than acting against it. The same goes for representation and consultation. In the best-run enterprises, consultation – and innovation – should run from top to bottom and back again. I don't want to deny that, in the hands of ruthless employers, 'flexibility' can be a code name for a more or less total denial of workers' rights. Yet, when properly developed, 'flexicurity' can mesh in a productive way with wider trends in everyday life in contemporary society. Many employees – men as well as women – want flexible working, and also part-time work, in order to accommodate family demands. Most people are accustomed to a much wider range of lifestyle choices than a generation ago, at all levels of society and in all age groups.

FROM WELFARE TO SOCIAL INVESTMENT STATE

As with so many other areas of the EU, the ESM – in all its diversity – has to be restructured and revamped. Beginning about fifteen years back – in common with many others – I started to think about what should become of the welfare state in contemporary social conditions, so different from the early post-war period during which it was first constructed. I believe that, with some rather crucial addenda, the framework I elaborated at that point remains valid today. The founders of the post-war welfare state, such as William Beveridge, did not give much thought to connections between the welfare system and wealth creation. Today those connections must be regarded as central. The welfare state should transmogrify into a social investment state.[7] A social investment state is one that deals in wealth creation, not just a system concerned with picking up the pieces after things have gone wrong.[8] In a social investment state there is a transition from *negative* to *positive* welfare. Beveridge spoke of correcting pre-existing social and economic maladies. Thus he emphasised above all the need to counter the 'five evils' of ignorance, squalor, want, idleness and disease. The aim today should be to turn these into positives – aspirations to pursue. In other words, the point is to promote education and skills, prosperity, active life choice, social and economic participation, and the pursuit of healthy and fulfilling styles of life.

Beveridge also concentrated overwhelmingly on rights, as

did his celebrated successor T. H. Marshall.[9] Today we must recognise that welfare presumes not only rights but also obligations on the part of citizens, obligations that should be to some degree enforced by sanctions, whether these are incentives or more punitive measures. Unemployment benefits, for example, were once upon a time defined largely as rights, but the results were to some degree counterproductive. 'Welfare dependency' is a very real phenomenon. The introduction of active labour market policies, where welfare recipients after a certain period are obliged to seek work or engage in training, have proved successful in reducing unemployment. The classical welfare state was a risk management system. It provided insurance against risks, in health, work or personal circumstances, for example, which individuals couldn't handle for themselves. The point was to minimise risk, the minimising of risk being defined as 'security'. However, risk is a more nuanced and subtle notion than that when we consider positive life opportunities. Risk-taking clearly often has positive aspects to it, especially in a rapidly changing world. We are back to the complex relation between opportunity and risk. Security may quite often be furthered more by an active embrace of risk than by attempts to reduce or avoid it. This statement is as true for the bulk of the labour force as it is for entrepreneurs. The very concept of 'flexicurity' is an attempt to capture this interplay.

Many authors, especially those on the political left, have seen the welfare state as defined in terms of 'de-commodification'. In an essentially market-based economy, money, price and profit inevitably have a dominant role in most spheres of life. In other words, goods, and human labour-power too, are commodities to be bought and sold. The welfare state, it is said, creates a separate sphere where other values can flourish. Any involvement with market forces hence sullies its essential character. Yet, expressed in such a way, the distinction is unhelpful. The workplace, for example, may be dominated by economic considerations, but many other values can and should come into play there too. Even when in menial jobs, many people value the satisfactions they get from their work other than just the revenue it generates. Conversely, many services provided by the welfare state may be 'free', but this word always means 'free at the point of delivery' – provided at no cost to the individual who utilises the service in question. The welfare state, obviously, has to be paid for. What is 'free' at the point of use is usually not even free to the person making use of the system, since that person will have covered part of the cost through his or her taxes.

In today's circumstances, over and above taxation there must be direct contributions from the users of welfare systems. Services designed to be 'free' embody a noble ideal but are prone to well-known difficulties. They tend to be overused and undervalued, creating in some cases a sort of vicious cycle of decay. Even where relatively small, direct contributions can help with these issues by promoting a responsible attitude to the use of services without creating a deterrent effect for the poor. A system supposedly designed to lessen inequality can otherwise end up creating it. The tendency is for two-tier arrangements to develop, in which the more affluent simply opt out. In health care, education and other areas, private and public provision become separated, with those who can afford to pay enjoying a different level of care and resources from the rest of the community. The contributory principle – direct contributions from users – must hence become more common, especially under current conditions. One of the main aims of reform should be to minimise the inequalities thus produced. Keeping those able to opt out within the broad umbrella of public services is as important as creating the conditions in which those from poorer groups don't become marginalised.

Social justice remains fundamental to the social investment state. However, investment for the future is seen as just as important for reducing inequalities as redistribution after the event. For instance, we know that the chances of educational

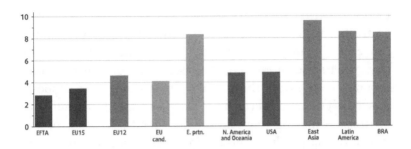

Figure 9 Wages in Europe are less differentiated than in other regions (earnings ratio between top and bottom deciles, 2007–9)

Note: The differential is measured by decile ratios (D9/D1 = wage level of the top 10 percent of workers divided by the level of the bottom 10 percent). 'EU cand.' refers to EU candidate countries and 'E. prtn.' refers to EU eastern partnership countries. EU candidates are represented by Albania only. The data for 2001–2006 are used for France, Luxembourg, the Netherlands, and Sweden (EU15), Hungary (EU12), and the Philippines (East Asia). For Albania, the period covered is 1995–2000.

Source: World Bank: *Golden Growth: Restoring the Lustre of the European Economic Model*; International Labor Organization, 2012.

success are often laid down by what happens early in a child's life. Pre-emptive investment in helping children from disadvantaged backgrounds can be of key importance here. Much the same is true at the very top. As discussed in the preceding chapter, inequality has grown sharply in most of the industrial countries, including the EU states, over the past twenty or so years, much of it the result of the staggering level of revenue accumulated by a small elite. Such inequalities can't be remedied simply through the tax system. They can only be reduced by active intervention into the economic order that has generated them.

Reform of the welfare state – or its transformation into a social investment state – has to give attention to the 'state' part of the equation. In the classical welfare state, the individual tended to be treated as a passive subject – as in the 'Doctor, doctor!' joke

I quoted earlier. A person registering as unemployed might be treated with condescension or indifference by the officials concerned. State systems tended to become vast bureaucracies, where the interests and concerns of officialdom could become remote from those of the citizens they were supposed to serve. The empowerment of users and the decentralisation of decision-making must be on the agenda. These processes should be sharply distinguished from privatisation as such. The fostering of human and social capital is, or should become, a key part of welfare systems. Educational reform, stretching from early years schooling right through to higher education and lifelong learning, hence becomes fundamental. Human and social capital is vital not only to active citizenship but to success in the labour market too. The social investment state therefore has to be much more interventionist than the classical welfare state was.

CONSEQUENCES OF THE CRISIS

In most of its incarnations the ESM was in trouble even before the financial crisis came along. What hope for it now as austerity policies start to bite? In most parts of the EU cuts are being made in welfare programmes, often hitting some of the most vulnerable members of the population. In an interview published in February 2012, Mario Draghi stressed the need for labour market reform in different parts of Europe, criticising particularly the persistence of divided labour markets. He was then asked, not in the purest English: 'Do you think that Europe will become less of the social model that has defined it?' His answer was, 'The European social model has already gone when we see the youth unemployment rates prevailing in some countries.'[10] As I interpret it, he was not saying that the ESM is dead but implying that it will become so if quite sweeping reforms are not made, at least in many member states. The same point is made in a recent study of the impact of austerity programmes on the ESM, where the first sentence in the text reads: 'It is an open secret that the welfare state has become a basket case . . .'[11]

The research in question looks at how the welfare commitments of the EU states have been affected by the need to cap or reduce borrowing. We have to remember that the point of austerity policies is not just to borrow less but to help force through structural change. The research covers seven different European countries, including Germany. Germany has relatively robust economic statistics, but the government has been obliged to set up a programme of retrenchment, dating from 2011, 'one of the biggest austerity plans in the history of the Federal Republic'. The aim is to make annual savings of 0.8 per cent of GDP in welfare expenditure. Reductions in social spending make up nearly a third of the package. Cuts have been instituted or are planned in unemployment, family and childcare benefits. Significant pension reforms are not on the table, but state pensions were restructured before the financial crisis. Health care under Germany's insurance-based system will cost patients more. The stated aim of these reforms – mild by the standards of the rest of Europe – is to contribute to growth by fostering a greater sense of social responsibility and initiative on the part of those most dependent on state benefits. Whether this happens or not, as elsewhere the effect in the short term is certainly to reduce the living standards of those already struggling.

Elsewhere the picture is naturally much more dramatic. Large cuts are being made in welfare programmes, again hitting some of the most vulnerable members of the population. Spain has long had a less developed welfare system than Germany. Social spending made up 21 per cent of GDP in 2007, only a little higher than the average of the Eastern European member states. Nearly a third of those registered as unemployed in Spain – and there are very many of them now – have no effective protection since the level of benefits is so low. Since 2010, the government has introduced pensions and health-care reforms, the main effects of which are regressive. As a result of the changes to the pensions system, for example, people in precarious jobs and those on low incomes will receive lower state benefits when they retire than those in more secure jobs.[12] Universal health care has been a preoccupation in Spain since the transition to democracy in the country. In 2000 the health system was ranked seventh in the world by the WHO. There are large numbers of primary clinics, even in small villages. Since that date, heavy cutbacks have been made as part of austerity policies: these have produced frequent clashes between the central government and the regions.

Spain's rate of joblessness is the second highest in the EU, after Greece. The overall unemployment rate has risen each year from 2008, although some now think it has reached its peak. Combined with cuts in benefits, it has led to large numbers of tenant evictions and mortgage foreclosures. Unlike in many other European countries, tenants in Spain have few rights. Banks have the right to reclaim their loans if a tenant is over a month in arrears in paying his or her rent. Should the bank repossess the property and then resell, it is able to keep the full sum even if the sale price is greater than the amount owed by the former incumbent. In response to the evictions, citizens have organised themselves to counter the policies of the authorities. For instance, *corralas* have come into being, whereby groups take over unoccupied apartment blocks.[13] They are not squatters, since they offer the landlord a low rent before taking over a building. Here the Spanish law acts to their advantage. So long as they show it is their primary residence, at least in some circumstances the courts can override any objections the owner might make.

As in Greece, in Spain there have been massive public protests against welfare cutbacks and lack of job opportunities. The *indignados* first took to the streets in May 2011. Besides contesting the welfare cuts, they set themselves against a variety of targets, including the orthodox political system, corruption and the excesses of the bankers and financial institutions. In some cities there were serious confrontations between the protesters and the police. The street protests later died down, in spite of the fact that the economic and social situation in Spain had worsened. However, sections of the movement remain and support citizens' initiatives such as the *corralas* mentioned above. They have worked upon setting up local currencies, barter systems and networks of cooperatives.

Rather than Greece, I take as a further example Ireland – before 2008 widely seen as one of the great success stories of the EU. Ireland's problems do not come from over-borrowing by government. They stem, as in Spain, from a property bubble fuelled by reckless lending on the part of the banks.[14] Public revenue came to depend substantially upon taxes on property transactions and hence dropped sharply when the bubble burst. Ireland ran a surplus in public spending between 2000 and 2007, but in 2009 government borrowing climbed to 14 per cent of GDP. The level of government intervention needed to prop up the banking system was so huge that, two years later, liabilities connected to the banks rose to 110 per cent of GDP. In November 2010 the government was forced to seek a bailout of €67.5 billion from the EU and the IMF. The loan was part of an €85 billion package, to which the Irish government contributed €17.5 billion.

The impact on the welfare system was immediate and radical. In the years when the economy seemed solid and healthy, the government set up a national pension reserve fund to generate revenue for pensions. However, in 2009 a substantial proportion was redirected to help prop up banks in difficulty. Unemployment went up from less than 5 per cent to some 15 per cent in 2012. Long-term unemployment (defined as people out of work for over a year) has been rising steeply. In that year it accounted for over 60 per cent of those out of work. As in Spain and some other EU countries, the burden of unemployment falls particularly upon the young. There is the same talk in Ireland as in Spain – and indeed across much of Europe – of 'a lost generation' whose members may be on the fringes of the labour market for the rest of their lives.

WEALTH, POVERTY AND INEQUALITY

As with other welfare indices, inequalities of wealth and income differ substantially across the EU countries. In most of them, however, those inequalities had been growing for some two decades before 2008. As of 2007, there were some 79 million people living in poverty in the EU, many of them children. The North–South division was marked. Child poverty rates were below 4 per cent of the total population in Sweden, Denmark and Finland. In Greece they were 20 per cent and in Italy 18 per cent. In most countries both poverty and child poverty were highest in lone-parent families. In some of the Southern states, by contrast, a much higher proportion of the poor lived in 'standard' families.

Poverty is often spoken of as though it is a unitary and unchanging condition – people get stuck in poor communities and there is no way out. There are some situations like that, but in fact they are relatively uncommon. 'The poor' are very diverse, both within and between countries. Many types of deprived regions, areas or neighbourhoods exist, even in one society, let alone across Europe as a whole. They are driven by different, sometimes contradictory dynamics. Thus the very trends that create prosperity in one area might generate poverty in another, as when rural poverty is heightened by the impact of supermarkets in the towns. Recent research has also shown that there is far more movement in and out of poverty than used to be thought. In the EU-15 countries in 2007, about 40 per cent of spells of poverty ended within the space of one year. In the light of such research we have to look at 'poor communities' in a different way from in the past. An area which 'stays the same' can have a large number of people moving in and moving out. This finding mostly applies just as much to immigrant groups as to the indigenous population, in some cases in fact even more so. It hadn't come to light previously because most research is carried out over a short period of time. Thus time-based studies of Bolton and Bradford in the UK, where there are substantial proportions of East Asian groups, showed that the majority of immigrants moved on from the inner city. In particular they sought to move out into the suburbs or into the countryside, a goal achieved by many.

Studies carried out in Germany have shown how much mobility there is in and out of poverty in that country. For some individuals there is a 'carousel effect' – they move out of poverty, only later to lapse back, and may repeat the cycle across their lives. Yet the majority who escape from poverty do so permanently. The German researchers distinguished three sets of circumstances that affect individuals' experience of poverty: 1) how long it lasts, what happens between spells of poverty and at what time time of life the individual is; 2) whether the person has social support to draw upon rather than becoming marginalised; and 3) whether or not the experience of poverty is 'biographical' – that is to say, the result of specific life events, such as divorce or illness. The effects of such happenings can be more difficult to shake off than simple loss of income.

The classical welfare state focused upon improving people's lot once they had fallen into poverty. This emphasis is inadequate today. Pre-emptive welfare is targeted more at trying to keep people out of poverty in the first place and preventing relapses once they have escaped. 'Flexicurity' is important here since, in contrast to traditional benefits, it has an activist approach to a return to work through an emphasis upon retraining. Pre-emptive policies pioneered in the US are relevant in Europe too. One that has been deployed successfully, for example, is a scheme to allow workers in threatened industries to apply for retraining before their specific jobs disappear. Local colleges offer training on the internet, backed up by weekend classes. Another is that of flexible education accounts. In some cities in the US, lifetime learning credits were introduced, according to which workers could get 20 per cent of the costs paid by the state for learning and retraining while in work. Such schemes have proved to be especially important for the crucial issue of keeping older people in work.

Investment in children is especially important, not only because of child poverty as such, but because there is an accumulation of research now showing how decisive early years can be in shaping later capacities. As in so many other areas of social life, the nature of childhood is changing. In the developed countries, this is the era of the 'prized child'. Children still do 'come along', but for most parents, of all income levels, the decision to have a child is just that. This is one of the reasons why teenage pregnancy, once the norm, is felt to be such a threat. The average age of marriage is so much later now than it was a generation ago, contraception is easily available, and it is widely assumed that having a child will be a conscious decision. Thus the teenager who 'gets pregnant' is violating a range of taboos. She is likely to come from a poorer background and, without support from parents or a partner, will inevitably struggle.

The dynamics of poverty have been greatly affected by the entry of women into the labour force in large numbers over the past twenty to thirty years. There is very little poverty where there are two wage-earners in the family, regardless of whether there are children present. On average, women move in and out of jobs more than men, a factor that influences the pattern of poverty across the life course. Policies aimed at reducing child poverty have to focus on households and the nature of early care. Households with no one in work are most prone to child poverty, followed by those with only one earner, whether a lone-parent household or not. Few of the EU states achieved the Barcelona targets set for 2010 for child-care spaces.[15] These

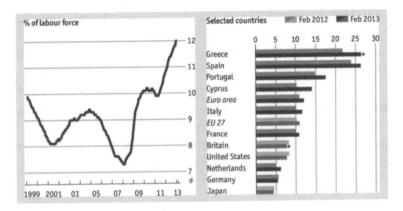

Figure 10 Unemployment in the euro area and beyond

Source: *The Economist*, 2013.

were that at least 90 per cent of children aged between three and
mandatory school age, and at least 33 per cent of those under
three, should have available day care by that date. However,
unless provided publicly, child care accentuates poverty rather
than helps limit it. In almost all EU countries, households with
the highest incomes also have the highest usage of child-care
services.

The recession and the return of high unemployment in
Europe are bound to increase both poverty and inequality
unless remedial measures are somehow put in place. According
to the latest Eurostat indicators, 24 per cent of the European
population were 'at risk of poverty or social exclusion' in 2011 –
the so-called AROPE measure. That phrase is defined as those
at risk of being below the poverty threshold in a given year,
those in a situation of 'severe material deprivation', and people
living in households where no person is in stable work. AROPE
figures vary a lot across member states. The highest rate in the
EU is that of Bulgaria, at 49 per cent, followed by Romania
and Latvia, at around 40 per cent. In Greece the figure is 30
per cent. Even among the best-performing states the levels are

quite high – around 16 per cent in Germany, Austria and the Netherlands, for example. The clear danger is that poverty will mount especially rapidly in the Eastern and Southern countries. Most have had weaker welfare systems than the more affluent states, but even these now threaten to unravel. As benefits are cut back, individuals and families are left more and more exposed. László Andor, the European social affairs commissioner, has quite rightly said that those out of work will face 'an enormous poverty trap' if current trends continue.[16]

IS COST-CUTTING COMPATIBLE WITH BENEFICIAL REFORM?

The position of the different EU states today differs according to a range of factors – how hard a given country has been hit by the recession and in what specific ways; whether it had a developed welfare system before 2008 or was concerned with constructing one; how far it had reformed before that date; and the level of austerity measures imposed upon it. A fundamental question is: in a situation of deep crisis, can changes be instituted that will not inevitably undermine the ESM? Can the social model be saved?

To do so, reforms have to be well thought through and pursued with vigour. I have to re-emphasise points made earlier. The social model in many EU states was as much an aspiration as a reality. That aspiration should remain a guiding principle of European life today. It was always an evolving set of ideals, strategies and practices. Even when well developed, the classical welfare state was the very source of some problems, not only a means of resolving them.[17] Once established, welfare systems have a strong tendency towards inertia. Those who receive a given set of benefits organise to resist change, even when such change is in the interests of wider social justice. Welfare dependency is real, not just a figment of the imaginations of right-wing political commentators. Even free health care can have unintended consequences of a negative kind. These problems can be attacked with greater vigour and determination at a time of crisis than otherwise.

In most countries the pressure to innovate is much greater than it was some years ago. As in the economy, the status quo is no longer an option. Reforms this time cannot be put off but have to be pushed through. The question of austerity versus investment comes up again with full force here. Cost-cutting is certainly necessary, especially in the countries whose economies are struggling, but to some extent everywhere. Yet such an exercise should be a basis also for long- as well as short-term investment, aimed wherever possible at conjoining welfare reform and a return to growth.[18] Special provision must be made for those hardest hit. Fire-fighting in this sense is vital, but it is clear that restructuring must be much more profound.

Plainly in many cases there will be hard choices to be made. There is again a lot to be learned from the Nordic states, even for countries in the EU which have quite different welfare systems. Even through the recession the Nordics have sought to preserve social solidarity, restrain growing economic inequality and, at the same time, be responsive to the demands of citizens for more influence over decisions taken. Sweden is a key case in point. Not far short of 30 per cent of Sweden's health-care system is now in the hands of private providers, subject, however, to careful state controls. The results so far have been encouraging, although of course there are drawbacks and difficulties too. For instance, average hospital waiting times have dropped by some 25 per cent over the past fifteen years.[19] Swedes can take charge of their own investment accounts for their retirement and can choose from hundreds of providers. Small charges have been introduced for visits to the doctor and to hospital, which have led people to think a little more about how far their visit is necessary, but have also created expectation of a personalised service. The not-for-profit sector is strong and has also expanded significantly.

Cost-effectiveness now matters a great deal. The difficulty in many countries is the tendency to pluck the low-lying fruit – to cut, for example, where public resistance is likely to be weak. Yet a cut isn't really a cut if its consequences undermine the up-front savings that are made. Thus cost-cutting should be integrated with a wider vision for the area in question. Wherever economies can be made but at the same time the quality of a service improved, that is the route which should be taken.

The health sector again provides interesting examples. A high proportion of overall health expenditure is taken up today by services for older people, especially the so-called frail elderly who may need long-term care. Pre-emptive policies, however, directed towards supporting healthy and active lifestyles can actually save a great deal in terms of economic costs. Research shows that the outcome is not just to postpone the date at which a person might require care, but actually to close the gap in years between health and chronic illness. Average life expectancy at birth in the EU countries in 2012 was seventy-seven years for men and eighty-three for women. The aim should be to use public health policies to close the gap between those figures and 'healthy life expectancy' – the point at which someone suffers from a chronic illness or disability. That figure at the moment stands at an average of fifteen years for men and nineteen years for women. The objective is to narrow the differential considerably, which will both improve quality of life and produce significant cost savings. New technologies in principle offer the possibility of large areas in which patients, healthy and otherwise, can monitor their state of health and act accordingly in a pre-emptive way to avoid possible pathologies. As in other contexts, the current crisis has served to expose inefficiencies in existing forms of health care which there is the chance to remedy. For instance, in some countries there are enormous levels of over-prescription; care is not well integrated within or outside hospitals, so that there is a great deal of duplication of effort; administrative processes are not computerised and hence are slow and inadequate. Quite often there has been no attempt whatsoever to try to assess cost-efficiency.

Annika Ahtonen provides a cogent list of reforms that could not only help cut costs but also revitalise some key aspects of Europe's health-care systems.[20] One is to coordinate health and social services much more effectively than is often the case today. There are many fields open to improvement in most countries, among them diagnosis, treatment, after care, rehabilitation and health promotion. A second is improving health outcomes and quality of care. This category covers dealing with over-prescription, but it includes also assessing the effectiveness or otherwise of varying health technologies, reducing waiting-lists, and dealing with other inefficiencies at the point of contact between patient, doctor and place of treatment.

The third is strengthening public health. As befits the social investment state, there should be a strong emphasis on promoting health rather than simply treating diseases. Although Ahtonen does not mention it, a crucial element here is confronting the fast-food, cigarette and alcoholic drink companies. So far they pay for only a minute proportion of the harm their products cause, the cost of which has to be borne almost wholly by the taxpayer. Some countries have mounted vigorous programmes directed towards reducing fat and sugar consumption and cutting smoking and alcohol consumption, especially among young people. For others there is a long way still to go. Next, the means should be provided for both patients and professionals to compare different providers. Such comparisons tend to drive up standards but also promote efficiency. Finally there is empowering the patient – as I have already stressed, a fundamental part of the reform of public services more generally. Both high- and low-tech innovations are important here. For instance, internet or telephone consulting can be widely deployed, subject to clear quality controls. Computers which have simplified codes of access can be used by patients suffering from even quite advanced forms of dementia, allowing them to escape from isolation.

At the moment there is little chance of building more than the rudiments of a pan-European welfare system, although that should be a longer-term goal. However, best practice can be widely shared; and where the need is especially acute, direct interventions can be attempted. An example of the moment is the Task Force for Greece, which offers the country technical assistance in restructuring its health-care system. That same endeavour, disturbingly, has revealed that cuts have been made mostly without reference to a wider vision of the future. Some of the worst aspects of the pre-existing system have actually become accentuated. For instance, bribes are offered to medical staff to allow people to jump the queues as the services become overstretched. Yet the system could be radically improved if a properly thought-out strategy is adopted; and there are indeed many positive changes happening. Thus a new online prescription service was introduced to help limit the chaos and corruption that had existed for years, whereby doctors and pharmacists would write bogus prescriptions and pocket the proceeds.

Moves towards common standards of welfare across the EU could have positive effects in terms of one of the desiderata for the future – the creation of a European-wide labour market. When workers leave Spain or Greece today to go to other parts of Europe, it is often said that they are 'fleeing the country'. And there are very real worries should needed groups of professionals up and leave in too large numbers. Yet to be successful the single market, and an integrated eurozone, will need quite high levels of labour mobility. The news that Finland is actively trying to recruit health-care professionals from Spain, announced in February 2013, has provoked mixed responses in both countries. In Finland, which has an unemployment rate of 7 per cent, there are not enough nurses and health-care workers to cope with the demands of an increasingly elderly population. Finland has actively campaigned to draw in workers from other parts of Europe; 4,000 Spanish nurses have applied for posts. Several months' training, including learning new language skills, is provided for them in Spain, together with further training options when they arrive.[21]

FUTURE SHOCK

Led by digital technology, we might be on the verge of a transformation of welfare systems as fundamental as those affecting other institutions of our society. Some of the changes happening in this context could undoubtedly contribute to lowering the costs of welfare services at the same time as making a step-change in their efficiency and coverage. Consider, for example, what is happening in the spheres of higher education and medicine. In the early years of the spread of the internet, many believed that orthodox universities would be undermined by the spread of online learning. A number of attempts were made to set up institutions based on courses provided on the internet. The campus university, it was widely thought, might be coming to the end of its life. Some online universities, such as the University of Phoenix in Arizona, had a period of dramatic success before more recently entering a period of decline.

In the meantime technology has advanced dramatically, as has the number of users worldwide. New forms of teaching and learning are emerging which look potentially much more revolutionary than the earlier prototypes. As a prominent scholar has observed, 'The solid classical buildings of great universities may look permanent but the storms of change now threaten them.'[22] Higher education, and perhaps education more generally, could be shaken to its roots by the global trends that feature so strongly in this book. Because of shifts in the nature of work in almost all employment settings, educational and vocational qualifications are probably going to be more important for reducing unemployment than ever before. Lifelong learning might become a prerequisite for continuous employment rather than an empty slogan. Yet, even with the widespread introduction of student fees, costs are mounting beyond the capacity of either individuals or the state. In the United States, total student debt now stands at just under $1 trillion. As much as 30 per cent of it may never be paid off. Yet a university degree is no longer the passport to ready employment it once was. In many of the EU states, the rate of unemployment for recent graduates is worryingly high.

It is very likely that the value of getting a degree in the traditional universities will decline compared to other forms of qualification and modes of learning. The distinction between full-time and part-time education will start to break down as new forms of digitally based learning come to the fore. Some universities in the United States have decided to reorganise their teaching models completely. They have scrapped terms and operate continuously through the year. Online learning has replaced much of the traditional lecture system. Students are more responsible than in the past for organising study groups on- and offline. The costs are much lower than in old-style universities, while faculty still have excellent research opportunities.[23]

Both the content and the form of higher education are becoming globalised. Online courses, involving interactive components and quite often delivered for free, can not only reach vast audiences but also provide for intensive course-work. Debates and discussions can be carried on with others anywhere in the world, rather like the open-source collaboration common in the universe of digital manufacture. Where courses are paid for, students can interact directly with some of the world's top scholars and researchers. The notion of a 'global classroom' has moved out of the realm of fantasy. Numerous innovations are in the pipeline, such as the World Education University in the US. The university offers a variety of courses leading to degrees and diplomas. It claims to be the first free online institution of higher education in the world and has no support from state sources. Revenue is derived from advertising and endowments. Students, who can be of any age, can apply and begin at any time and study at their own pace, although there are recommended hours of work each week. The university's mission statement says that it 'welcomes anyone who has a desire to learn, regardless of the level of education, age, nationality, location or any other factors'.[24]

A parallel and even more intriguing story is unfolding in the area of medicine. Many people now wear a wrist bracelet that continually monitors the state of their bodies, including heartbeat, energy expended, sleep patterns and other medical data. It marks one more stage in the progressive integration of man and machine, but presumptively a beneficial one. Medical diagnosis and treatment, like education, are beginning to become more and more detached from the exigencies of time and place. Digital medicine at a distance could revolutionise medical treatment and could be part of the solution to overburdened medical services. A whole variety of convergent developments is unfolding. New broadcasting technologies make possible the 24-hour monitoring of vulnerable people, including the elderly living at home. Remote surveillance of medical conditions can be carried on, with an interactive facility between the individual and medical staff. The most recent pacemakers, for example, do not just act on the heart but send a stream of data back to the hospital or doctor. Advances in imaging and processing power have been dramatic in recent years, allowing exchanges of treatment information from any one point in the world to any other.

Robots can be used to carry out operations over indefinite distances using new forms of data collection and imaging. The surgeon can be in one location and the robot and patient in another. Software is now available to translate CT images into three-dimensional models. These can have colour added and can be rotated so as to be viewed from any position. Major cost-savings and patient benefits can in principle be achieved.[25] It is not uncommon at the moment, for example, for a patient to have to see a doctor at one place for a diagnosis; travel to another location, perhaps miles away, for a scan; go somewhere else for a biopsy; visit another medical expert for an interpretation of the findings; and have surgery at yet another time and place. All of this can today be handled in an integrated way on one site. Most can be accomplished at one time, not at removed intervals.

And then there is the case of prisons, worth commenting upon briefly here, even if they are not usually thought of as part of the welfare state. Incarceration of offenders is both extremely costly and of dubious utility in producing law-abiding citizens. 'Prisons without walls' might help in both of these respects. Electronic surveillance might be a better option for prisoners not deemed to be dangerous to the public. New devices are much more compact than their forerunners, can be made tamper-proof and can be run continuously, including in the shower. If combined with active rehabilitation – very difficult to achieve in prison – the result could be to help cut the tie between gaol and persistent criminality.

In making these points, I do not mean to appear a naive technophile. Low-tech or minimalist approaches can often be as or more important than the most stunning technology. Thus studies of procedure before operations showed that lives could be saved if every surgeon ticked off the points on a simple list before commencing a procedure. All technologies can have noxious uses, including for the perpetration of violence or war. The same advances that make possible remote medical diagnosis and treatment have also produced military drones. Yet it is hard to resist the conclusion that we are at a turning point in many areas of social and economic life, with deep-rooted consequences. Michel Foucault pointed out that hospitals, schools, universities, prisons and factories are all products of modernity.[26] As such they have similar characteristics, among them surveillance and the need for discipline. The prototype of them all, he suggested, was Jeremy Bentham's Panopticon, a model prison in which the guards occupy a central tower with the prisoners in their cells ranged round them in a circle. The prisoners can therefore be kept under 24-hour surveillance. The same arrangement can be produced through the electronic surveillance of offenders at distance, except that surveillance can be even more continuous and complete.[27] Much more radical developments could be to come. Could it be that at some point in the future the organisations which Foucault discussed might become more or less wholly deconstructed? In other words, action at distance may replace the need for people to be clustered in specific institutions. Hospitals, prisons, schools, and so forth, may become disassembled and scattered across time and space. It wouldn't be a reversion to previous history but a leap beyond the organisations that have become so familiar over the past two centuries.

AGEING . . . AND 'YOUTHING'

On the demographic front the EU states are caught in a pincer movement. On the one hand the population is ageing. Unless far-reaching reforms are made, large numbers will become impoverished, pension systems will crack under the strain, and quality of health care will diminish. The changes involved are long term and pre-date the financial crisis but, as elsewhere, further accentuate an already difficult situation. On the other hand, the younger generation in many EU countries is shrinking, and today a growing number are without jobs. In 1995 the younger generation – those aged under twenty-four – made up 31 per cent of the EU population. Today that proportion has declined to 27 per cent. These trends are intimately related, since the younger generation have to contribute to supporting their elders. In countries with pay-as-you-go pension systems, they will bear the large part of the burden unless reforms are made.

There are major differences across Europe both in terms of the extent of these changes and responses made to them. Largely because of the effects of immigration, for example, the UK has a

Table 1 Percentage of population aged 65 and over, selected European countries (1985, 2010 & 2035)

Country	1985	2010	2035
Sweden	17	18	23
United Kingdom	15	17	23
Germany	14	21	31
Belgium	14	17	24
France	13	17	25
Italy	13	20	28
Netherlands	12	15	26
Finland	12	17	26
Spain	12	17	25
Ireland	11	11	19

Source: Office for National Statistics, 2012.

higher birth rate than most of the other EU countries. In other member states the birth rate is at the lowest ever known in history. According to these and other differences, there are large variations in the impact of population ageing, visible before the crisis struck. Some of the states suffering the most from the recession are in the group where, without reform, the highest burden will fall upon the public purse. They include Italy, Greece, Spain and Ireland, alongside the Netherlands, Romania and Slovenia. For a second group of countries, such as the UK, Germany, Belgium, Hungary and the Czech Republic, the cost of the ageing population will still be very high. These states, however, have initiated pension reforms which have helped trim their obligations. A third group, the Nordics among them, has pushed reform further, but these states still have a significant shortfall to cover.

While longevity has been increasing, the average at which people in EU countries retire from the labour force has been dropping. Over the past forty years or so, average length of life has increased by ten years; and there has been a comparable drop in the average age of retirement. In some countries until recently that trend was actively fostered by public policy. As

Bernd Marin has pointed out in his very comprehensive study of ageing and the welfare state, the proportion of people in Europe who are non-employed is much higher than those who are registered as unemployed.[28] There are four times as many people over eighteen in the first category as compared to the second. Unemployed men make up less than a fifth of non-employed men as a whole. The proportion of women outside the workforce is six times as high as those who are unemployed.

Pension systems were originally built upon the expectation that most workers would stay in the same job for much or all of their working lives, at a time when the male working career was the standard against which needs were determined, and for a world of stable family life. A radically increased proportion of women in work and the advent of more fragmented labour markets, together with rises in rates of separation, divorce and people living alone, have altered this situation dramatically. The Southern countries mostly lagged behind the Northern states in the development of their pension systems, trusting more in the family to deal with the support of older people. Even so, or perhaps because of this fact, the average age of retirement in some such countries has been among the lowest in Europe.

Significant gender differences have emerged as a result of this composite of trends. In almost all EU countries older women are most likely to be living in poverty and in isolation from the wider community. Their pattern of leaving paid work is also different from that of male workers. A study was carried out in 2011 by the OECD of people aged fifty to sixty-four who left the labour force in the previous year.[29] The results showed that retirement (that is, taking a pension) accounted for a high proportion of men leaving the labour market in countries with low pension ages or early retirement options (Italy, Hungary, Greece, France, the Czech Republic and Belgium). In other EU countries included in the research (Spain, Sweden, the UK, Finland and Slovakia), by contrast, the majority left work through either long-term unemployment or disability. Women leave the labour market to care for other family members in far greater numbers than do men.

Raising the age of retirement for both sexes is an essential strategy in countries, still by far the majority, where it is too low to make ends meet, and this forms a key part of the adjustment programmes enforced on those member states that have been obliged to accept bailouts. Everywhere, however, it meets with fierce resistance from those affected. Reform of pension schemes themselves is another obvious necessity and has been initiated by now in most of the EU countries, although with mixed results. Thus in Britain a goodly chunk of the pension system was turned over to the private sector. The approach has encountered numerous problems – low and variable levels of coverage, structural inefficiencies, problems as people move from job to job, and lack of coverage for the poor. The most important strategies, however, depend upon what I have earlier called positive welfare – they involve recasting the nature of ageing itself. In some respects, if the reader will forgive the clumsiness of the term, we live in a *youthing* society rather than an ageing one. In other words, some of the discrepancies between youth and old age have disappeared. Fauja Singh, an Indian-born immigrant to Britain, ran his first marathon aged over eighty. He has since taken part in numerous others. Aged 101, he decided to give up marathon running and turned instead to runs of a mere 10 kilometres. Many older people keep fit in a regular way, travel the world, begin courses of study – and work, either for pay or in the third sector. Their patterns of sexuality, marriage and divorce are similar to those of younger age groups.

Positive encouragement of lifestyle change is going to be a big part of the solution to the 'ageing problem' because it will directly affect attitudes towards retirement on the part of those involved, as well as the attitudes of younger people towards their elders. It is important to combat ageism, inside and outside the workplace. As far as possible, the view that retirement is a privilege that 'compensates' for ageing should be turned on its

head. Older people should have the right to work, and governments should encourage them to stay on in the labour force by
putting in place appropriate programmes. Lifelong learning
for both sexes should become a reality, along with acceptance
of the importance of part-time work. The state should lose
its monopoly over such programmes, since both businesses
and not-for-profit organisations can have important roles. For
example, business firms can ensure that retraining schemes are
available for people of all ages in the workforce to help them
adapt to technological or market changes.

The Nordic countries are once more in the lead, although
the details of their various policies vary. They were the earliest European states to alter their pension systems with a view
to introducing greater flexibility in working options. Many
policies have been introduced to entice older people either to
continue their careers or to move to part-time work. They have
adopted a stringent attitude towards the large numbers of older
people who used to claim disablement benefits and therefore
were out of the labour force – so-called disability pensioners.
Special attention has been given to finding jobs for people with
reduced work capacity. The same applies to those claiming
long-term sickness benefits. There has been considerable success in increasing the employment rates of older people previously on such benefits, mainly by using incentive schemes rather
than simply punitive policies. Across much of the rest of Europe
there is still a long way to go.

If the proportion of older people in work goes up, does it
mean that those in the younger generation find it even more
difficult to find jobs? The answer is unequivocally no. Countries
that have the highest levels of older people in work also have
the lowest levels of youth unemployment. Youth unemployment in Europe has attracted lurid headlines since the advent
of the financial crisis. Levels of youth joblessness in the EU are
indeed highly disturbing, especially among the countries in the
greatest economic difficulties. Yet some of the figures talked of

are almost certainly exaggerated. Measuring the rate of youth unemployment presents difficulties because of the high proportion of those aged under twenty-five in education or training and therefore not 'in work'.

To calculate the real level of worklessness among young people, it is best to use what economists call the unemployment 'ratio' as well as the unemployment rate.[30] It is in fact the more accurate statistic. It measures the share of the unemployed for the whole of the youth population in a particular country or region. The results are very different from the employment rates that are usually quoted. The unemployment rate for those under twenty-five in the EU in 2012 was 22.8 per cent. The unemployment ratio, however, was only 9.7 per cent.[31] In Greece in the same year, the unemployment rate for young people was 55.3 per cent, a seemingly quite shocking statistic. However, the unemployment ratio was 16.1 per cent, a very different figure. The statistics for Spain were 53.2 per cent for the unemployment rate but 20.6 per cent for the unemployment ratio. Of course there are complications, because it may be that, in the more depressed countries, some young people who stay in education or take up some sort of training would otherwise be looking for a job.

These considerations actually affect comparisons often drawn between the EU and the US at the current time. The rate of unemployment for young Americans in 2012 was 16 per cent – high, but seemingly a lot lower than that in Europe. However, the contrast is misleading because of the larger numbers of young people in the United States who are in education or training programmes. The unemployment ratio was actually higher in the US than in Europe.[32] Perhaps the most telling figure to use in making comparisons is the proportion of young people who are not in employment, education and training (NEETs); the percentage in the US in 2012, at 14.8, also outstrips that in the EU, where it was 13.2 per cent. In both cases, however, the figures were and are rising. As in most other statistics, there are big differences between the European countries. In Germany and (again) the Nordic countries, the figure is less than 10 per cent. Those for Spain and Greece in 2012 were 18.8 per cent and 20.3 per cent, with Italy the highest at 21.1 per cent.

It makes sense in the situation in Europe today to target policies especially at the NEETs, with a particular focus on the struggling economies of the South. It isn't as if relevant policies are difficult to find, as can be seen by looking to countries where rates are low. They all have a range of job training programmes for young people who are neither out at work nor in higher education of some sort. The best known are the apprenticeship schemes in Germany. Young people enter them at age fifteen or sixteen, and combine work on the shop floor with classroom teaching, for a period ranging from one and a half to three years. It is clear, however, that action on many fronts will be needed, and in short order too, to make a serious reduction in the figures for the countries which are suffering most. The prime overall objective, of course, has to be higher levels of wealth and job creation in those economies as a whole. Policies such as reforming divided labour markets are vital both to that aim and to the specific difficulties of young people.

Based upon the schemes in play in countries with low levels of youth joblessness, the EU has initiated a 'grand plan' to get young people into work. The idea is that all the EU states should offer what a few – the usual suspects – already do. The programme would offer a 'youth guarantee' for everyone up to age twenty-five. All young people would be offered a job, an apprenticeship or a traineeship within four months of leaving education, or becoming unemployed, if no other opportunities come their way. So far a pilot scheme has been funded to the tune of €4 million, a minor amount. A recent Franco-German proposal is of interest, because of its provenance as much as its content, which echoes ideas in wide circulation.[33] It builds upon the 'youth guarantee'. The new proposal has three elements. The first is funding commensurate with the scale of the problem. €60 billion would be made available for small and medium-sized enterprises to borrow at favourable rates and thereby generate jobs. The resources will come from the European Investment Bank, European structural funds and a one-off investment by the EU. A Europe-wide training scheme will be set up covering schools and in-work training. The Erasmus programme for higher education will be extended to allow those in vocational training to take part – an 'Erasmus for everyone'. François Hollande has affirmed that Angela Merkel will support the plan, which will be presented to the various EU institutions. EU2 strikes again, or at least we have to hope so. Otherwise it's yet more paper Europe.

Most of the issues discussed in this chapter overlap heavily with that of immigration and wider problems of multicultural-ism. I move onto these in what follows.

Chapter 4
The Cosmopolitan Imperative

The EU has a significant, indeed irreplaceable, role in coordinating border management and connecting it with neighbourhood and foreign policy initiatives. The Commission recognises the need for 'a coherent, balanced EU migration policy', while accepting that it does not yet exist.[1] It denies that a 'fortress Europe' is being built. Dialogue with what is somewhat quaintly called the 'outside world' is necessary, not just to police the borders from unwanted migrants but to help show the attractions of Europe for those who are actually sought after. There is a new strategic framework in play, the Global Approach to Migration and Mobility. The EU immigration portal has been launched and proposals have been made to establish a European border surveillance system. The 'smart borders' programme will help simplify border crossings for those frequently travelling in and out of the EU. Another innovation is the 'Single Permit Directive', designed to ensure that legal migrants enjoy rights on a par with established citizens. A variety of initiatives exist to promote social cohesion in the increasingly diverse European population. However, as with the social model, most of the significant powers remain in the hands of the member states.

I shall not offer an analysis of this cluster of policies in what follows. Necessary though they are, they treat migration mainly on the technocratic level, as a series of problems to be managed. I shall concentrate my attention on the debate surrounding multiculturalism, where the fiercest controversies are to be found. I want to argue for what I call the *cosmopolitan imperative* not just as essential to coping with large-scale immigration but as integral to Europe's future as a whole. By the cosmopolitan imperative I mean the exigency of learning to live in a globalised world, where the intersection of divergent beliefs and ways of life becomes an everyday occurrence. Migration, I shall argue, has changed its nature as a result of the ubiquity of everyday electronic communication. We have moved into an era of 'super-diversity'. I see this transformation as deeply connected with problems of European identity as a whole, but also as directly influencing Europe's economic future. Most of the debate about whether or not immigration brings benefits to host countries concentrates upon its direct impact on jobs, welfare schemes, and so forth. In this chapter I want to develop a much more ambitious argument – that the greatest economic benefits to the EU states will come from their capacity to respond in a positive and constructive way to the new world of super-diversity.

GLOBALISATION AND MIGRATION

When Europeans migrated en masse to the Americas and elsewhere a century ago, they essentially cut themselves off from their countries of origin because communications were so slow. Today, no matter how many thousands of miles a person travels, he or she can keep in daily touch with those left behind. It makes little difference if that individual is poor and deprived, since electronic contact can be made virtually for free. Moreover, there are innumerable websites that can supply needed information or exchanges of views, wholly independently of the physical and social milieu in which that individual exists. It is perfectly possible for a second-generation immigrant, who has never been outside his or her country of birth, to become politically radicalised in the context of a state or region on the other side of the world. It used to be called the *brutal bargain*: immigrants coming into an alien country or region had to give up many traits and customs close to their hearts. This situation still applies to some degree, of course, but it is tempered by the fact that today in an important sense we all live in 'one world', whatever our differences. It can mute the feeling of shock, but in some cases work the other way and exacerbate it – on the part of both the new arrivals and the established population.

Alongside its economic problems, immigration has been called Europe's 'other crisis' and even its 'most significant chronic problem'.[2] As globalisation takes hold, people are on the move all over the world. The changes that have affected Europe, however, are unprecedented because they mark a reversal of an historical pattern. Population movements have always taken place; enforced migration has been an elemental part of the continent's violent history. During the two world wars, millions of people were displaced from their homes, many forcibly transported elsewhere; refugees took shelter wherever they could. However, in terms of more voluntary migration, for some two centuries the European countries have been emigrant nations. Millions of people left Europe for the Americas in particular. Some 5 million Germans migrated to the US between 1850 and 1930; 3.5 million Britons and 4.5 million Irish immigrants entered the country between 1820 and 1930. In all, 25 million Europeans made the journey over that period of a century or so.

In recent times it has been Europe's turn, although of course migration to the Americas from across the world proceeds apace. During the 1960s and early 1970s, since they were short of labour, some of the European countries made active attempts to attract workers from abroad. An example is the Turkish

Table 2 Top ten citizenships of immigrants to EU-27 member states, 2008

EU citizens (including nationals)		EU citizens (excluding nationals)		Non-EU citizens	
Country of citizenship	(1 000)	Country of citizenship	(1,000)	Country of citizenship	(1,000)
Romania	: (a)	Romania	384	Morocco	157
Poland	302	Poland	266	China	97
Germany	196	Bulgaria	91	India	93
United Kingdom	146	Germany	88	Albania	81
France	126	Italy	67	Ukraine	80
Italy	105	France	62	Brazil	62
Bulgaria	92	United Kingdom	61	United States	61
Netherlands	81	Hungary	44	Turkey	51
Spain	61	Netherlands	40	Russian Federation	50
Belgium	48	Portugal	38	Colombia	49

(a) At least 384 000.

Source: Eurostat, http://epp.eurostat.ec.europa.eu.

immigrants who arrived in Germany at that time. They came as 'guest workers', on the presumption that they would at some point return to their country of origin. The large majority, however, stayed on and others later joined them. Today there are over 3 million people of Turkish origin living in Germany. Legislation was passed in 2000 making it possible for the children of foreign parents living in the country to become German citizens after eight years' residency. However, dual nationality is not on offer, and individuals of Turkish origins, when aged between eighteen and twenty-three, must choose of which country to be a citizen. Similar practices existed in other countries where migration was also seen as temporary, long after such was clearly not the case. Although several major European states at that time sought immigrants, unlike in the United States, there was no idea of a 'melting pot' or even of the acceptance of diversity. When in more recent years migrants started to arrive in large numbers, with the exception of Britain and one or two other countries, the European states were mostly poorly prepared.

Before the financial crisis, immigration into the EU was running at between 3 and 4 million a year. Precise figures are impossible to obtain because the true scale of illegal immigration is unknown. There is a lot of movement out of the EU countries too, so the level of net migration up to that time was probably of the order of 2 million annually. Many came from ex-colonial countries in North Africa, the Middle East, India, Pakistan and elsewhere. There are 'migration corridors' linking specific countries. For example, two-thirds of Moroccans who moved to Europe in recent years went to Spain. In 2012, the latest year for which detailed statistics are available, 1.6 million immigrants entered the EU legally, while an unknown number arrived illegally. The UK, Germany, Spain and Italy received the largest numbers. However, the proportion in relation to population size was higher in some of the smaller states.

The chaos in the Middle East and parts of North Africa is leading to a sharp rise in the pressure on the EU's borders. Millions of people have been rendered homeless by the conflicts in Syria, Iraq, Libya, Mali, Sudan and elsewhere. Many of them cast their eyes towards Europe as a place of refuge and as offering the chance of a new beginning. Again, Europe is not in a unique situation here, since the issue is to some extent worldwide. The United States, Canada and Australia, for example – countries that have welcomed generations of immigrants across the years – are adopting more draconian policies designed to limit the influx. All are seeking to cope with pressure from people desperate to enter, frequently risking their lives in making the attempt. All are clamping down upon illegal immigration while at the same time actively trying to attract qualified and skilled migrants to their shores.

The Mediterranean countries are particular targets for those fleeing from disaster areas. Italy is a prime case in point. In the first half of 2014, 65,000 migrants crossed the sea to try to gain entry. Many have to be saved at sea before reaching lands, having been seriously at risk while attempting the crossing. The numbers are almost certain to increase in future years, perhaps dramatically. Here is another area that will demand far more cohesive policy-making at an EU level than exists at present. The current situation is haphazard and full of unintended consequences. The headquarters of Frontex is in Warsaw, far from the southern border. The main source of migration twenty years ago was perceived to be from the former Soviet satellite countries in Eastern Europe. No one anticipated either the Arab Spring (a name too positive to be any longer current) or the disasters that would follow in its wake. Yet EU policy towards North Africa and the Middle East more generally had long been not much more than a weak veneer of good intentions – an instance of paper Europe if ever there was one.

In lieu of effective EU policy, in 2002 the government of Silvio Berlusconi introduced a strategy of intercepting the migrants at sea and returning them to their countries of origin. The attempt was a manifest failure both in practical terms and in terms of the absence of any sort of ethical asylum policy.[3] A more accommodating strategy was introduced subsequently, but has been undermined by the sheer number of those trying to make the crossing. Because there is little effective action at European level, with countries like Italy being left to deal with the issue locally, such countries seek to accommodate by taking a lax attitude towards at least some of the asylum-seekers who arrive on its shores. They are quite often issued with temporary permits and allowed to pass through the country. There is currently no effective form integrated asylum system in the EU, so many either become vagrants or work illegally. This situation in turn prompts public resentment against migrants more generally.

A Common European Asylum System (CEAS) has been agreed. A meeting of the European Council in June 2014 agreed that its full implementation 'is a necessity'. The same meeting emphasised that robust and effective cooperation agreements with countries of origin is a necessity – such as the provision of assistance to help them strengthen the management of their borders. Regional protection and resettlement programmes in countries suffering from internal conflicts will receive expanded funding. Following a tragedy in which a boat carrying 500 migrants sank off the coast of Lampedusa, a Task Force Mediterranean was set up to seek to minimise further such incidents.

The Union is in an odd and paradoxical situation because, while external immigration is tightly regulated and limited, internal migration is encouraged by the EU authorities, since people should migrate to where the jobs are and interaction across Europe is needed to help create a stronger European identity. The Schengen Agreement was set up precisely to promote ease of movement. Well over a million people living in an EU country migrated to another in 2013. As one would expect under current economic conditions, considerable numbers of internal migrants are moving from South to North. There was a 40 per cent increase over the previous year in those coming into Germany from Spain, Portugal, Greece and Italy. However, emigration out of the EU altogether from Southern countries now seems to be growing. Thus significant numbers over the past three years have moved from Spain and Portugal to countries in Latin America. Some smaller European states until recent years were quite closed and homogeneous. Norway is an example. In 2012, however, 12 per cent of the population were classified as immigrants. They come from no fewer than 220 different countries. Most live in urban areas, as is generally the case across Europe. Oslo has 26 per cent foreign-born inhabitants. In many European cities there are neighbourhoods where over 50 per cent are first- or second-generation immigrants from outside the EU.

Immigration ranks highly among the preoccupations of citizens in most European countries today. It is one of the prime concerns of far-right and populist parties, but it also figures highly among most voters when they are asked to rank the issues that worry them. In one of the most debated recent books on the topic, the Dutch author Paul Scheffer argues that the shock-waves produced by mass migration into the EU are real and worrying:

> We're in the middle of profound changes and it's unwise to pretend they're inconsequential or simply to close our minds to them. How often do we hear the unanswerable 'immigration has always been with us', the notion that people are always on the move and our time is no exception? . . . The guest workers from Morocco and Turkey who are changing Dutch neighbourhoods aren't simply counterparts to the seasonal workers from Germany who spent time in the low countries in seasons past. The fact that Jews from Portugal fled to the Netherlands to escape the Catholic Church's Inquisition doesn't make it a matter of course that refugees from Islamist despotism in Iran and Afghanistan should come to live here.[4]

Like many others, including prominent political leaders, Scheffer sees multiculturalism as having failed. Its essential idea, as he interprets it, is that the interaction of different cultures is a mutually enriching learning experience. Yet how can that be the case if many people simply live in closed-off neighbourhoods, following values and norms not only different from, but perhaps actively hostile to, those of the large majority in the host society? Immigration is often thought to produce greater openness and tolerance, but how is that so if migrants hold deeply intolerant attitudes – for example, towards freedom of speech or the equality of women and men? When Scheffer says that 'There's a need for a more candid approach to the frictions and clashes that always result from the arrival of sizeable migrant groups', he is right – although the seriousness and direction of such clashes vary a lot depending upon economic circumstances, the level of cultural difference between newcomers and hosts, and how far racist attitudes are involved.

Migration in contemporary times is no longer only a local or a regional issue but an outcome and a medium of globalisation.

Table 3 Numbers travelling each year: a hyper-mobile world – but unevenly so

	1990 millions	2007 millions	Market share 2007 %
World	436	903	100
Europe	252.7	502	55.6
Asia and Pacific	58.9	181.9	20.1
Americas	99.8	149.7	16.6
Middle East	8.2	27.8	3.1
Africa	9.9	26.7	3.0

Source: Data from UNWTO, 2008.

The models of reception and assimilation that applied to mass migration in earlier times, such as from Europe to the US in the early part of the twentieth century, no longer necessarily hold good. Where electronic communication is available to everyone, and instantaneously, to anywhere, all sorts of new permutations are possible. For instance, the 'two-step' process of assimilation so common in former times – where second-generation immigrants become more like the indigenous population, might not apply. A recent book on Europe, for example, concentrates upon what, in respect of Muslims in Europe, the author calls precisely 'the revolt of the second generation'.[5]

There are other consequences too. Globalisation has an uprooting effect for almost everyone, a phenomenon which has both negative and positive sides. It is often said that, as a result of immigration, many Europeans feel like strangers in their homelands. Yet the pace of change is intense for almost everyone. A neighbourhood or town can alter its character almost completely over a few years depending on vagaries of the world economy. It is not surprising that there are 'back to the future' sentiments everywhere, fuelled by nostalgia – quite often for an idealised past. Indeed, religious fundamentalism is essentially a back to the future phenomenon related to an idealised past, as are some versions of resurgent nationalism. All sorts of ambiguities and contradictions need to be teased out. The very same people who complain about too much immigration will cheerfully go out for a Chinese meal. They will avidly support football teams in which most, or sometimes all, of the players, as well as the managers and training staff, are foreign. People who want to be free to travel the world now that air fares can be very cheap want strict controls on those coming into their own country, but might resent having to wait two hours going through passport control in their country of destination. Immigrants, first or second generation, unless they are very poor, can now travel around just like anyone else once they have official documents. This is an era of mass fluidity.

Scheffer describes a visit he made to Tangiers, where he met a man of his acquaintance, Moroccan by origin, but who lived in Amsterdam and spoke Dutch with an Amsterdam accent. He said to Scheffer, 'This is my country. What do you think?' The man spoke as a compatriot but was now in 'his' country. In his welcome, Scheffer perceived not only a ritual greeting, but 'bittersweet vengeance'. The roles back 'home' were reversed and also the likely feelings of superiority/inferiority. His welcome 'was almost a challenge, drawing the attention of Dutch visitors to shortcomings in their own dealings with outsiders.'[6] Or at least, Scheffer concludes, that's how it felt to him.

UNTRADITIONAL TRADITION

Just as Yogi Berra famously said that the future ain't what it used to be (not just a good joke, but actually a complex socio-logical truth in today's world), so tradition ain't what it used to be. Tradition, of course, was always invented and reinvented: many customs and practices often thought to be age-old are in historical terms very recent.[7] Christianity may have a 2,000-year history, but what a diversity of changes, innovations, reversals and schisms are contained in that evolution! Yet tradition today is more malleable and changeable than ever before, and in the very short term, because of the constant interaction of different values and influences. Thus the wearing of the full veil in Islamic communities might seem like a return to tradition. Yet it is often a reconstructed one. Many women who now adopt the practice are in fact the first generation in their families to do so. The 'conservatism' in Islam today is sometimes very new-found indeed and mostly prepared to embrace the modern, even to accentuate it. The supposed 'conservatives' may make full use of mobile phones, the social media and the internet in their daily lives and see no problem in doing so. The full veil is no doubt usually associated with a repression of women's rights, but at least some women who wear it say they do so in the interests of female liberation – freedom from the sexual gaze of men and from being stylised as objects of male desire. The fiercest debates and confrontations in Europe centre around Islam, seen by many to be incompatible with 'Western' values. Yet Islam is just as 'Western' as Christianity. Each emerged in the same part of the world, and their histories are interwoven.

Migration always to some extent created global diasporas, but today they form both real and virtual communities, normally in a far more self-conscious way than in the past. Their subdivisions and nuances are sometimes national or regional, but often stretch indefinitely across the world. The case of jihadists who are second- or third-generation immigrants in a Western country, or who are attracted to the cause having been converted to Islam from a secular background, are just the most visible edges of what has become a ubiquitous process. Mohamed Merah, born in France, but whose family was of Algerian origins, went on the rampage in March 2012. He shot and killed three unarmed French soldiers, as well as a rabbi and three small children at a Jewish school.

When Merah attacked the soldiers he shouted 'God is great' in Arabic. He wore a small video camera around his neck to record the killings and sent the footage off to the TV station Al Jazeera, although the station did not air it. Initially it was thought that he was acting on his own, although it was known that he had made several journeys to the Middle East and Afghanistan, supposedly as a tourist. Later it was found that he was in contact with many like-minded groups and individuals in different parts of the world. His phone records showed that he had made 1,800 calls to 180 different contacts in twenty countries. Many of those of North African origins disavowed Merah's acts, which terrorised the Toulouse region and ended in a shoot-out in which he was killed by a police commando. Yet he received a good deal of support too, from the local community and his family. Merah's mother would not try to persuade her son to surrender to the police. His brother said that he was proud of him, while his father brought a case against the French government for unlawful homicide.[8] It has become commonplace to argue that Europe's 'second crisis' is weakening the Union in an even more profound way than economic recession. As Richard Youngs puts it: 'The prominence of . . . Islamic radicalism, migration and the flailing "European identity" has probably done more than anything else to ensure that fear is the dominant emotion when Europe looks out on the emerging world order. It is this nexus which has engendered the most hyperbolic talk of "the end of Europe" and the continent's "cultural death".'[9]

ANXIOUS MOMENTS

In 2010 Thilo Sarrazin, a member of the left-of-centre Social Democratic Party and a prominent banker, published a book called *Deutschland schafft sich ab* (Germany Abolishes Itself)[10] which became a sensation and sold over 1.5 million copies in the space of a year. Germany, he proclaimed, risks becoming undermined by immigration, and specifically by the presence of so many Muslim communities in its midst. Because of their higher birth rates, such communities will bring about a 'conquest by fertility'. The magazine *Der Spiegel* labelled Sarrazin 'the man who divided Germany', since his views seemed to polarise the country. He argued forcefully that multicultural-ism is a failure. Muslim communities are largely separate from the rest of German society rather than in any sense integrated into it. Many have low levels of education; birth rates are higher than those of the indigenous population. Sarrazin implied there might be genetic factors involved in the backwardness of Muslim groups. In a newspaper interview he observed that 'all Jews share a certain gene like all Basques share a certain gene that distinguishes them from other people' (he later expressed his regrets about the statement).[11]

Many immigrants choose to depend on the state, he wrote, and are not interested in connecting up with the wider society. The Turkish and Arab population in Berlin mostly live on welfare while at the same time denying the very legitimacy of the state that provides it. Sarrazin has said about Islam: 'No other reli-gion in Europe makes so many demands. No immigrant group other than Muslims is so strongly connected with claims on the welfare state and crime. No group emphasises their differences so strongly in public, especially through women's clothing. In no other religion is the transition to violence, dictatorship and terrorism so fluid.' Most political leaders condemned Sarrazin, and he stepped down from his position at the Bundesbank. He was widely accused of being a racist. Yet his book tapped into a groundswell of public opinion. Some of his critics agreed with the popular sentiment that he raised issues that previously were being swept under the carpet.[12]

In 2012, Sarrazin published a follow-up work, *Europa braucht den Euro nicht* (Europe Doesn't Need the Euro).[13] Germany is being pressurised to support the failing countries of the euro-zone and is conceding because of Holocaust guilt. To atone for its past, Germany is called upon to put its money into European hands. Specifically, the support that is being given to Greece demonstrates Germany's 'psychopathological guilt complex that makes it fulfil almost every wish of self-interested foreign countries even sixty-seven years after the end of the war'.[14] The euro, Sarrazin says, has not helped promote German exports. Thus since the launch of the single currency, Germany's trade with countries external to the eurozone has increased far more than it has with the other eurozone states. Germany is being penalised for its success; it is held liable for all other countries in the single currency whenever they need help. Sarrazin opposes closer political union and advocates a return to national currencies.

Not long after Sarrazin published his first book, Chancellor Angela Merkel intervened publicly in the debate. In the 1960s, she admitted, Germany had actively recruited foreign workers to come into the country. It was presumed that they would return to Turkey and their other countries of origin. As Merkel put it, 'We kidded ourselves for a while. We said: "They won't stay, sometime they will be gone", but this isn't reality.' While disavowing views of the sort represented by Sarrazin, she added that the German attempt to build a multicultural society 'and to live happily side-by-side, and to enjoy each other . . . has failed, utterly failed'.[15]

In March 2012 an extensive report produced by the Interior Ministry on the situation of Muslims in Germany was published. It was based on a wide-ranging set of interviews, plus an analysis of media coverage of Islam. According to official statistics, there are some 4 million Muslims living in the country, about half of whom are German citizens. The results showed that almost 80 per cent of those with citizenship were favourable towards integration, and just over 50 per cent of those who were not citizens took the same view. At the same time, a significant minority of Muslims overall – some 20 per cent – were characterised as 'sceptical'. A proportion of the 'second-generation' age group between fourteen and twenty-two was described as 'strictly religious'. They showed 'strong antipathy to the West, a tendency to accept violence and with no willingness to integrate'. This group was found to amount to 15 per cent of Muslim citizens and 24 per cent of non-citizens – sizeable numbers. The report discussed the possibility that Sarrazin's book on immigration may in fact have contributed to the attitudes of those who discounted integration. Some of the interviews on which the ministry's study was based were carried out before the publication of the book and others afterwards. The results in fact did show distinct differences. The public outcry the book provoked might have had the 'undesirable effect' of making non-German Muslims feel they were regarded in a hostile way by the rest of society.[16]

Angela Merkel's claim that multiculturalism has 'utterly failed' has been echoed by many other political leaders across Europe, especially of course those on the extremes. Is she right? I don't think so. I would put things almost completely the other way around. Far from multiculturalism having failed in Germany, and in Europe more widely, it would be more accurate to say that it has *hardly been tried*. More accurately put, it has been tried only in limited contexts and in a few countries. As developed by its academic initiators, multiculturalism is almost the opposite of what it is taken to mean in most public discourse. It does not imply value relativism – that there are no standards by which different cultural claims and activities can be judged. It does not mean accepting, let alone accentuating, the physical and moral barriers that separate communities. On the contrary, it implies bringing those communities together in active and everyday contact.

Dutch and French policies on immigration might seem quite opposed – two contrasting experiments, as it were. The Dutch practised 'minority policy'. It was a system based upon 'separate and parallel lines'. A policy was pursued that almost encouraged immigrants to retreat into their own areas with their own radio, TV and newspapers. This 'positive encouragement of non-belonging'[17] was almost the very opposite of multiculturalism, and it produced difficult repercussions. The new 'integration policy', introduced in the late 1990s, although widely seen as a backlash against multiculturalism, was in fact rather more in line with multicultural policy as it should be understood. Citizenship classes, combined with the compulsory learning of the Dutch language, were instituted. Little was done, however, to set up effective programmes to try to remedy poverty, neighbourhood isolation or racism. France did not recognise the existence of ethnic minorities but pursued a policy of 'citizenship for all'. Statistics of ethnic origins were simply not collected, while active multicultural policies were notable for their absence. As a result, the actual degree of separation between minorities – especially those of North African origin – and the rest of the population became greater than in almost any other EU country. The two sets of policies seem to be at the opposite ends of the spectrum, but in fact were functionally similar.

WHAT MULTICULTURALISM IS

Multiculturalism has its political and intellectual origins in Canada – in the writings of authors such as Charles Taylor, whose exposition certainly remains relevant today.[18] Taylor argues that two concepts are involved whenever cultural divergences within a society (or wider constellation) are debated. The first is that all people should have equal dignity, whatever cultural traits they follow or whatever lifestyle they adopt. Multiculturalism hence implies a principle of universal citizenship within a society. The second is that multiculturalism presumes 'a politics of recognition'; it is not about separate identities, but about mutual recognition and therefore interaction. It is exactly when groups are treated, or treat themselves, as 'separate and alien' that problems arise. Multiculturalism presumes, not that groups should go their own way or be left to their own devices, but that action should be taken to remedy such developments. In Taylor's words, 'the societies we are striving to create – free, democratic, willing to some degree to share equally – require strong identification on the part of their citizens.' Multiculturalism in a national context, he argues, 'requires patriotism'.[19]

Equality of status (backed up by law) does not imply an uncritical acceptance of the beliefs and practices of others. 'It is how we do things' is not an acceptable justification of a given item of behaviour if that behaviour seriously impinges on the rights or the dignity of others. Where there are serious infringements of that sort, they always have to be dealt with in law, where the legal system embodies the principles that Taylor mentions. However, given the intricacies of cultural inter-changes in a globalised world, we should always be alert to the tangles they are likely to involve.

The 'headscarf wars' in France provide a good example. The laws that limited the wearing of the headscarf or veil among schoolgirls formed one of the grievances that motivated Mohamed Merah in his killing spree. According to those laws, the headscarf was regarded as a symbol of women's inequality under Islam and hence flouted France's insistence on equal gender rights. The original case, which prompted much anguished public debate, dates from October 1989. Three girls at a school not far from Paris were expelled because they refused to take off their headscarves. Many saw in this stance a refusal on the part of the Muslim community to accept French secularism. A subsequent public enquiry concluded that no 'significant' form of religious symbolism could be worn in schools, including not only the headscarf but also such items of apparel as a Sikh turban or Jewish skull cap. This principle eventually became adopted in law, but only much later. The girls did not wear their headscarves to school because of pressure coming from their families, or indeed from any religious figures in their neighbourhoods. They did so in fact self-consciously against the wishes of their parents. In another interesting turn, two of them eventually agreed not to wear them in the classroom after Muslim community leaders per-suaded the king of Morocco to intervene to that end. Other schoolgirls in France took to wearing headscarves decorated with the French flag and inscribed with the words 'liberty, equality, fraternity'.[20]

The actions of the three schoolgirls were just one moment in the endless interplay of the local, the personal, and the global that is now part of everyday life. Because of this global edge, the controversies around Islam in Europe are mostly not like those of a generation ago.[21] The controversy about the headscarf and full veil is going on in a diversity of countries in different parts of the world. Some are largely Muslim in their composition, while in others there are hardly any Muslims at all. For instance, the practice and the debate have surfaced in Japan. Until recent years Turkey, a majority Muslim country, had a more extensive ban on headscarves than France.

The idea that Muslim minorities living in Europe form a threat to the core values of the European countries is risible, whatever the very real dangers posed by terrorists, 'home-grown' or otherwise. Muslims in Europe are a diverse group in terms of their origins and beliefs. Insofar as one can in fact generalise, most Muslims in Europe are not religious, if this term means regular participation in ceremonies and prayers. Among those who hold conservative views, most want integration without assimilation. They want to be active in the wider society but without abandoning their religious views and practices. We should remember that the Christian and Jewish churches have their share of the ultra-orthodox. We do not judge these religions by the ideas of their extremist groups, and nor should we do so in the case of Islam.[22]

IMMIGRATION AND SOLIDARITY

In the UK, a more reasoned account of the same sort of issues discussed by Sarrazin was published by David Goodhart several years before Sarrazin's work appeared.[23] Goodhart subsequently wrote a fuller and more subtle version. So far as immigration into Britain goes, he says, the country 'has had too much of it, too quickly, especially in recent years'.[24] His writings have given rise to a very lively debate, although, being less raucous, they provoked nothing like the public controversy associated with Sarrazin. Largely as a result of immigration, Goodhart argues, British society has become so diverse that many people constantly interact with strangers. Feelings of solidarity become diluted, creating a threat to the continuity of the welfare state. Citizens become less willing to support progressive taxation and the need for a developed welfare system if they sense they have little in common with many of the welfare recipients. Just as in the case of Sarrazin, Goodhart's ideas were widely condemned as racist. One critic wrote: 'Nice people do racism too . . . some very nice folk have decided that the nation's real problem is too many immigrants of too many kinds.'[25]

Is Goodhart's thesis correct, though? The evidence tends to suggest not, although the questions involved are clearly complex. A major piece of research carried out on the issue involved a detailed study of several different countries: Britain, Germany, the Netherlands, the US and Canada. According to its authors, Will Kymlicka and Keith Banting, there are two claims made in the position represented by Goodhart. One is that it is ethnic diversity as such that undermines feelings of solidarity. It would follow that, the larger the size of ethnic minorities in the population, the more difficult it is to preserve a robust welfare state. The second is that policies based on recognition of the special needs of minorities diminish trust in other aspects of the welfare system. If either of these should turn out to be the case, not just the EU countries, but most of the other industrial societies, would face huge problems. Many such countries today apply strict restrictions on entry for immigrants, except for those (mainly skilled workers) they are actively trying to attract. Yet there is good reason to suppose that immigration will continue to be substantial, since the ageing population can't be supported without a thriving younger generation and because neither the

EU nor its member states are able to block immigration completely. Indeed, some in the future may need to make up for workers who, in the current situation, are emigrating out of the EU altogether.

Using a variety of measures, Kymlicka and Banting conclude that an ethnically heterogeneous population does not in fact inevitably weaken welfare systems. No relationship exists between the proportion of the population born outside a given country and level of social spending. To measure possible policy connections, a list of different policy strategies was drawn up and compared across countries (for instance, exemptions from dress codes, allowance of dual citizenship or the funding of bilingual education). Twenty-one democratic countries were compared in terms of the adoption of such policies. There was no evidence of any systematic connection between the introduction of such policies and the weakening of welfare states.[26]

INTERCULTURALISM

The debate about multiculturalism and migration in Europe has become stale, revolving around the same themes for many years now. It is time to break free and to consider it afresh, starting from different premises – ones bound up with the changing world in general. Following a recent trend in the literature, I suggest that the word 'multiculturalism' at this point is dropped. There are three reasons. One is that it has become too contaminated by years of misuse. It has been construed as what some have called 'laissez-faire multiculturalism' – let a thousand flowers bloom – rather than the rich and sophisticated notion it should be. It might never be possible to bring its proper meaning into public discourse. The second, however, is much more important. It is that the notion of multiculturalism was created before globalisation had reached the levels it has attained today – and which is now receiving a massive further boost through the universalising of the internet. The interaction of cultures can no longer be treated as internal to a society, or even to an entire region such as the EU as a whole. Global today means global, even though globality might be expressed in the smallest of actions (e.g., using a mobile phone). At the same time it is intensely local, with thousands of complex levels in between.[27]

Reason number three is that, even in its sophisticated form, multiculturalism used the word 'culture' in a way that might have had application thirty years ago but does not now. Its proponents tended to assume that cultures, including ethnic cultures, have clear-cut boundaries, are unchanging over time, and are not internally divided – or even essentially contested. If that was ever true it certainly is not now. Finally, there has been a marked inclination to assume that 'Western' culture developed indigenously and shares little with cultures in other parts of the world. Hence, the West (or the EU, with its 'civilising mission') has to propagate ideas that are ill-developed or non-existent elsewhere – more on that below.

Interculturalism is a better term to express the fact that we – collective humanity – are in a new era of diversity and social cohesion. That era is obstinately local yet fundamentally global, not only in the sense of 'worldwide' but in the sense of capable of transcending specific contexts of time and space. It is the cultural dimension of the high opportunity, high risk society. Interculturalism is not just about finding a place for 'alien' cultural groups within society, fostering interaction between minorities and host communities and nations, or reducing inequalities, important though all those aims are. Rather, it focuses attention upon processes of negotiation and dialogue that can positively reconstruct public space. Even sophisticated multiculturalism was mainly about improving the position of 'minorities', not about how shared identities, including those of the cultural majority, should be renegotiated. Thus the invocation of 'freedom, equality, fraternity' by the French schoolgirls in *l'affaire du foulard* poses a question to the majority, and to the principles of law that majority endorses. Universal standards and transcultural institutions (such as courts of human rights) are a prerequisite but are (or should be) themselves subject to ongoing dialogue, whereby those institutions can be routinely examined and recast.

A super-diversity of contacts and involvements is replacing the simple alignment of cultural groups within cities, regions and the wider society. In some of the major European cities there are now over 300 language groups.[28] The heterogeneous nature of London's population was revealed in the bombings of July 2005. The fifty-two people who died included individuals from all over the world. Among their number were five Muslims, who came from Tunisia, Bangladesh, Afghanistan and Indonesia. One young woman was described as 'a thoroughly modern Muslim, a girl who loved her Burberry plaid handbag and fashionable clothes while at the same time respecting her family's wish that she sometimes wear traditional *salwar kameez* at home. She went shopping in the West End of London with friends, but would always be seen at the mosque for Friday prayers.'[29] Others who were killed came from Romania, Italy, Nigeria, Israel, New Zealand, Vietnam, Mauritius, Australia, Sri Lanka, Grenada, India, Ireland and Jamaica.

When super-diversity reigns, many individuals – or perhaps the large majority – no longer feel themselves to have single identities. Their allegiances may be mixed and fluid and their patterns of behaviour not intrinsically predictable from the boxes that are ticked on a census return. Whether a person is black, white, Christian or Muslim may show very little about what kinds of lives they have, or what their social needs are, in terms, for example, of welfare provision.[30] 'Home-grown terrorists' are usually part of this hybrid pattern. The London bombers, for instance, on the surface appeared well integrated into their local communities. Muslims in Western countries are not homogeneous groups, sitting outside the larger social order, in the way they are so frequently portrayed in the media.

Figure 11 After the London bombings: Muslim women register their protest against violence

Extremists exist, of course, and the threat of terrorism is real. Yet in the case of Muslims these facts are used to make absurd generalisations. A piece of research carried out at the University of Cardiff analysed a thousand newspaper articles in which Muslims featured. There were seventeen times as many references to radicals as to more moderate groups – which are in fact far and away the large majority. 'Terrorists,' 'militants' or 'Islamists' were the words most frequently used.[31] Extremists, in fact, can be and are of many different hues. In one of the most lethal attacks in Europe in recent years, in Oslo, the perpetrator, Anders Breivik, was a member of the political far right. Seventy-seven people were killed and a total of 260 injured.

The danger with otherwise well-meaning government initiatives is that they could reinforce the very traits they seek to change. Targeting the whole Muslim community as a source of potential terrorism encourages exactly the 'them versus us' mentality that has to be overcome. As Amartya Sen has stressed: 'The confusion between the plural identities of Muslims and their Islamic identity is not only a descriptive mistake, it has serious implications for peace in the precarious world in which we live.'[32] The term 'immigration' itself needs deconstruction in relation to changes affecting society, from the local to the global and back again. The positive and negative emotions surrounding it, experienced by newcomers and host communities alike, overlap with so many other changes in a sort of swirl. 'Immigration' can become a code for other transformations affecting identity and community, for example. Thus mass immigration into Europe has largely coincided with the hollowing out of the old working-class communities as heavy industry either disappeared or was transferred overseas. Immigrants frequently moved to such areas because they were cheap and there was housing available. They can become scapegoats for feelings of lost identity and community spirit that in fact stemmed largely from these other causes. A range of intersections between the local and the global are going on here, perhaps to a large extent invisible to those most centrally affected by them.[33]

Immigration today also coincides with deeper mutations. There is a quite fundamental sense in which we are all migrants now, adrift in a world with an imponderable future, where old identities are under strain and new ones elusive. We are pioneers along new social and technological frontiers, even if at any point in time they are integral parts of our everyday behaviour. All sorts of issues to do with identity, individual and collective, arise from these circumstances. The internet is as contradictory and complex as human society itself, which it reflects but also trans-forms. It promotes active dialogue, freed from the constraints of context, but at the same time it carries, and perhaps ampli-fies, the full range of emotions, including hatreds. Migration intersects with all these changes, producing a complicated set of consequences for identity, personal and collective.

'EUROPEAN' VALUES?

The harsh line now taken by most EU states against migra-tion is reproduced at the European level. The EU's Return Directive of 2008 damaged the Union's standing in the eyes of many countries. Patrolling migration now makes up some 60 per cent of the EU's budget in its programme for Freedom, Security and Justice. EU governments – and to some extent the EU institutions – 'deceive themselves in thinking that a kind of Euro-chauvinism represents a viable and enlightened means of dealing with the non-Western world order.'[34] The principles of interculturalism should be applied to Europe itself and the idea of Europe's 'civilising mission' reappraised. Take the core idea of democracy, which, together with those such as the rule of law, the freedom of the individual and tolerance, is often thought to have its origins in Greece and Rome and hence to be intrinsically 'European'.[35] John Keane's magisterial work on democracy has thoroughly discredited this idea. The stated objective of his study, he says, is to 'democratise the history of democracy'. Democracy has many origins and has taken a variety of forms. The popular assemblies found in Greece had their antecedents two millennia previously, in the civilisations of Mesopotamia. Keane is critical of the tendency to idealise Athenian democracy. In the conjuncture of *demos* ('people') and *kronos* ('rule') the second was the more important. 'Rule' actually referred to power, backed up by military might. The Athenians' sense of destiny was the prime motivating force of the ruling groups.

Keane vigorously refutes the notion that, with the fall of the Greek city-states, democracy went into hibernation for centuries, to be rediscovered in Europe and the newly emerging United States. To the contrary: across this long period, democracy continued to develop in other parts of the world, in the Middle East and the Far East, as well as in areas of sub-Saharan Africa. Democracy came back to Europe via the Muslims. The first European parliaments emerged in the south of Spain in the twelfth century and were a direct response on the part of the Christian monarchs to democratic Islam, which at that point was spreading widely. Keane refuses to celebrate the coming of representative democracy, which he regards as a mixed bag at best. He analyses democracy in the nineteenth and twentieth centuries in Latin America before coming to Europe. Violent and corrupt though they might have been, he does not see states such as Brazil, Argentina or Mexico at that period as aberrations. They were in fact the forerunners of representative democracy in Europe, which was steeped in violence and shaped by war. Mass democracy, and its association with citizenship, was bred in conjunction with 'the brazen murdering' of whole peoples – in Europe and in Europe's colonial domains.

The same applies to 'Western values' in other areas besides democracy. Tolerance is a good example. It is in no way a purely Western notion. A well-articulated discussion is to be found, for example, in the work of Ashoka, an Indian emperor who wrote in the third century BC. The Ottoman empire practised religious tolerance; different religious groups flourished at certain periods, allowed to have their own areas of jurisdiction.[36] These observations – and a multiplicity of others could be adduced –

are extremely important. It is quite wrong to see immigrants from other cultures as pre-modern – as constituting an intrinsic threat to values cultivated distinctively in the West. The values that underlie 'the good society' come from many sources and rest upon something of a universal foundation. They do not have to be simply 'exported' from the West to more barbaric parts of the world.

In policy terms, an interculturalist approach contrasts in some clear ways with multiculturalism, even in its sophisticated versions. It seeks not simply to integrate minorities but to provide a vision for the society as a whole, as well as communities within it – and one with clear transnational dimensions too. It is not only the EU that has identity problems today: many or most nations do too. In some part this is because of fragmentation or because of the resurgence of local nationalisms; but it is also because of the diversity of options available at national level. Consider the US, Russia and China. In each of these cases there are competing versions of what the identity of the nation should be or should become. National identity might still involve what Benedict Anderson famously called an 'imagined community' – history reintegrated as myth.[37] Yet it is also increasingly composed of competing future options. In the US some works echo the anxieties of Sarrazin. Samuel Huntington's book *Who Are We?*, for example, is concerned with the impact of mass immigration into the US from Latin America.[38] The legal creed of the United States is a creation of English settlers, an expressing of 'a dissenting Protestant culture'. The influx of Latin American, especially Mexican, immigrants, concentrated in the South, is introducing other cultural values, essentially those of Catholicism. Some states in the South could come to form a distinct cultural bloc within the US – a threat to the nation's key values.

Very different interpretations of US identity have been put forward by others. The dilemmas and possibilities are multiple, externally as well as internally. How far should the US be turning towards Asia? Is the country becoming a Pacific rather than an Atlantic one? What is its role in the Middle East following the Arab uprisings? In the case of Russia, the dilemmas are just as problematic. Russia suffered a traumatic loss of identity and power following the collapse of the Soviet Union – how best to respond? 'The West treats us like we just came down from the trees', Vladimir Putin once remarked. Is Russia a European country or not, since it stretches all the way to the fringes of Japan? It is an age-old dilemma, but one that is now appearing in new form, partly because of the rise of the 'new China'. And then there is the issue of the fractured relation of the country to its own diverse Muslim groups.

China's accelerated rise to global prominence has opened up a very lively debate about the country's identity. Many inside and outside China in recent years have spoken of the nation's 'identity crisis'. One of the myths many Chinese have cultivated about their society is that it is the harmonious outcome of thousands of years of continuous traditions developed in separation from other cultures. However, except for one or two periods, Chinese civilisation has always been shaped through interaction with the wider world. Moreover, Chinese history has been as violent and brutal as that of the West or anywhere else. What it means to be 'Chinese' has been as contested as what it means to be 'European', in the past and today. In his book *The China Wave*, Zhang Weiwei has put forward the argument that contemporary China is pioneering a model of social development distinct from and superior to that of the West. China, he says, 'is now perhaps the world's largest laboratory of political, economic, social and legal reforms in the world.' And, he continues, 'we have looked beyond the Western model . . . we are exploring the political, economic, social and legal systems of the next generation.' 'What the West is practising is increasingly an election system which I sometimes call "showbiz democracy or "Hollywood democracy", and it's more about showmanship than leadership.'[39]

Zhang is critical of Western views of democracy. The Chinese way of democratic decision-making is superior to the parliamentary system of the West. Every five years a national development plan is prepared. It is the result of tens of thousands of discussions at many different levels of Chinese society. According to Zhang, this process is a real form of democratic involvement and, moreover, one which allows for more rational forward planning than is possible in Western countries. So far as democratic decision-making is concerned, he says, the West is at the 'undergraduate' or perhaps even 'high-school' level, whereas China has progressed to 'graduate' level. Not many in the West would support such an interpretation, given the repression of dissent in China. Francis Fukuyama has vigorously contested Zhang's views.[40] Yet it is not as if democracy in Europe or the US were in a sound state, even in its heartlands. On the issue of corruption, Zhang makes some pointed remarks about Greece, as well as other European countries such as Italy. He once joked to a Greek friend that China could send a team from Shanghai or Chongqing to help Greece with good governance. The public debate between Zhang and Fukuyama is an example of a fruitful open dialogue in which in fact neither party came out clearly on top.

Creating a coherent identity for the EU is obviously a rather different task from that of established nations, since the very point is to find a transnational narrative. 'Europe' has a continuous history of 2,000 years or more, including several centuries of colonialism. Yet before the establishment of the EU – a very short period in historical time – Europe as it now is never had a clear institutional form of governance. The empires that arose in Europe from the Romans onwards covered only part of that (admittedly vague) territorial entity that we now define as 'Europe'. Where does Europe begin and end? On its eastern flank, it is to a large extent an arbitrary matter. Václav Havel produced some compelling reflections on European identity.[41] The question 'what is the identity of Europe?', he pointed out, is normally asked today in relation to debates about how much sovereignty should be transferred from member states to the institutions of the European Union. In that sense it has an artificial quality to it; it is not a question that flows from natural roots but is of almost a technical nature. 'When I pose myself the query "to what extent do I feel European?"', Havel continued, 'my first thought is, why didn't I ponder it a long time ago? Was it because I regarded it as of no importance, or was it something I simply took for granted?' It was essentially the second of these, he says, but there is an additional factor: 'I have a feeling that I would have looked ridiculous if I had written or declared that I was European and felt European.' Such a declaration would have appeared 'pathetic and pompous'.

This sort of attitude, Havel adds, is shared by very many living in Europe. They are so intrinsically European that they don't even think about it. In everyday life they do not describe themselves as 'Europeans', and when asked a direct question about their European identity in opinion polls they feel a sense of mild surprise when they declare that affiliation. Why is it that, until very recently, Europe paid so little attention to its own identity? The reason, Havel says, is because Europe felt (falsely) that it was the world. Or, put another way, Europeans considered themselves so superior to the rest of the world that they felt no need to define Europe in relation to others. Hence 'conscious Europeanism' had little tradition until recently. Havel welcomes the fact that a reflexive European awareness 'is rising from the indistinct mass of the self-evident'. Through enquiring about it, by bringing it to the surface, we contribute to its formation. Such a process is immensely important in current times, exactly 'because we find ourselves in a multicultural, multipolar world, in which recognising one's identity is a prerequisite, for coexistence with other identities.' A critical self-examination has to recognise that many European values and principles may be 'double edged'. If carried too far or abused, they can in fact, Havel declares, 'lead us to hell'. Moreover, a self-conscious identity cannot be built upon economic, financial or administrative considerations.

Following the Second World War and the rise of communist totalitarian rule, there was no need to debate the values being defended, because they were self-evident. (Western) Europe needed to be united in order to prevent a reversion to previous conflicts and to halt the spread of dictatorship. Those values did not need to be spoken of because they were so taken for granted. Only when the military threat to Europe disappeared was there the drive to engage in deep-rooted reflection about 'the moral and spiritual foundation' of its reunification and the objectives of a united Europe.

Havel argues – surely completely correctly – that it is essential when considering 'European values' to reflect on the double-edged legacy that Europe has left the world. There are the values of human rights, freedoms and the rule of law. Yet those rarely applied to the peoples living in Europe's vast colonial domains. Moreover, the 'worst events of the twentieth century – World Wars, Fascism and Communist Totalitarianism' – were largely Europe's doing. In considering the further unification of Europe, he concludes, we 'must demonstrate that the damages generated by its contradictory civilisation can be combated.' The fact that nations across the world – and those that make up the EU – are busy rethinking their identities, and producing diverse interpretations, suggests that aiming for a single narrative for the Union will not work. Rather, the point is to create discursive space in which different themes can be argued about, in ways that grip the interest of citizens. Identity doesn't just depend upon what a political entity says about itself, because it has also to resonate with the rest of the world. European leaders may imagine that Europe has put its colonial past behind it, and is therefore free to preach high abstract values to countries it previously oppressed. Yet the past is not buried so easily. The EU's efforts to arbitrate in the Middle East, for example, come up squarely against the fact that the seeds of the core conflicts in the region were in some large part sown by the Europeans themselves. Looking in from China, Zhang Weiwei makes exactly the same point.[42]

Chapter 5
Climate Change and Energy

The EU has sought to be at the forefront of the world community in combating global warming. It is an urgent and necessary ambition. Human-induced climate change is without precedent in history and is one of the most formidable problems humanity has to face in this century. No other civilisation could intervene in nature even remotely to the degree to which ours does on an everyday basis. It is awesome to recognise that, as collective humanity, we are in the process of altering the world's climate, and very likely in a profound way. Moreover, so far as we know, climate change is irreversible. Some of the main greenhouse gases, including the most important one – CO_2 – will be in the atmosphere for centuries. The cornerstone of the EU's approach to climate change is its 20:20:20 strategy. Member states must reduce their greenhouse gas emissions by 20 per cent by 2020 as compared to 1990 levels; increase their share of renewables in their energy mix to 20 per cent by that date; and achieve a 20 per cent increase in energy efficiency. To help keep the average rise in global temperature to no more than 2 degrees centigrade, the aim is to reduce emissions by at least 80 per cent by 2050.

THE ETS

Among the Union's many initiatives related to these goals, the most ambitious has been the introduction of a European Emissions Trading Scheme (ETS), which began operating in 2005. As part of its climate change agenda, the EU originally considered the possibility of establishing a carbon tax. It was not able to do so because the Union does not have the capacity to intervene in the fiscal affairs of member states. Although in fact it is a tax under another name, emissions trading could be introduced more easily. Emissions trading markets actually originated in the United States, where they were first applied in the context of controlling emissions of sulphur dioxide, a prime cause of acid rain. The scheme met with success and inspired some political figures, most notably Vice-President Al Gore, to seek to apply the idea of a trading market in permits to help limit carbon emissions. In the US, however, on a federal level, carbon trading proved a non-starter. It was the EU which picked up the baton.

The ETS was set up to cover emissions coming from certain forms of energy production (fossil fuels, by and large) and energy-intensive industries. Intense lobbying from those industries and from some of the member states sank the project of having a full auction. A hybrid system arose from the negotiations. Some credits were allocated for free. The member states were allowed to construct their own national allocation plans. Not all of them at that point had precise measures of their CO_2 emissions. They tried to create the most favourable conditions they could when the individual countries' targets were allocated. A market was created, but one far removed from that which the American initiators of the idea of 'cap-and-trade' had in mind, which was an auction of all permits.[1] Huge amounts of money changed hands in the early years of the ETS, but the scheme proved ineffective for its prime purpose – reducing CO_2 emissions. The carbon price rose sharply first of all, but soon dropped in a catastrophic way. There was a large surplus of allowances because of the slack built into the national allocation plans and the number of free permits given out. Some companies made windfall profits by passing on the price of the carbon credits to consumers at the point when it was high, even though the credits were allocated free of charge. Such profits were estimated to have reached almost €14 billion over the period from 2005 to 2008.[2]

It is difficult to estimate with any precision what effect the first phase of the ETS, which lasted across this period, had on CO_2 emissions, because so many other factors were in play at the same time. One quite detailed study concluded that emissions across the EU were about 7 per cent lower than they would have been otherwise.[3] Yet most of that apparent gain dissolves when one takes into account the inflated reporting of their emissions made by some EU nations in the run up to the creation of the scheme. The Commission accepted that the first stage of the ETS was deeply flawed and described it as a 'learning phase'. A second version, initiated in January 2008, was designed to close the loopholes that had rendered its forerunner so ineffective. The allocation of allowances was carried out in some part centrally instead of being in the hands only of the member states and was scrutinised much more carefully. A considerably higher percentage than before was auctioned. Aviation emissions of planes flying in and out of the EU were to be covered by the ETS, but because of resistance from the world's airlines this proposal was not introduced until 2012. In spite of the changes made, the second phase of the ETS, which lasted up to the end of 2012, continued to experience enormous problems.

Phase three of the ETS is due to run from January 2013 to the end of 2020. It features a number of further innovations. The emissions cap is more stringent. The scheme is extended to cover new areas and a greater range of greenhouse gases than before. Most importantly, free allowances are to be phased out. Auctioning will become the prime means of making allocations:

88 per cent of allowances are to be distributed among member states according to either their emissions in 2005 or their average for the period from 2005 to 2007, whichever is the higher. There is a redistributional element: 10 per cent are to be allocated to the poorer EU countries to encourage investment in low-carbon technologies. The remaining 2 per cent are to be given to member states which attained emissions reductions of 20 per cent or more over the fifteen years after 1990, the base year for the Kyoto Protocol. So-called carbon leakage received special attention in phase three. Carbon leakage occurs when one country or region has higher carbon costs than another, such that companies are tempted to move to those with more relaxed regimes – in this case, countries outside the EU. The extent to which such an outcome has happened as a result of the ETS is unknown, but carbon leakage had been in the minds of the creators of the scheme since its early beginnings. The Commission has initiated studies of the phenomenon and intends to apply the results within this phase of the scheme. Sectors thought to be particularly at risk from carbon leakage could be exempted from the auctioning requirement, in order to prevent industry from simply migrating elsewhere.

The only problem with all of this ambition is . . . a very large one indeed. The ETS in fact appears close to collapse. The successive revisions of the scheme have made it forbiddingly complex. To the nations and companies that must operate within its framework, it is enormously cumbersome. Each revision has brought new clauses and sub-clauses. To the ordinary citizen it surely must be completely impenetrable – the opposite of what is needed in moves towards greater transparency and accountability in the EU. Greenhouse gas emissions have been substantially reduced over recent years, but the bulk of this reduction comes from the effects of the recession, not from policy. Without relatively stable prices, and at a fairly high level, the whole point of the scheme is lost. The surplus of emissions in the market for early 2013 was put at 2 billion tonnes of carbon, the same as

one whole year of output for the EU states combined.⁴ At a time
when they are most needed, no effective price signals are being
given for investment in the relevant industries.

Among other problems, the ETS has shown itself to be vulnerable to fraud. In order to create marketable carbon units,
a range of proxy measures has to be used to standardise the
measurement of emissions. In 2010 a huge scam within the
ETS came to light, responsible for losses of €5 billion. At a
later time, ETS trading had to be suspended when credits from
the Austrian and Czech governments were stolen.⁵ A key vote
on the future of the ETS was held in the European Parliament
in February 2013. At that point, because the carbon price had
dropped so low, the scheme was said to be 'on life support'.⁶
A group of large companies signed up to a petition for further
reforms designed to raise carbon prices and revive the programme. However, the method suggested was complex and
would have added to its already arcane nature. In an effort to
prevent the price being subverted, the Commission came up
with another proposal – so-called back-loading – which would
postpone the regular auctioning of credits in some areas for a
number of years.

The idea was voted upon in the European Parliament in April
and was first of all rejected. The carbon price immediately fell
to its lowest level ever. Subsequently the proposal was endorsed
by the Parliament, although at the time of writing it still has
to be sanctioned by the Council. Yet the change does no more
than take the ETS off life support for the while. It is not just
that the ETS is floundering; it has become actively dysfunc-
tional. A recent study showed that the scheme is likely to cancel
out 700 million tonnes of emissions reductions delivered by
other policies.⁷ It is also suffering from being a means whereby
companies are rushing to dispose of offset Kyoto credits, which
are set to be excluded from the ETS through new regulations.
The failure of the ETS is an enormous headache for the EU, as
well as a fundamental setback in attempts to limit emissions. It

was designed to be a vanguard policy that would blaze the way for other countries and regions to follow, thus making way for a worldwide carbon market. That prospect at the moment looks as remote as an effective agreement in the endless UN negotiations, although a number of countries, including the most important of them all in terms of volume of greenhouse gas emissions – China – are proposing to introduce emissions trading schemes. As many observers have noted, the ETS may have a useful impact on the wider world, but one very different from what its initiators originally envisaged. It is a lesson in how not to do it and hence indicates the pitfalls that have to be avoided. Thus, after years of lack of progress, the state of California has introduced an emissions trading scheme. In contrast to that of the EU, it contains a price floor and a price ceiling, to limit wild price fluctuations.

The EU has invested enormous effort, as well as resources, in the endeavour. For that reason, it has a good deal of inertia behind it, and the temptation is to keep on tinkering in the hope that it will all suddenly go right. Yet, if it is allowed simply to limp along, Europe's prestige, already so damaged in other areas, will take a further blow. The dilemma is a bit like that of the euro. Either the ETS needs to be strengthened in a very substantial and effective way or it should be shut down. A further major consequence of the malfunctioning of the scheme is that coal becomes a cheap option for energy production. Coal is the most lethal of the fossil fuels in terms of carbon emissions. I shall discuss the implications further below.

THE UN PROCESS

The EU has been a strong supporter of the activities of the Intergovernmental Panel on Climate Change of the United Nations (IPCC). The IPCC is charged with summarising and interpreting the current state of scientific knowledge about climate change and proposing strategies to curb its advance. Its first assessment was made in 1990 and preceded the Rio Earth Summit that was held two years later. In 1997 the UN established the Kyoto Protocol, whereby the developed countries agreed to cut their greenhouse gas emissions by an average of some 5 per cent over 1990 levels over the period 2008–12. The US declined to ratify the agreement, the sole major exception among the industrial countries. The EU declared targets well ahead of the rest of the world. A whole diversity of other measures were set up under the auspices of the European Climate Change Programme.

Committed to the rule of international law, the EU has invested a great deal of its kudos in the United Nations climate change negotiations that followed on from the signing of the Kyoto Protocol. The EU authorities had high hopes that the UN meetings held on its own territory, in Copenhagen in December 2009, would prove a breakthrough in getting the nations of the world to commit to emissions reductions. Before the event, there was an atmosphere of high optimism about what might be achieved. President Obama led the US back to the negotiating table after years of disengagement under the administration of George W. Bush. China, as an emerging economy, was not required to make any commitments at Kyoto. Yet, in the run up to Copenhagen, the Chinese government announced that the country would set itself the goal of reducing its energy intensity by 40 to 45 per cent by 2020. Because of the level of expectation, the Copenhagen congress was the largest UN meeting of its type before or since. Over 40,000 delegates, from virtually every country in the world, attended: 122 prime ministers and presidents came, the largest number ever assembled in the history of the UN outside of New York. In the event, however, the meetings turned out to be a more or less complete debacle – because of poor organisation on the part of its Danish hosts but as a result of other mishaps too. President Obama arrived only at the last minute. On meeting up with him, Hillary Clinton said: 'Mr President, this is the worst meeting I've ever been to since eighth grade student council.'[8] There were quarrels within and between the developed countries and the developing ones, as well as divisions within the host government. The negotiations began to break down amid widespread acrimony.

Obama met in closet with the leaders from China, Brazil, India and South Africa to produce an informal agreement that would prevent the whole enterprise from becoming a fiasco. The deal they worked out was labelled the Copenhagen Accord. It was a humiliation for the EU. Far from showing the rest of the world the way in seeking to combat climate change, the Union found itself excluded from the meeting that produced the document. It was the same story that has haunted the Union from its beginnings: who speaks for Europe? Many within Europe subsequently played down the exclusion of any EU member from the key decision-making process. Yet, in a conference supposed to demonstrate Europe's lead in regulating carbon emissions, it was a serious setback. Following the meeting between Obama and the four other leaders, the Accord was taken back to the conference hall as a whole. Under extreme time pressure, as the meetings were due to end very shortly, what turned out to be an acrimonious debate ensued among a wider group of states. The Accord was not formally endorsed; all that the nations present were prepared to do was to 'take note' of it. The provisions in the document had no binding force. Those nations which signed up to it did so on a voluntary basis, agreeing to submit their national plans for carbon reductions to the UN. Many eventually did, but in the majority of cases what was registered was thin and inadequate.

Three further rounds of UN meetings have been held so far – in Cancun, Durban and Doha. Following the flop in Copenhagen, only a small group of leaders of state or government attended any of the conferences. Progress was made, at least in principle. At Cancun, the UN for the first time officially adopted the 2°C target which the EU had endorsed years before. A fund to help the poorer countries adapt to climate change and switch to renewable energy, due to amount to $100 billion annually by 2020, was endorsed (no money has been forthcoming to date). Partly because expectations were more modest, many pronounced the meetings in Cancun a success, and similarly those held subsequently. In the normal way of such congresses, agreement in Durban was reached only at the last minute, in discussions that ran over 30 hours beyond the point at which they were supposed to close. As had happened in Cancun, the EU this time played a significant part in contributing to the outcome. No treaty was signed, but the countries present agreed to set up a legally binding treaty by 2015 to confront global warming. In terms of actual obligations, it would take effect in 2020.

The agreement, which was labelled the 'Durban Platform', included the developing countries as well as the EU and the US. EU representatives were enthusiastic. At the conclusion of the conference, the presiding figure at the meetings, Maite Nkoana-Mashabane, declared the enterprise a great success and proclaimed: 'What we have achieved in Durban will play a central role in saving tomorrow today.' The meetings at Doha in December 2012 added very little to the Durban Platform. After years of indecision it was agreed that the Kyoto Protocol should be kept alive; however, the United States, Russia, Canada and Japan did not sign up. One can have legitimate doubts as to whether the negotiations, in which the EU above all has placed such faith, are in fact ever likely to produce any substantial results at all. They could be seen as a version of paper Europe writ large. The meetings have been going on for over twenty years and the tangible results they have produced have been small indeed. With the exception of Copenhagen, they regularly end with a declaration of a breakthrough. One is reminded of the film *The Matrix*, in which the characters inhabit a day-to-day world in which everything seems normal and secure. In fact, it is a computer simulation. The world outside, the real world, is nasty and violent, and human beings live a marginal and embattled existence.

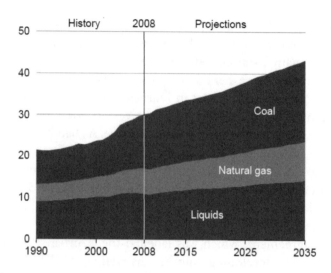

Figure 12 World energy-related carbon dioxide emissions by fuel, 1990–2035
(billion metric tons)

Source: US Energy Information Administration (September 2011).

In a somewhat similar way, the climate change negotiations take place in a surreal universe of formal discussions and supposed agreements. Success is defined not in terms of substantial achievements in the real world, but in terms of whether the meetings are kept going and paper commitments made. Meanwhile, outside, things are turning nasty. Climate change, it should be pointed out, because of its cumulative and permanent character, is not like most other global problems. The greenhouse gases that are now accumulating in the atmosphere will be there for many years – in the case of CO_2, for centuries.

At the moment the world is making no dent at all upon greenhouse gas emissions. As measured by the Mauna Loa observatory in Hawaii, CO_2 emissions in May 2013 for the first time topped 400 parts per million (ppm), the highest level for at least 600,000 years. The average pre-industrial level was 280 ppm. Emissions are going up more steeply each decade than the decade before. If one excludes hydro and nuclear, the proportion of the world's energy delivered by renewables is minute. On a global level we are more thoroughly in hock to fossil fuels than we ever were. I used to believe that the melting of the Arctic ice in the summer – now proceeding at a far faster rate than was believed possible only a few years ago – might be a wake-up call to the world to do far more to combat advancing climate change. It has proved to be the other way around. Countries surrounding the Arctic have endorsed drilling for oil and gas, as well as prospecting for other minerals, and have started to contest one another's territorial rights in the region. There are now serious worries about what is happening in the Southern Ocean, which could be contributing to a global change in air circulation patterns.[9] The Southern Ocean is warming twice as fast as the Earth's other oceans. The International Energy Agency (IEA), which usually takes quite a conservative line on future risk, suggests that the world might be in for an average rise in land temperature of at least 4°C. However, land surface temperature might no longer be the best way to assess the likely overall progression of climate change, exactly because the ocean deeps are absorbing an increasing amount of heat.

I fully support the EU's aim to be a world leader in climate change policy. Yet the two endeavours in which the Union has placed its faith, the ETS and the UN process, to put things bluntly, thus far have failed. Major rethinking is needed in almost all areas of EU climate change policy and indeed in its environmental efforts more generally. The situation in climate change politics looks quite different now from what it was twenty years or so ago when the Union started out in its mission. The UN meetings will go on and the EU states should continue to take part, although in hope rather than real expectation. The real action is likely to happen elsewhere, especially in terms of what the EU and the major state actors do in terms of substantive policy. Especially important are the US and China, which between them generate over 40 per cent of total global emissions.

CONFESSIONS OF AN UNGREEN GREEN

Rethinking the EU's climate change and energy strategy should
at this point start from fundamentals. The green movement in
its modern guise began in Europe and has had a significant influence on EU thinking. That influence has in many ways been for
the good. Yet is also conceals major problems and limitations. I
describe myself as an ungreen green. By this I mean that I share
some of the aspirations of the green movement, especially the
overriding importance of limiting the impact of climate change.
However, at least some sections of that movement are driven by
ideas incompatible with countering the environmental dangers
we face today. Climate change is a huge, huge problem, but it is
part of a raft of new risks that have to be confronted. Examples
are the likely rise of the global population to 10 billion and the
accelerating disappearance of animal species, forests and plant
life.

　The green movement had its origins long before we became
fully conscious of the destructive side of industrialism as it has
spread across the world. It was born from a romantic reaction
against the invasion of the countryside by cities and mechanised
production. Its driving force was conservation and restoration – to protect the countryside and keep large areas of nature
in a pristine state. The name of one of the prominent green
groups, 'Friends of the Earth', captures this orientation perfectly. Nature has to be shielded from the ravages of human
beings and their invasion of its eco-systems. Yet the Earth has
no need of our friendship – it will continue on whatever we
might do. It is not the Earth's future that is at stake, it is ours.
We have to move far beyond the notion that we can protect
'nature'. Much of what we call 'nature', including large aspects
of the climate, is no longer natural at all. We have moved into
what geologists have started to call the *anthropocene* age. It is an
age in which nature has become everywhere invaded by human
influences: 'We humans are becoming the dominant force for

change on earth.'[10] Green philosophy is anchored in a world that has now disappeared, with the consequence that some of its core beliefs and values are suspect. The concepts at stake are those of *conservation*, *sustainability*, and the *precautionary principle* – core emphases of the green movement that have entered the mainstream.

The founder of 'reconciliation ecology', Michael Rosenzweig, argues persuasively that we have to move far beyond the conservation and restoration model if environmental disaster is to be avoided. Today, he says, 'We stand at the edge of an abyss as deep as the greatest known catastrophe in the history of life, the Permo-Triassic mass extinction, which, some 225 million years ago, exterminated more than 95 per cent of the earth's species.'[11] Using current approaches, he continues, no ecologist believes that more than 5 to 10 per cent of species and plant diversity can be saved. Remedial measures must start from the reality of the human domination of the natural world rather than from the traditional conservationist view of the separation of humanity and nature. Conservationists should no longer focus only upon the 'pristine wilderness' but rather upon the totality of lived environments in which human beings exist, including the most 'artificial'. Not only protection but reinvention should be the goal. Species diversity should be re-created by active policy in the spaces that seem most removed from 'nature' – forests and fields, to be sure, but also the totality of urban environments.[12] Biotechnology can be used to increase the diversity and hardiness of different species, protecting those that otherwise might be lost by extending the range of environments in which they can survive and prosper – diversity by design.

The idea of sustainability, so widely used, should be reformulated along somewhat similar lines. Sustainability was famously defined in the Brundtland report as the ability of humanity 'to ensure that it meets the needs of the present without compromising the ability of future generations to meet their own needs'.[13] The difficulty with the definition is not so much how it is framed but how it has been interpreted, which is usually in terms of limits. Thus attempts have been made to define the Earth's 'carrying capacity', a term that in fact originates in traditional biological ecology. Yet it is almost impossible to say what that capacity is at any one point in time – and in this respect human beings differ massively from the animals. The joker in the pack is human ingenuity and innovation, together with the pace at which both can now move. Who would have thought, for example, even a decade ago that the US might become self-sufficient in energy? It would be best to redefine sustainability in terms of creative challenge. To say a given trend is unsustainable is to accept that it is necessary to alter it. The answer might sometimes be to try to limit or reverse that trend, but just as often a better strategy is to seek to redefine or transcend it. As I have stressed throughout the book, opportunity and risk are entangled in complex ways.

The complexities of opportunity and risk bring us directly to the precautionary principle, an official part of the EU's policy framework, but a notion that is deeply flawed. The most widely quoted definition comes from the Rio 'Earth Summit' in 1992: 'Where there are threats of serious or irreversible damage, lack of full scientific certainty shall not be used as a reason for postponing cost-effective measures to prevent environmental degradation.'[14] In somewhat different wording, it was officially endorsed by the EU and incorporated into the Lisbon Treaty. Many other definitions of the precautionary principle exist, and there is a large academic literature on the subject, including on how the EU has sought to put it into practice.[15] Yet, closely examined, the precautionary principle turns out to be incoherent. It in effect prioritises one common-sense saying against another, when they always have to be examined contextually. The two sayings are 'Better safe than sorry' (the precautionary one) versus 'He who hesitates is lost'. In everyday 'common sense', the two are usually applied *ex post facto* – neither has any predictive value. That obviously won't do when we confront an open future and have to decide which to apply as a decision with real consequences. If a person were always to apply the maxim 'Better safe than sorry', he or she would necessarily be cautious, unadventurous and conservative. Yet that attitude might itself be extremely risky. It is a great mistake to suppose that inaction carries no risk. In every situation there is always a balance of opportunities and risks that has to be calculated, and there will almost always be grey areas where a chance has to be taken one way or another.[16]

The 'precautionary principle' must be replaced with open-ended risk assessment. Consider, for example, the use of GM crops, or biotechnology more generally, in relation to the growth of the world's population. The risks of environmental contamination should clearly be reduced as far as possible, but those risks have to be set against that of being unable to feed the world's rapidly growing population. There is no simple 'principle' that can determine the decision. The same applies to our efforts to contain climate change. Renewable forms of energy should certainly be a key part of the EU's strategy for reducing carbon emissions. Yet, as I shall say in the next section, unconventional gas may be just as important, at least for a transitional period. The reason is that, if its production is carefully regulated, it produces considerably lower greenhouse gas emissions than coal. That advantage has to be balanced against the local environmental effects its production can have, but the balance is quite strongly positive because curbing climate change is one of the overriding goals of our time.

These ideas should drive new thinking in the EU. Renewable technologies that seem 'close to nature' – such as wind or solar power – are not necessarily more 'green' than gas or nuclear. It depends on what the balance of opportunities and risks is at any one point, in this case in relation to the consequences for the level of carbon emissions. In sum, how should EU climate change policy be restructured? I would summarise as follows.

As just mentioned, the precautionary principle should be abandoned and replaced with a more nuanced treatment of opportunity and risk. Quite rightly, in my view, the US has never accepted it. (The difference could affect the progress of the talks on the proposed transatlantic free trade area, since there are knock-on consequences for regulation.) Assuming that it is to survive, the ETS must be thoroughly reformed and the political difficulties such a process will face overcome.

Greater political and economic integration in the EU will make a major difference to the Union's capabilities to limit climate change. The United States has announced significant measures of its own to seek to cut down emissions, and so has China. In lieu of any results of substance from the UN negotiations, these states, together with Brazil and India, will hold a great deal of responsibility in their hands, since their national policies will determine whether real progress can be made. Projections of a linear kind suggest that the EU will be well ahead of its target of reducing greenhouse gas emissions by 20 per cent by 2020. However, as mentioned, studies show that much of the reduction achieved so far comes from the effects of the economic slowdown. What will happen if and when economic growth resumes? Moreover, even using existing figures, only half of the member states will reach the target with existing measures they have in place. The positive changes have been accomplished by the other states. For renewables, the situation is worse and has been significantly affected by the crisis. The majority of member states at the moment look unlikely to reach their targets. Some, like Germany, however, will exceed them. The EU renewables target has a significant deficiency. What matters so far as emissions reductions are concerned is not just the proportion of renewables but what makes up the remaining 80 per cent of energy production. A country which had 20 per cent of renewables but obtained the rest of its energy from coal would not be making much contribution to combating climate change.

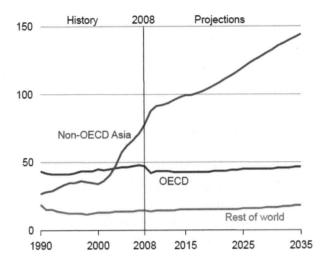

Figure 13 World coal consumption by region, 1990–2005 (quadrillion Btu)

Source: US Energy Information Administration (September 2011).

Progress with energy efficiency lags well behind the other two 20:20:20 targets. Quite apart from that, there is good reason to doubt that energy efficiency is as effective in reducing emissions as is ordinarily assumed. Everything depends upon how the money that is saved is spent – the so-called rebound effect. People who insulate their homes, for example, might spend the money they save on buying bigger cars or going on foreign holidays. The result could be higher emissions than were being produced in the first place. Studies of the subject suggest that most rebound effects are in the range from 10 to 80 per cent.[17] Since some of these operate on a macro-economic level, their impact can be very large. The EU should consider publishing consumption-based accounting of emissions alongside its internal targets. Research shows that about a third of Chinese greenhouse gas emissions derive from production for export, very largely to the industrial countries. If transportation is included, about 9 per cent come from net exports to the EU.

In Germany, France, Spain, Italy and the UK, net 'imported emissions' make up between 20 and 50 per cent of consumption emissions. If these are included in the figures for carbon reduction targets, they make a lot of difference. The UK, for example, has reduced its emissions by some 18 per cent since 1990 as measured in the usual way. If net imports plus transportation are included, emissions have in fact risen by more than 20 per cent over that period.

The rapid rate at which the sea ice in the Arctic is melting could have direct consequences for the jet stream, which influences weather throughout Europe. It is possible, even likely, that such an impact is already being felt, given the erratic weather patterns of the past few years in many parts of the continent, in Canada and in Russia. Yet a report of the European Environmental Agency, published in 2013, found that only half of the thirty-two countries that form its membership have any plans in place at all for adaptation. No more than a handful had actually started to institute specific projects to that end. Yet the implications are formidable. Changing temperatures and patterns of rainfall and drought will affect agriculture in all areas; water shortages will alternate with flooding; forest fires will become more frequent and intense in the Southern areas; and forms of disease previously unknown in Europe may become commonplace. It will not do to wait until these conditions become more and more extreme before investing in adaptation measures.

Geo-engineering has been a controversial topic in Europe. Some civil society groups have been forcefully opposed to it as a matter of principle. It has also been argued that taking geo-engineering seriously would have the effect of reducing the impetus to cut back on emissions more generically. Yet, given the fact that no progress has been made in curbing emissions on a global level, promoting research into geo-engineering is no longer a possible option, it is a necessity. The EU should be supporting more research of the type being carried out by the

Max Planck Institute of Meteorology.[18] That research brings together scientific organisations from Germany, Scandinavia and France. The objective is to study the possibilities offered by different forms of possible intervention into the climate and assess the benefits and risks.

THE ENERGY TRILEMMA

Energy policy is crucial to the Union's future because it straddles three key concerns – emissions, economic prosperity and resource security. Reconciling these, against the backdrop of failing growth, is the 'energy trilemma' facing the EU at the current time.[19] Climate change commitments have to be reconciled with the need to maintain security of supply and ensure that energy prices do not further erode competitiveness. The EU states are major importers of oil and gas and therefore distinctly vulnerable to price fluctuations. Some of the Eastern European countries import 100 per cent of their gas from Russia. Europe consumes a great deal of oil, but until recently oil security has not been high on the agenda. The reason, discussed in more detail in the following chapter, is that the member states of the Union have been content to shelter under the US umbrella, especially as regards security of supply from the Middle East. Many European leaders have been highly critical of aspects of US policy, and often rightly so. Yet, should the US run down its military presence as it moves towards energy self-sufficiency, Europe will be vulnerable.

Coping with these difficulties won't be an easy task, especially since energy policy is still largely in the hands of the member states. In the shape of the European Coal and Steel Community, energy was a core element of the EU from the very beginning. However, unlike agricultural and competition policy, it was not subject to direct EU influence. That situation changed to some degree with the signing of the Treaty of Lisbon which, at least in principle, transferred significant powers to the Union. However,

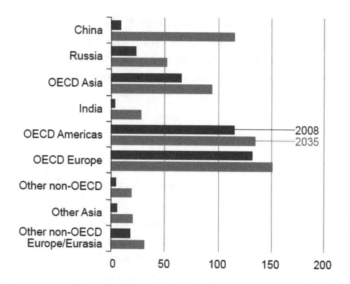

Figure 14 World nuclear generating capacity, 2008 and 2035 (gigawatts)

Source: US Energy Information Administration (September 2011).

the Treaty also stated that any measures instituted by the EU should not compromise the right of member states to choose between different energy sources and to determine their overall energy mix. Hence the EU states more or less tend to go their own way, with large differences existing between their energy systems. One of the biggest contrasts is between Germany and France. France is heavily dependent upon nuclear power, which generates not far short of 80 per cent of its electricity. Germany is committed to phasing out its nuclear energy completely, a decision that was taken in the wake of the 2011 Fukushima disaster in Japan. The 'red–green' coalition that was in office up to the year 2005 had already announced that the country's nuclear plants would eventually be closed down. In 2008 Angela Merkel's government, when it came to power, reversed that policy and committed the country to a continuation of nuclear energy for a substantial period. Following Fukushima, however, the policy was altered yet again. All nuclear reactors are to be decommissioned by 2022.

A number of other countries in Europe and elsewhere have decided to adjust their nuclear policy. Italy has voted to keep the country non-nuclear. No new reactors will be built in Spain or Switzerland. In France there is public discussion of whether some of the country's nuclear plants should be decommissioned. Other states are proceeding with building nuclear plants or have plans to do so. As of June 2013, four reactors are under construction, one in Finland, one in France and two in Slovakia. Sixteen others are planned, among them four in the UK and two each in Finland, the Czech Republic, Poland and Romania. There are no fewer than 132 operating reactors in the member states as a whole. Nuclear power will therefore be part of the power mix in Europe for a long time to come, regardless of what individual states decide to do. It currently generates about 30 per cent of the electricity produced in the EU. Those countries which are rejecting nuclear for safety and wider environmental reasons hence will be dependent upon EU regulation for their protection from accidents or leakage deriving from neighbouring countries. The Euratom Treaty has been designed to maintain high standards of safety and security across the continent. Nuclear power makes a significant contribution to lowering emissions in Europe. Although emissions are released in the construction of nuclear plants, once built their emissions are close to zero. The Commission has made no move to suggest that nuclear power should eventually be wound down in Europe as a whole. It is right not to do so. I am a reluctant supporter of nuclear power – reluctant because there are hazards and because of the problems of the disposal of nuclear waste. Yet cutting emissions is an overriding concern. Moreover, continuing investment in nuclear might promote the development of thorium-powered plants and perhaps that elusive holy grail, nuclear fusion.

In the case of thorium, there is no chance of a Fukushima-type disaster. Thor Energy in Norway has begun a four-year test to see if thorium could be used in a conventional reactor near Oslo. Other experimental programmes have been deployed in Germany, the UK and the Netherlands. Yet the EU is in danger of falling behind China and India so far as research investment is concerned. China is planning to build twenty-six orthodox reactors by 2014 and has plans for a further fifty-one. At the same time the country is investing heavily in nuclear-linked research, including especially thorium. China has large thorium reserves – as does India. India is developing a thorium-based reactor expected to be in operation later this year.

The German experiment of abandoning its nuclear power is nevertheless being widely scrutinised not just across Europe but by countries across the world. The aim is to create a massive expansion of renewable energy sources – and in short order. The *Energiewende* (energy transformation) is well under way. The existing nuclear power stations will be closed down in a progressive fashion. The agenda builds upon previous accomplishments, since Germany had already established a large presence in renewable energy, particularly in wind turbines and solar panels. On days where it is both sunny and windy, wind and solar can generate as much as 85 per cent of Germany's electricity needs; 22 per cent of the country's overall electricity supply is now generated from renewable sources. The figure is projected to rise to 40 per cent by 2020. Much thought has been put into how to deal with the intermittent nature of wind and solar energy. The idea is that, eventually, base-load plants will disappear. Gas and coal will be used only on a part-time basis.

Germany's energy planners recognise that, as the energy delivered by solar and wind mounts in volume, completely new requirements will be needed for future power plants. Such plants must be capable of being rapidly ramped up and down over short periods of time. Fluctuations in weather patterns cannot be forecast in detail in advance. Hence a great deal of flexibility must be built into the power stations that are not powered by renewable sources. Biomass plants are scheduled to replace many of Germany's coal-fired plants in the longer term. Substantial funding will be made available for research into energy storage, since a breakthrough in this field could be transformative for renewable energy.

The German government envisages that, by 2022, total energy output will be covered by renewable energy alone during many hours of each day.[20] Significant subsidies are needed to support the introduction and operation of wind and solar plants. Both need high capital expenditure initially but, once in operation, running costs are extremely low. However, the decision to close down its nuclear plants means that, at least during the long transitional period, Germany depends to a substantial degree upon coal, the most lethal of the fossil fuels in terms of greenhouse gas emissions. Some power stations still burn lignite, which is worse still than conventional coal in this respect. A significant number of new coal-fired power stations are due to be built in the country over the next few years, although some may not go ahead because of legal battles which they face. The overall impact of German policy remains to be seen, especially in terms of its consequences for greenhouse gas emissions.

TRANSITIONAL TECHNOLOGIES

Investment in renewable energy on an EU-wide level is absolutely demanded – it is the future. Moreover, such investment may bring competitive advantages to Europe. However, we should also think very seriously about transitional technologies. In combating climate change, there are two overlapping imperatives. One is to cut emissions in a serious way; the other is to do so in short order, given that global warming is cumulative and we know of no way of getting the greenhouse gases out of the atmosphere once they are there. A widespread turn to natural gas should be elevated much higher up the agenda, so long as it replaces coal, and especially lignite, in energy production. In combining energy innovation and emissions reductions in Europe, nothing is more important than sharply reducing the role of coal and lignite. Poland still gets some 90 per cent of its energy from coal, the Czech Republic 56 per cent, Greece 55 per cent and Germany 44 per cent. Moreover, coal is staging a comeback in countries where its use had started to decline. These countries include Germany, the UK and France. The EU should break away from the simple equation 'carbon reduction means renewables'. Coal is by far the most polluting fuel in terms of emissions. The overriding objective should be to put an end to the building of coal-fired power stations and close those which currently exist. EU policy on this issue should be radicalised. Yet many such plants are under construction and even more are in the pipeline. Some countries have started to import coal from the US, where prices have dropped because of the impact of shale gas.

In terms of lives lost, injuries and chronic diseases, 'King Coal' is far more dangerous than nuclear. Across the world annually, coal kills 4,000 more people per unit of energy produced than nuclear power. Even within Europe's regulated, mechanised and health-conscious coal industry, thousands of people die each year from air pollution, toxic conditions in the mines, and the leaking of mercury. A study of the 300 biggest coal-fired power stations in Europe showed that they contribute to 22,300 deaths a year.[21] In 2010, a total of 240,000 years of life, plus 480,000 work days, were thereby lost in the EU – at great cost to health systems, quite apart from the suffering caused. The 300 plants in question generate a quarter of the EU's electricity. Yet they are responsible for over 70 per cent of European sulphur dioxide and more than 40 per cent of nitrogen oxide emissions.

The EU and most of its member states have adopted a conservative (i.e., precautionary) attitude towards the shale gas revolution. France and Bulgaria have banned the production of shale gas altogether, and by and large it is frowned upon in Germany. The French decision is significant because it is estimated that France has the largest shale gas reserves in Europe after Poland.[22] Poland has been the country most determined to exploit its shale gas reserves, which would be a progressive step given its extreme reliance upon coal. The Polish government anticipated being able to produce shale gas by 2015, but so far progress has been limited. Britain is the other EU state to have taken a strong interest, but progress there too has been slow. Its reserves nevertheless appear to be considerable. The EU cannot stand aside from what has become a revolutionary force in the energy industry and must ensure that there is a clear regulatory structure in place.[23] Shale gas is heavily controversial in Europe as a result of the local environmental problems that can surround it. Moreover, it is often pointed out by critics that population is much denser in Europe than in the wide open areas of America. Yet, given appropriate regulation, those problems can be dealt with; they are insignificant in comparison with the overriding issue of making cuts in emissions. Not-in-my-backyard issues arise with shale gas, but they do also with all other forms of energy production and distribution.

Several years ago the US seemed to be totally out of the game in terms of reducing its greenhouse gas emissions. Over the past five years, however, these have come down by 13 per cent, in some substantial part because shale gas has replaced coal. In the United States shale gas has been described as a 'coal killer'.[24] It poses significant environmental problems, but these are less critical than those associated with coal. In the US the proportion of electricity derived from coal declined from 50 per cent of the energy mix to 37 per cent between 2005 and 2012. Studies comparing the two fuels on a life-cycle basis show that unconventional gas has half the level of greenhouse gases compared to coal – although it is essential that leakage of methane is prevented.

The economic benefits of the shale gas revolution in the US have also been very considerable, not only because of net new jobs created in the energy industry but because of the knock-on effects for American manufacturing production. Shale gas production means the building of unattractive local plants, but they are much more limited in their effects on the landscape than coal mines are – even more so in the case of strip mining, still common in some parts of Europe. Shale gas is a game-changer not only in the US but around the world. Very large reserves exist in China, which has set under way an impressive-looking programme to try to exploit it. There it could be of huge consequence in terms of reducing emissions, given the fact that the country still gets 70 per cent of its total energy consumption from coal, and mostly from antiquated plants at that. Not only within the EU but around it – especially in Algeria and Ukraine – the available resources look to be extremely extensive. The gas price looks certain to become permanently decoupled from oil, and in a substantial way. Gas can in principle be widely used in transportation, which at the moment is almost completely dominated by oil, although electric vehicles can also play a part.

The Commission has published three recent studies on the subject of shale gas.[25] They concern its potential effects on energy markets, its impact on emissions, and the local environmental hazards which its extraction can create. The findings are broadly positive so far as possible development in Europe is concerned. Because of the EU's hesitant approach to unconventional gas, the precise extent of its reserves remain unknown. The estimates so far are based on geological data and not on exploratory drilling. If the EU states cannot make progress in their own territories, they will have to turn to the countries in North Africa and the Middle East to get access to their reserves. At the moment the history of shale gas exploitation is another instance where Europe produces papers and reports while the US acts. So far as climate change objectives are concerned, the main difficulty surrounding a move to gas is the issue of lock-in. Gas is not a long-term solution in terms of the scale of carbon reductions that will ultimately be required. Hence there will

later have to be either a move away from it or the transformation of carbon capture and storage (CCS) into an effective and
cost-competitive strategy, or a combination of both. CCS would
appear to be a necessity for the future. Fossil fuel will dominate
the energy mix in Europe for many years to come. The main
prerequisite is CSS for gas rather than coal, presuming at least
that coal production in Europe can be radically pared back. Yet
none of the CCS plants that were supposed to be built in the
EU by 2015 are in fact under construction.

ENERGY INVESTMENT AND
ECONOMIC RECOVERY

Getting energy policy right is as important as almost any of
the many difficult issues confronting the EU at the current
time. Intensive investment in energy should be a key part of
any stimulus package aimed at revitalising the EU economy. At
the moment there is even more paper Europe around in energy
policy than in most other areas. The gulf between plans and
real achievement, especially against the backdrop of the performance of the ETS, is creating dangerous uncertainties about
Europe's energy future. It is a very significant issue, because
most funding will have to come from private sources, which
will want to see much more clarity before making significant
investments. The initiatives that exist on an EU level are many
indeed. They include a series of internal market energy packages, various climate and energy projections stretching back
for some years, the 2012 Energy Efficiency Directive, proposals for a Connecting Europe Facility, the Industrial Emissions
Directive, the Renewable Energy Roadmap and the Energy
Roadmap. Is all this morass of plans and proposals the right
way to think ahead? I don't believe so, for reasons I gave in my
discussion of the notion of sustainability. Climate change and
energy security are prototypical examples of what it means to
live in a society with such a tangle of opportunities and risks.

Scenario thinking rather than roadmaps is the way to seek to deal with such an uncertain future. A single major discovery – such as a way of storing electricity in the long term and in an economical way – could alter the whole nature of existing energy systems.

According to the Commission's projections, upwards of €1 trillion at today's prices will be needed to refurbish the EU's energy system by 2020, against a baseline of 2010. That sum would cover significant aspects of generation and transmission, including the modernisation of the grid. Upgrading the grid is fundamental. It offers the chance of making the best use of inter-mittent energy sources and of making a step-change in energy efficiency – itself a goal of EU policy. The cost of power would be lowered because large areas could share the output of the most efficient power plants. It would also make possible a shar-ing of European hydro-power resources, which can cover about six weeks of full-load European output. Many proposals have been made about transforming the grid on a European level. They include, for example, the possible creation of a network among the Baltic countries, involving Germany alongside the Nordic states, Estonia, Latvia, Lithuania and Poland. Among other ideas are the Low Grid, which would link countries in Central Europe, especially Germany, the Netherlands, Belgium and France, and the High Grid, linking Europe and North Africa. A version of the latter, where concrete progress has been made, is Desertec, which involves transporting electricity from solar power from North Africa and the Middle East to Europe. The project has, however, been threatened by divisions between the two main partners involved.

A specific but highly important issue, in part because of its geopolitical ramifications, is the existence at the moment of 'energy islands' within the EU, among them the group of Estonia, Lithuania and Latvia, dependent as they are on Russian gas. They have few infrastructural connections with the rest of the EU. The same is true on an individual level of

Slovakia, Bulgaria, Hungary and Romania. Even Germany is to some extent in a similar position, having set up the Nord Stream pipeline. The Commission has argued that Germany should increase the connectivity of the pipeline. Oddities have emerged from Germany's *Energiewende*. The Netherlands, the largest gas producer and exporter in Europe, has extensive energy connections with countries nearby, including Germany. The Netherlands has liberalised these market ties as part of its contribution to the single market. On some occasions Germany has been exporting electricity to the Netherlands at negative prices – the customers were paid for what they consumed rather than the other way around. The reason was that the subsidies set up by the German state to support the expansion of renewables meant that producers continued to supply energy regardless of the price.

The conflict in Ukraine has shown that energy security needs to move high up on the EU's agenda. Over 30 per cent of the natural gas used by the EU states comes from Russia; nearly half of that flows across Ukraine. In general the EU is heavily dependent upon energy imported from abroad. The Union imports 88 per cent of its crude oil, 66 per cent of its natural gas, 42 per cent of its solid fuels, including coal, and 95 per cent of the uranium used in nuclear plants. In a hurried response to the confrontation with Russia, the Commission announced a new energy security strategy in May 2014. Short-term measures proposed include increasing gas storage capacity, developing capabilities for coping with emergencies, reducing erratic energy demand and switching to alternative fuels. In the medium term, possible strategies include increasing energy efficiency, completing the internal energy market, increasing energy production in the EU states and 'speaking with one voice' in external energy policy.[26]

Perhaps the newfound sense of urgency will help mobilise greater collective will – and investment – than has been visible hitherto. The disparate nature of energy policy among member-states until now has been a major source of inefficiencies as well as vulnerabilities. If mobilised in the right way, enhanced energy security could also go along with positive economic benefits, short- and long-term.

There is little doubt that investment on the large scale in upgrading the grid would have significant multiplier effects as part of a stimulus package. Could the money be found in the straitened circumstances of today? As one would expect, there are significant difficulties. A sounding by the Commission of possible investors, including large pension funds, showed clear stumbling blocks. The financial institutions approached responded that they would consider investment in only a limited number of EU states, as the economic circumstances in the others were too adverse. It is essential, nevertheless, that a realistic package be put together. At the moment, most of the endeavours under consideration are partial, if worthwhile in their own terms. An example is the project bonds initiative agreed upon in July 2012. It will offer enhanced conditions of credit for specific projects, supported by contributions from the European Investment Bank. EU2 will certainly have to get involved. Investment in energy infrastructure in the Southern countries, particularly Greece, could have a double multiplier effect. It would help recovery in the country but also be a stimulus to the wider EU economy if it were integrated with plans for the overall development of the pan-European grid. The EIB has provided €215 million for investment in natural gas and upgrading the national grid. It is at least a beginning.

Estimates suggest that about 85 per cent of the investment required to modernise the grid will have to come from private sources. Institutional investors, especially pension funds, have an obligation to provide stable income for their stakeholders. Hence a clear and credible policy framework is indispensable. At the moment, because of flaws in existing policies, such a framework does not exist. The issue is not primarily that of targets: it is how they should be reached. There are too many uncertainties around the ETS, the impact of shale gas, and the ambivalent attitudes across Europe towards nuclear power, compounded by the overall economic uncertainties of the crisis. In a recent survey of institutional investors, fewer than 10 per cent agreed that the ETS provided a worthwhile incentive to switch from carbon-intensive to low-carbon investments. Not a single respondent believed that the ETS provided long-term price signals. These uncertainties directly affect the likelihood of investments in the upgrading of the grid.[27] There are plenty of plans for the top-down reconstruction of the grid. In terms of attracting investment, however, this is almost certainly the wrong way to go. The most effective method would be to construct a pan-European grid in an incremental and localised way. The different clusters would have to be 'grid-ready' – open to interconnection. A super-grid constructed in such a fashion would be compatible with a diversity of micro-grids, based on local energy sources. The construction of new grid systems, of whatever type, however, could meet with significant local opposition. Thus in Germany a substantial amount of wind energy needs to be transported from the north to the south of the country. Public disquiet about local environmental consequences has caused the project to be delayed for several years so far.

The EU absolutely must not abandon its attempt to be a pioneer in climate change policy. Yet, compared to its level of ambition – to deal with a problem that cannot wait – concrete results so far have been limited. Part of the reason is the familiar one that the Union is largely in the hands of whatever its member states decide to do in respect of their energy needs and their consumption patterns. Yet, as I have tried to show, there are major problems with the strategies and policies adopted too.

Chapter 6
The Search for Relevance

The conclusion of the Second World War marked the end of Europe's worldwide hegemony. It was a momentous transition. The antagonism between the United States and the Soviet Union that was to define global politics for close to half a century came into existence. The United States established a military presence in Europe which continues to this day in attenuated form. France and Germany, plus the other Western European states, were little more than bit players in a much larger global drama. The major wars in that rivalry occurred outside of Europe, but things could have been different. Tensions at some points were very real and dangerous. History is quite easily reconstructed after the event, but it is fair to say that no one imagined that Soviet power would dissipate almost overnight and with virtually no violence. I remember walking through Prague in 1990 with the anthropologist and philosopher Ernest Gellner, who was brought up in Czechoslovakia but spent most of his career in Britain. Gellner was one of the foremost students of the Soviet Union. He told me that he was in the city when the Soviets came, but he never expected to be there when they had left. He had believed that the Soviet Union would last a hundred years.

The proper flowering of the European Community, and therefore the creation of the EU, owes an enormous debt to someone from the outside – Mikhail Gorbachev. Without *perestroika* and *glasnost*, without his decision not to intervene militarily to suppress the movements in Poland, East Germany and Hungary, there would be no European Union in the form in which it exists today. It is surely right and proper that Mr Gorbachev is a Nobel Peace Prize winner alongside the Union itself. History flowed towards the reunification of Europe, but in fact the continent could have been riven by warfare all over again had the Soviets tried to deploy military force. The expansion of the European Community to the east was a hinge of history by any reckoning. The EU was for the first time 'on its own' – potentially a more influential actor in the world than before, but no longer the precisely bounded entity it had been for over forty years. The problem of 'finitude' came into being: where should the European Union's boundaries to the east lie? Is the EU, as currently constituted, a process rather than a fixed entity? The Union now could be seen, and was seen by many, as a possible model for transnational governance in an era of advancing globalisation, where individual nations had lost many of the powers they once had.

Free trade organisations had sprung up in other parts of the world, such as in South-East Asia (ASEAN) and in Latin America (Mercosur). Would they follow a similar path? Was a new form of power developing, discarding 'Westphalian' norms and abandoning violence in favour of respect for human rights, democracy and the rule of law? Could the EU's peaceful approach even rival the influence of the US, which continued to engage in military adventures? Following the attacks of 9/11 on the twin towers and the Pentagon, how should the EU respond?

THE POWER AND THE WEAKNESS

The period just after the turn of the millennium spawned a large literature influenced by these questions. I mention here only the works of Robert Kagan and Mark Leonard, both written shortly after the time of the second invasion of Iraq by the United States and its allies. The conflict polarised Europe, and most of the EU states refused to participate. Kagan compared the EU and the US using an analogy from a best-selling self-help book. His typology became almost as famous as the original. The EU is 'from Venus' and the US 'from Mars'. 'Europe', as he put it, 'is turning away from power' towards a 'post-historical paradise of peace and prosperity', taking its guidelines from Kant. The US, on the other hand, 'remains mired in history'. True security, as well as the means of promoting a liberal order, depends upon the capability to deploy military force. Kagan admitted that the contrast is to some degree a caricature but insisted that it expresses a core truth. The divide between the EU and the US may in fact 'be impossible to reverse'.

Kagan pointed out that the military weakness of the European states – such a dramatic contrast to the centuries of their imperial dominance – was masked by the unique situation of the Cold War. Once the bipolar world had disappeared, the European Union fell at the first hurdle, unable to handle war in the Balkans without help from the Americans. If the EU could not cope with a conflict on its own doorstep, and, in spite of its savagery, a relatively limited one at that, how could it make any pretension to superpower status? The EU's attachment to multilateralism, Kagan argued, is driven by its own incapacity. Its tactics and its goals 'are the tactics of the weak'; 'Europe's new Kantian order could only flourish under the umbrella of American power exercised according to the rules of the old Hobbesian order.'[1]

The ripostes were not slow in coming, and there were many of them – Kagan's analysis touched on some sensitive nerves. Mark Leonard sought to chart out a very different position. Arguing almost exactly the opposite of Kagan, he observed that the limits of American military power have become clear. Iraq is not pacified, and the US, together with the rest of NATO, is also bogged down in Afghanistan. Europe is shaping a different kind of power, more profound and with far greater long-term potential. Kagan's attempt to subvert European idealism, and see it as a cover for weakness, is itself misconstrued. The EU has managed to pacify large chunks of a continent 'without becoming a target for hostility', as would have happened if this goal had been achieved by conquest. When the EU becomes directly involved in conflicts in different parts of the world, Leonard continued, it does not act on its own but operates under the aegis of international organisations. Precisely because its influence is exerted to some degree 'invisibly', the Union is able to get results without provoking hostile responses from others. Lack of a visible leader is in fact a source of strength. Operating as a network allows a whole group of nations to have a diffuse but worldwide presence.

Moreover, the Union is not a closed entity but one open to new members in its vicinity. Rather than threatening to conquer, it exerts a magnetic power of attraction. What we have observed since 1989 'is regime change on a scale never before seen in human history but without a single shot being fired'. The influence of the EU goes well beyond those countries which might one day be accepted as full members; the European Neighbourhood Initiative, Leonard argued, could draw almost a third of the world's population into its orbit. Mars versus Venus – well, for Leonard, Venus comes out ahead. Compare, for example, the EU's involvement in the previously warring states of Croatia and Serbia with the relationship of the Americans to Colombia. The US has, or had, a strong military presence there and sought to influence its local politics as part of the war on drugs. There was some development assistance, but no programme of structural funds such as the EU offers, or the appeal of becoming involved in a wider framework of democracy and stable economic development.

The limits of military power are well demonstrated by what happened in Iraq and in Afghanistan. Military victories are transient and ineffective unless there is a positive chance of reconstruction and the introduction of the rule of law. 'The lonely superpower can bribe and bully and impose its will almost anywhere in the world', but as soon as it turns its back its potency starts to wane'. The EU is a model for other regions, including East Asia and Latin America.

Europeans have played a disproportionate part in creating some of the major international agencies of the recent period, Leonard pointed out, often against the resistance, or in the face of the indifference, of the Americans. It was the Europeans who pushed for the World Trade Organisation, the International Criminal Court and the Kyoto Protocol. The nation-state was invented in Europe in the eighteenth and nineteenth centuries; today Europe is pioneering a new global model. In the twenty-first century, 'the European way of doing things will have become the world's'. Leonard accepted that his work sounded out of tune with the situation on the ground in the EU at that time. At that point the European Constitutional Treaty looked dead and buried. There should, he said, be a five-year moratorium on new treaties. The Lisbon Treaty was in fact signed on 13 December 2007, a year after Leonard wrote this. The Union, he added, should develop more limited packages of reform. 'We should lose this idea of a single European Union and move towards a notion of many Europes.' We should abandon the 'European dream' of a federal future analogous to the United States.[2]

Let me first go back to Kagan and consider his attempt to subvert the European project by arguing that it is essentially based on hypocrisy, the attempt of the weak to gain a moral superiority over the strong – Nietzsche comes into his own, as it were. Is there any validity in the idea? I would say definitely yes. The early origins of the EU were inspired by the thoroughly laudable and essential project of putting an end to wars between the European nations – wars in which many millions of people died. Yet the reasons for its success weren't just the determination and persistence of the key players but the shelter provided by American military strength. Since the early years after the Second World War, and the period of decolonisation, the EU and its member states have been trying to cope with a radical loss of power, especially vis-à-vis the United States. They have sought to do so by inventing, or promulgating, a new type of influence, the opposite of their bellicose past. Virtuous and significant though this attempt may be – and it is both – virtue here comes in part from necessity. Leonard observed that the US has no comparable mechanism to the EU's *acquis communitaire*, which is true. Nevertheless, Latin America, which he pointed to as an example of the ineptness of the US, over recent years has seen at least as extensive a process of democratisation as Eastern Europe and the ex-Soviet states adjacent to the EU. I don't say that democracy in Argentina, Brazil, Chile and other Latin American countries is the result of direct US policy, which was often reprehensible. Yet the Latin American example suggests that democratisation is a process resting on a wider foundation than any influences specific to Europe. Neither Mercosur nor ASEAN have moved beyond being free trade zones. The African Union too remains a fledgling enterprise.

The EU is not a pioneering form of governance, the vanguard of a new model of transnational cooperation that others can learn and copy from. Its future is likely to be in a regionalised world system. A federal model is not compatible with the idea that its distinctiveness lies in its form. Nor does the EU stand in any kind of privileged position with regard to the promotion of world peace. Kagan was not the only one to spot that Europe's commitment to pacifism and to international law, genuine though it may be on the level of good intentions, hides weakness. Other blocs and nations see it too. Valid though some of Kagan's points may have been, it is time to drop the dualism on which they – and the works of Leonard, Robert Cooper and other authors at that time – were based.[3] The contrast between

Venus and Mars is very much like that drawn by Joseph Nye between soft and hard power. Yet Nye has always been careful to stress that these intersect in many different ways. There are very few forms of persuasion, for example, that do not depend upon sanctions of one kind or another. The opposite is also true.[4]

Moreover, some of the claims Kagan made ten years ago now sound more than a little archaic. Kagan wrote that Americans and Europeans 'understand one another less and less' and that 'the reasons for the transatlantic divide are deep, long in development, and likely to endure.'[5] Yet the United States and the EU are now cooperating directly in the conflicts both in the Ukraine and the struggle against Islamic State in Iraq and Syria. A key argument in this book is that we in Europe should seek to establish new transatlantic ties. This time they should be built upon a partnership between equals, not an ambivalent relationship of dependence. A transatlantic free trade area is an appropriate beginning. The notion goes back to President John F. Kennedy in the 1960s. He used the notion of a 'transatlantic partnership', and this remains the best term to employ today, since trade should be only one part of strengthening EU–US connections. Kennedy's interest in transatlantic free trade was prompted in part by the superior economic performance of the European Community countries at that time. In his 'Grand Design', he spoke of Europe as 'a partner with whom we can deal on a basis of full equality'. The idea lapsed with Kennedy's death and in the face of hostility from some European nations, especially France under de Gaulle. Indeed, it may have been one factor prompting the French to begin their disengagement from NATO.[6]

The project of creating a transatlantic free trade area was endorsed in Obama's State of the Union address of 2013. The EU and the US have established a High Level Working Group for Jobs and Growth to help consider the possibility. It is by no means a straightforward endeavour, and there are major political and economic hurdles on both sides. Will Obama be able to steer such a programme through Congress? A dash of EU2 no doubt will be needed in Europe. This time there cannot be endless negotiations of which the Union is so fond. The Americans have said that a deal must be shaped and implemented quickly, on 'one tank of gas'. Will the Europeans be able move on a swift time-scale? The potential advantages are difficult to contest, especially if they form an avenue to other types of collaboration, such as improving the security relationship. The transatlantic economy generates some \$5 trillion in turnover from commercial sales each year and keeps some 15 million workers in mutually 'on-shored' jobs.[7] Levels of foreign direct investment are especially high. Surveys show that there is widespread public support for a transatlantic free trade area on both sides of the Atlantic. A Pew Foundation poll in 2010 indicated that 58 per cent of Americans think that increased trade with Europe would be good for the United States, compared with 28 per cent who believed otherwise.[8] Similar figures are found in Europe-wide surveys.

Various possible criticisms must be confronted. Would there be adverse consequences for the emerging economies? How would thorny issues such as France's *exception culturelle* – its commitment to protect its own cultural heritage – be handled? Would it be more logical to pour effort instead into negotiating free trade areas with the rising Asian countries? Each can be readily responded to, at least in principle. It is not in the interest of the emerging economies for the US and Europe to relapse into economic stagnation. Moreover, the world economy is not a zero-sum game. The French economy is facing huge problems and would gain significantly from a transatlantic partnership. Part of the negotiations would involve exceptions to be balanced against the common good. And the reasons for establishing the transatlantic partnership in new guise go well beyond free trade itself, as I have emphasised at many points in this work.

THE COLD WAR AND AFTER

The EU has taken many years to get anywhere close to clarity of purpose supplied by the Cold War. All its limitations reappear here. The uneasy relationship between EU1 and EU2 is very evident, as are the large areas of paper Europe that surround them – schemes, projects and proposals, produced by the nations as well as the EU agencies. There have been many plans for reshaping the relationship between the EU and NATO, as well as for moving towards common foreign policy. Progress has been slow and halting, even since the Lisbon Treaty supposedly conferred more cohesive foreign policy leadership. The EU states that intervened in Libya two years ago could not have done so without American logistical back-up, supplied through NATO. The same was true of the French in Mali. American aerial tankers flew more than 200 missions to support the French intervention. The French would not have been able to get to Mali, or to deploy their air force, without American help. It is not as if the Union lacks a military presence, looked at in terms of resources and numbers of personnel under arms. Combined military expenditure among the member states runs at over €200 billion a year. There are some 1,600,000 personnel under arms, more than the US possesses, plus a fleet of warships of disparate kinds. The main problem here is the persisting legacy of the bipolar period. It is not only that the national armies are uncoordinated; much of the weaponry is relevant only to a land invasion from the East.

A string of attempts have been made over the past twenty years to draw together the military forces dispersed across Europe and to modernise military technology, on both counts with only limited success. At a European Council meeting held in Helsinki in 1999 a plan was mooted for a European Rapid Reaction Force, consisting of specific battle groups. It was instituted in 2004, building upon a joint Franco-British initiative proposed at St Malo a year earlier. The EU countries undertook to provide a force of fifteen brigades – some 50,000 to 60,000 personnel – capable of full deployment at sixty days' notice. It was to be able to operate for a minimum of a year and to be backed up by replacements. In 2010 the concept was extended to incorporate a range of humanitarian and peacekeeping missions. The battle groups have been declared operational, although on a lower scale than originally envisaged. So far, however, they have not seen any action. Camille Grand, a French defence expert, has commented wryly that, in military affairs, Europe is moving towards 'a combination of the unable and the unwilling'.[9] The two most prominent military powers in the EU, the UK and France, are both starting to look ragged because of the economic situation and the cutbacks it has brought.

At a Lisbon summit in 2010, NATO's 'new strategic concept' was adopted and new areas of cooperation with the EU debated. The two organisations agreed to meet regularly, with staff contracts at a range of different levels. Conflict prevention, the management of conflict situations and their stabilising after the event were on the table. A crucial part of the agenda was the agreement to cooperate in a more wide-ranging way, to save costs and facilitate greater integration. However, the EU's rather hypocritical dependence on American military power continues. It is hard to escape the conclusion that the existence of NATO exposes Europe to systematic moral hazard so far as its own defence capabilities are concerned. The EU knows it has emergency back-up no matter how lax it is on its own behalf. Hence it can indulge its own lack of commitment and its internal squabbles. It is a situation that might not endure much longer. Like the European countries, the US is struggling to reduce its huge level of debt. In 2001 the Americans paid just over 60 per cent of the cost of NATO. Today that figure has risen to 75 per cent. The US is mounting pressure to create a more even distribution of funding.

At the turn of the century, during the period of enlargement

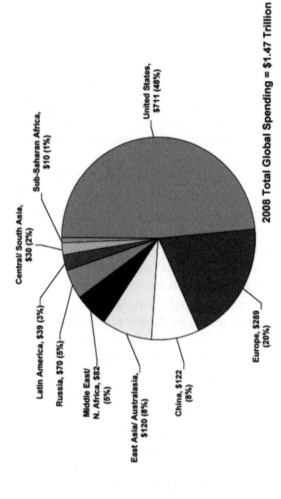

Sub-Saharan Africa, $10 (1%)

United States, $711 (48%)

Central/ South Asia, $30 (2%)

Latin America, $39 (3%)

Russia, $70 (5%)

Middle East/ N. Africa, $82 (5%)

East Asia/ Australasia, $120 (8%)

China, $122 (8%)

Europe, $289 (20%)

2008 Total Global Spending = $1.47 Trillion

Figure 15 US Military spending vs. the world in 2008 (in $US billion, with percentage of total global spending)

Notes: Data from International Institute for Strategic Studies. *The Military Balance 2008*, and DOD. The total for the United States is the FY 2009 request and includes $170 billion for military operations in Iraq and Afghanistan, as well as funding for DOE nuclear weapons activities. All other figures are projections based on 2006, the last year for which accurate data is available.

Source: Center for Arms Control and Non-Proliferation.

to what was Eastern Europe, it looked as though the EU might have areas of reasonable stability on its eastern and southern flanks. All this has now changed with the Russian incursion in Ukraine and the chaos in parts of the Middle East and North Africa. The threats to Europe are multiple. Whatever happens in the eastern part of the country, Ukraine faces an erratic and difficult future. The government will look to the EU and the US to provide more than just token support as the country seeks to chart a new path of development, break away from endemic corruption and modernise its economy. These are huge tasks, especially as Ukraine's energy dependence on Russia will continue.

THE EU AND RUSSIA

The EU has had a tense relation with Russia ever since Vladimir Putin came to power with the goal of rebuilding the country's authority in the world. The Union's extensive dependence on Russian oil and gas, however, has continued and grew even greater when Germany started to import more extensively than in the past. The Nord Stream gas project has been one of the most controversial energy innovations of recent years. It is a joint enterprise between Gazprom and German, Dutch and French companies, in which, however, Gazprom holds a 51 per cent stake. Two pipelines bring natural gas from Russia. The first was completed in 2011 and the second the following year. Both bypass the former communist countries in the EU, which are themselves mostly heavily dependent on Russia for their oil and gas. They objected very vociferously when the project was initiated, since they felt they were being outflanked.

One of the results is that German and Russian interests have become closely tied, giving Russia leverage in EU politics. At the same time, the relationship between the two countries is marked by a distinct ambivalence. Angela Merkel has been critical of Russia's human rights record and its lack of democracy.

Some of the problems came home to roost when Cyprus was on the verge of going bankrupt. Many affluent Russians kept their money in the Cypriot banks. The Russian government, however, resolutely declined to contribute to the bailout of Cyprus's economy and was at the same time critical of the German-led management of the issue.

While he was president, Dmitry Medvedev sought to introduce a European Security Treaty that would embrace security across a far wider area than the European Union itself, including Russia and the Caucasus. He opposed 'a bloc politics approach that continues by inertia'.[10] Medvedev mooted the idea of a summit meeting in which NATO and the EU security institutions would be represented – as well as Russia itself and other countries in what was labelled 'greater Europe'. He envisaged that the US and Canada would take part in drafting the new treaty and continue to figure in the new security architecture that would be created. As part of the proposals, the Russian government agreed to make progress with human rights issues inside its own country and encourage similar developments in surrounding states. It drew up draft versions of the treaty, which were circulated to a range of states and international organisations. All parties to the treaty would commit on an array of cooperative measures to minimise the possibility of conflicts.

The response from the EU institutions and states was, as so often, mixed and divided. The secretary general of NATO at the time, Anders Fogh Rasmussen, declared there was no need for a new treaty, as there was already a treaty framework in place – for example, the 1997 NATO–Russia Founding Act and the 2002 NATO–Russia Rome Declaration. The real question was to put the principles enshrined there into practice. Some of the leading EU countries, including Germany, France, Spain and Italy, believed the proposal should be taken seriously and a dialogue opened with the Russians. However, in the end the initiative was allowed to lapse.

Vladimir Putin's reassumption of the presidency in 2012 has been marked by some distinct policy shifts, partly consequent upon the internal opposition which he has faced from dissident groups. EU leaders had felt much more comfortable with Medvedev at the helm, even if Putin was still pulling the strings in the background. At a distance they were sympathetic to the street movements and bloggers who opposed his return. Following their repression, Putin's new period of rule has assumed more directly authoritarian overtones than was true before. He appears to consider that Europe is locked into a process of irreversible decline. The EU is no longer seen as a source of ideas relevant to Russia's future but as a cluster of weakened states. Far from contemplating new overarching treaties, the Russians are taking apart some of the agreements established in the 1990s. 'Moscow is "leaving the West" mentally by finally stopping to pretend that it shares the same values as EU countries and aspires to join them in some creative way.'[11] During its first term, Putin's government was able to engineer a progressive rise in living standards, based almost wholly upon rising oil and gas prices. The world economic slowdown, coupled to major changes in gas markets produced by the shale gas revolution, plus the progress of liquefied gas, which is easily transportable, have seriously eroded this tactic. Putin has introduced more hard-line policies both inside and outside Russia.

The Russians did not veto UN Resolution 1973, which made possible the NATO action in Libya in 2011 to protect the civilian population. The Russian leadership, however, was disturbed by what it saw as an unwarranted extension of the mission to remove Colonel Gaddafi. Russia's foreign minister, Sergey Lavrov, objected that 'The resolution does not provide for such actions and does not approve them, nor does the UN deal support regime change in Libya.'[12] The experience is one of the reasons prompting Russia's policy towards the Syrian conflict, whereby it has blocked a series of UN resolutions condemning the actions of the Assad government and has continued to supply arms to the regime. Having distanced itself from the US and Europe, Russia is looking to the East as its possible salvation. As in the case of Obama, Putin has made a 'pivot' towards Asia and the Pacific. One reason is that engagement with the West would inevitably focus attention on internal repression in his own country.

Germany remains highly ambivalent towards the deployment of military force. It stood aside from the intervention in Libya. The EU was initially unable to find a common line as regards possible action in Syria either. At a meeting of European foreign ministers in May 2013, France and the UK refused to renew the EU embargo on the supply of arms to rebel groups in the country, causing bitter reactions from some other member states. The two countries were later easily outmanoeuvred by the Russians, who moved swiftly to convey new missile defences to Syria. When, in August of the same year, the US proposed to launch missile strikes against Syria, Germany again declined to take part. After a parliamentary debate, so did Britain, leaving the United States and France temporarily isolated.

The EU was of course deeply involved in the events leading up to Russia's annexation of Crimea and its subsequent support for dissident groups in eastern Ukraine. Medvedev's European Security Treaty was designed to help stabilise the uncertain zones between the EU states and Russia, as well as to protect what were seen as Russia's strategic interests. The indefinite expansion of NATO in particular was and is one of Russia's major preoccupations. EU policy towards Ukraine, for better or for worse, largely ignored these concerns. The Union offered Ukraine an association agreement, but tortuous negotiations ensued about how to get it implemented. Putin stated his opposition to the deal and put pressure upon President Yanukovych to delay signing it, a situation that led to the street protests that forced him out of office. An agreement was finally endorsed in

March 2014. Russia's seizure of Crimea followed. Whatever is the outcome of the military confrontations in Ukraine, the responsibility that the EU has taken on is huge. The Ukrainian economy is weak and uncompetitive, levels of corruption are high and the country will be dependent upon Russian energy for a long while to come. Yet, given Russia's hope of drawing it back into its own ambit, there must be real substance in the help and guidance the EU must provide.

EUROPEAN SECURITY – OR THE LACK OF IT

Can the EU cut back its armed forces and at the same time improve and restructure its military capabilities? If so, how? The answer is clear and the same as elsewhere – it is the acceptance of greater integration, linked to a convincing future strategy. In other words, the much talked about but never appearing European army should come into being. It is the only way economies of scale can be made, modernisation achieved and integrated leadership created. Even in dire economic circumstances there are enough resources to go around if only they were to be deployed differently. A recent report on European security makes for interesting reading. It pulls no punches. Its author, Nick Witney, observes that the European Common Security and Defence Policy (CSDP) is 'all grin and no cat'.[13] Shifting the metaphor, he adds that it could be summed up as the "'3 Ts": timid, tardy and tokenistic'. In the aftermath of the financial crisis, pooling and sharing are upon everyone's lips, but in the real world 'virtually nothing changes'.

Could anyone seriously disagree with these observations, caustic though they are? The charade of European defence continues, even under current economic pressures. Foreign policy was supposed to have been given a new focus after the signing of the Lisbon Treaty and the appointment of Catherine Ashton as Europe's 'foreign minister'. Yet her hands have been tied by a characteristic mix of paper Europe on the one hand and EU2 on the other. In the background, and occasionally quite openly, the big states constrain what she says and does. States outside Europe don't have to try divide and rule, it has been said, because the divisions are already there.

There exists a plethora of organisations, strategies and acronyms exists – the CSDP, as mentioned above, an element of the CFSP (Common Foreign and Security Policy); EEAS (European External Action Service); HRVP (the High Representative, Catherine Ashton's official title, with the last two letters meaning she is a Vice President of the European Commission); the FAC (Foreign Affairs Council); the ENP (European Neighbourhood Policy); and the ESS (European Security Strategy). Some have also added ROTW (the Rest of the World: this is a place where people take Europe seriously only when it can act together in an integrated fashion). A publication of the EU Institute for Security Studies has argued persuasively that, although the EU states are worried about forfeiting their sovereignty in security matters, 'Europeans are already losing sovereignty by *not* consolidating, *not* optimising, *not* innovating, *not* regionalising, and *not* integrating their military capabilities.'[14] It is a judgement with which I fully concur and a telling way of expressing what I have called sovereignty+. A breakthrough is needed.

There are as many national security strategies as there are member states, but little in the way of an overarching sense of purpose. A comparison of the different versions speaks of Europe's 'strategic cacophony'. Most of the published strategies, its authors, Olivier de France and Nick Witney, conclude, are 'incoherent, derivative, devoid of a sense of a common European geostrategic situation, and long out-of-date'.[15] There seems no area where the inherent tendency of the leaders of the European nations to want to have their cake and eat it is more pronounced. Their strategic policies emphasise interdependence, but their concrete actions are national. Thus defence cuts in the various states over the past few years have been made without reference to a European sense of purpose. There are perhaps two underlying reasons for the 'cacophony', apart from the reluctance to concede formal sovereignty. One is the aforesaid moral hazard element: NATO is always there as an ultimate resource. The other is the divisions of outlook which security brings to the fore. Germany's position is still substantively different from those of the two most hawkish states in Europe, France and the UK. It hardly helps that the UK is actively debating exit from the EU altogether.

One possibility de France and Witney discuss is that a 'European Defence Semester' could be set up along the lines of the economic version that has been set up in the EU. However, the difficulties are the same in both instances – it means more bureaucracy, more meetings, perhaps more paper Europe. It is at least possible that the same forces that are driving economic integration in Europe might do the same for security, given the wastefulness of the 'cacophony'.

As of the first half of 2013, there are sixteen active CSDP missions in place. Four are mainly military in nature and twelve primarily or wholly civilian. All are limited in scope. Twelve others have been brought to an end in recent years. The European Union Rule of Law mission in Kosovo (EULEX) is concerned with training the population in policing, the law and administration. With well over 2,000 staff, it is the biggest civilian mission the EU has undertaken. The European Council has recognised that the Union must 'assume increased responsibilities in the maintenance of international peace and security'. Reorganisation of, and investment in, military capability could contribute to growth and economic competitiveness. Pooling and sharing are mentioned again without any detail being given. Much more flesh should be put on the bare bones of the Common Security and Defence Policy. Besides more traditional military concerns, an array of new risks has to be confronted. The most obvious is cyber-security, much talked about but with very little if anything having been achieved on

Figure 16 A restaurant in Pristina sporting the EU flag alongside the Albanian national flag on the day before the Kosovar declaration of independence, February 2008

a pan-European level. The very nature of warfare is changing before our very eyes. Automation and robotics are penetrating the military sphere just as they are becoming so widespread in industry and business.

The US now routinely uses drones as a means of waging remote war.[16] The drone, as it were, is the high-tech version of the suicide bomber, but potentially far more lethal. Both raise numerous ethical issues, but no doubt both will still be pursued across the world. Drones will not seem so 'remote' once other states have the capability of deploying them in the West should they choose to do so. How will the threat be countered? Well . . . in some part by other drones, used either for surveillance or to destroy the incoming ones. And so the robotisation of war proceeds. According to the American military, drones can project power 'without projecting vulnerability', but this is surely only

true if the US manages to stay ahead of everyone else techno-
logically. Germany has plans to buy drones and is currently in
negotiation with the Israeli government on the issue. The UK
has launched drones from its own territory; France is negotiating to buy American 'Reaper' (surveillance) drones and is also
in contact with Israel on possible purchases. In June 2013, three
of Europe's largest defence contractors, European Aeronautic
Defence and Space (the parent company of Airbus), the French
company Dassault Aviation, and Finmeccanica of Italy, proposed
a new programme for making drones.[17] If it goes ahead, they will
jointly produce a medium-altitude drone for use in combat situations. It will be used mainly for surveillance but can be set up to
carry missiles.

3D printing has entered the military arena. When warships
need to resupply with ammunition and other equipment, they
have to pull into port. The US navy is looking into whether,
instead of transporting parts, its ships might at some point
carry advanced 3D printers and their powdered ingredients.
Equipment would be printed as necessary. Echoing the MIT
Media Lab a military strategist, Michael Llenza, says that 'The
eventual goal is a drone that flies right out of the printer with
electronics and motive power already in place.'[18] These are all
remarkable developments, as in so many other areas carrying
us into new territory. The EU has no overall policy position
on the military use of drones, even though some of its member
states are bent on acquiring them. Polls show that many people
across the EU are opposed to the US policy of targeted killings
in situations where there is no formal declaration of war.[19]

A pan-European security strategy is surely an urgent necessity. There are still many local and regional concerns with
which Europe is ill-prepared to deal. As with the situation in the
Middle East and North Africa, they are evolving in potentially
dangerous ways. Yet security nowadays must at the same time
follow that very interpenetration of the local and global which
is the distinctive feature of our age.

THE HVRP AND THE ROTW

EU foreign policy more generally operates under the aegis of the CSDP, CFSP, ESS and EEAS with its HRVP (there are many more acronyms around to add to these). The second is supposedly the dominant influence. However, its mandate in practice is quite limited, since essentially it is an intergovernmental organisation. Competences were not transferred to the EU agencies and decisions require unanimity. Hence it is very vulnerable to the divisions of interest and outlook that separate the member states, and in most situations there are plenty of these not far from the surface. When the Lisbon Treaty was drawn up, the European nations were unwilling to see this situation change. Hence the position of HRVP was introduced, in tandem with the EEAS, to seek to produce more effective policy.

A group of commissioners concerned with external relations has been initiated, chaired by the HRVP. Real progress has been made in some diplomatic endeavours, especially in the Balkans. It is once more the attractions of EU membership that have driven the process thus far. A fifteen-point agreement was endorsed by the prime ministers of Kosovo and Serbia in May 2013 and also by both parliaments. There's many a slip. Kosovo Serbs oppose the move and some have reacted fiercely. The agreement does not mean that Serbia recognises Kosovo as an independent state. However, it does confirm that neither side will block or hold up the accession process of the other. In a key move, accession negotiations with Serbia have begun.

In some more far-flung parts of the world, the EU has met with some recent successes too. Such has been the case with some interventions in Africa and more recently in Burma. For years the Union deployed economic sanctions against the country and imposed visa bans. The sanctions of course had some adverse effect upon the ordinary population. Yet, along with similar action by the US, they also seem to have contributed to convincing the generals that they should step aside. For one thing, they served to keep European companies away from the country, together with the investment that could have been brought in. The EU did, however, keep up a commitment to humanitarian support to the needy.

So far as bigger countries are concerned, the EU's human rights record is less impressive. It has been remarked that, in the case of China, its policy efforts have proved 'the most embarrassing indication of the gulf between European rhetoric and reality'.[20] In 1990 the EU member states endorsed a resolution of the Human Rights Commission condemning China's human rights record. It did so each year for a several years. In 1997 several EU countries, with France in the lead, stopped doing so, as they were worried about the impact it might have on trade. The Dutch presidency recorded that the decision put 'the essence of the human rights policy of the European Union . . . at stake'. Supported by nine other member states, Denmark sponsored the resolution. The Chinese hit back by cancelling a scheduled visit to Europe by the vice-premier of the country. In 1998 the EU states pulled out of endorsing the resolution altogether. The Chinese, for their part, have encountered the familiar difficulty of 'who speaks for Europe?' in their attempts to forge various sorts of ties or negotiate common problems. In tandem with the Russians, over the recent period they have grown exasperated with the EU's failure to extricate itself from its economic difficulties. Various European leaders have visited China since 2007 to try to get financial help, but have been told in no uncertain terms to set their own house in order first. The then premier, Wen Jiabao, remarked that the difficulties of the euro revealed a 'long-term accumulation of internal problems within the EU and the eurozone' which it is the responsibility of the Europeans to sort out. He also pointedly said that 'emerging economies should not be seen as the EU's good Samaritan'.[21]

When the Chinese premier, Li Keqiang, came to Europe
for the first time very recently, whom did he choose to visit?
It was 'President' Merkel, of course, in the only EU country
where he stopped off, Germany. The Chinese managed to split
Europe on the question of the dumping of solar panels. The
Union has accused China of selling such panels below cost. As
a result, anti-dumping regulations came into play, resulting in
the imposition of large tariffs. Yet, even though its own solar
panel industry is seriously affected, the German government
informed the Commission that it opposed the tariff duties.
Germany instead called for a negotiated deal, but the whole
affair caused acrimony on all sides. One must conclude that, so
far, the EU is simply not a significant presence in global terms
so far as foreign policy goes. At the moment, the EU's economic
dilemmas are further dragging down whatever global influence
it did have. 'Why can't the Europeans get their act together?' is
the common refrain from different parts of the world.

The EU's struggle about where its borders should lie reflects
a fundamental and unresolved ambiguity about its nature. Does
it represent a 'method', a 'way of life', to which neighbouring
states can aspire, if they develop in appropriate ways? Or is it
a territorial entity, with geographical limits to its expansion?
The answer is that it is an uneasy mixture of the two. The
ambiguity is bound up with the unresolved tensions between
inter-governmentalism on the one hand and federalism on the
other. If it is a loose system of states, sharing certain principles
of governance in common, the Union could in principle expand
more or less indefinitely. The more it moves in a federal direction – as I have argued throughout this book is inevitable if it
is to survive – then at some point the boundary question has to
be confronted directly. For most purposes the Union is already
a bounded entity. It has accepted clear borders to the south.
They have no particular logic to them. After all, for centuries
the countries around the Mediterranean were not only a part
of Europe as it then was; the Mediterranean was the very

Table 4 Reasons mentioned why accession talks with Turkey should not proceed (up to three reasons were coded)

	French	British	Greek	Total Greek, British, French
Turkey is different culturally, geographically, religiously	102	42	103	247
	34%	47%	68%	46%
EU structures will not be able to cope with Turkey accession	40	33		73
	13%	37%		14%
Cyprus issue		5	18 1	23
		6%	2%	4%
France must just say 'No'	20			20
	7%			4%
Economic, cultural reasons, e.g. migration			20	20
			13%	4%
Turkey would become too influential in EU	12			12
	4%			2%
Turkey needs to deal with Armenian/ Kurds/ Cyprus issues	10			10
	3%			2%
The EU would become simply a trade zone	10			10
	3%			2%
The process is undemocratic on part of EU and French government	10			10
	3%			2%
Other	94	10	11	115
	32%	11%	7%	21%
Total	298	90	152	540
				100%

Source: Ralph Negrine et al., 'Turkey and the European Union: An Analysis of How the Press in Four Countries Covered Turkey's Bid for Accession in 2004', European Journal of Communication, 23 (2008): 47–68.

centre of European culture. Yet to the east it is still a 'method', whose ultimate range of application has been left obscure – that ambiguity being at the origin of the conflicts in Georgia and Ukraine. At the moment, full EU membership for Ukraine is a flickering light at the end of a very long tunnel.

But what about Turkey, a nation with which the EU has carried on a courtship for fifty years, and which is a long-standing and active member of NATO, as well as a range of other European organisations? The EU's attitudes towards the country have been so ambivalent that it is hardly surprising that support for the EU membership inside Turkey has dropped drastically. In terms of growth rates, Turkey has made greater economic progress since 2007 than the floundering EU. The Union is once more divided. Some European states have declared they will hold referenda if there is a serious prospect of Turkey becoming accepted as a member state. The stand-off in Cyprus stands in the way, as does the Kurdish problem inside Turkey, which has now taken on a new level of difficulty following the rise of Islamic State. Under its current government, France is unfreezing its opposition to progress with Turkey's accession. Yet, more than seven years after formal talks with Turkey opened, progress has been minimal. A further setback occurred with the coming of the street protests in Turkish cities in May and June 2013. In the light of the Turkish government's harsh response to them, the EU temporarily suspended talks on the country's future membership.[22] Recep Erdogan, Prime Minister of Turkey since 2003, has established a new presidential system and has been elected as its first incumbent. He has been accused of using the process as a way of keeping himself in power, à la Putin, thereby perhaps undermining some of the progress that has been made towards democracy.

The arguments for and against Turkey's accession are so well trammelled that I shan't repeat them here. My view, long held, is that the way should be open for Turkey to become a member state, not at some constantly deferred future date but according to a realistic timetable. My reasons are: to show that a cosmopolitan Union is not just another version of paper Europe but a reality; to recognise how far Turkey has progressed in a whole variety of areas; to help protect a secular and open society within the country – a continuing and problematic issue; and because both the EU and Turkey would be stronger as members of an integrated political and economic community.

All the flaws that limit the EU's capacities in other domains appear in its influence – its limited influence – in world affairs.

Because of its lack of leadership capacity and resources, the European Union is widely seen elsewhere as like a regional version of the UN – well-meaning and capable in many ways, but too divided to take really consequential decisions. Internally there is a large gap between the 'administrative' nature of the EU (the role of the Commission) and the high-flown values the Union proclaims.

The Union has sought to create the trappings of solidarity by copying some of the things nation-states have, but the emotional resonance they have on the national level is almost completely lacking. The EU flag commands respect among many in Europe, but nowhere can it be said to generate much feeling or emotion. Those who are hostile to the EU often feel passionate about it, but for most citizens the EU is seen in an instrumental way. Can more deeply held sentiments of attachment be built? It will be a fundamental question over the coming years should it happen that the Union survives its biggest test, the situation it faces at present. At stake is the EU's capacity to play a more assertive and influential role in the wider world than has been the case up to now. The issues discussed in this chapter are not take-it-or-leave-it ones. They are as important to face up to as are the reforms discussed in previous chapters. There is no area where the European states are as anxious to preserve their independence of action as in foreign relations. Yet the theorem of sovereignty+ applies just as forcefully here as in other contexts. Much real, as opposed to nominal, sovereignty has already been forfeited because of developments in the wider world but also because of the involvement of member states in NATO. The rationale upon which the EU has built its distinctiveness – the idea that its special influence in international relations can be the promotion of collaboration and the rule of law – is specious. Since its early inception through to the present day, what is now the EU has relied upon access to the means of violence in the shape of the 'American guarantee'.

It is useful at this point to summarise the implications of

the foregoing chapters. The EU faces fundamental challenges not only because of the incomplete project of the euro but because of a broad set of changes affecting the industrialised countries and, indeed, the wider world. It is a huge mistake, made by many commentators today, to concentrate only on the dilemmas of the eurozone, testing as they are. Welfare policy, profiting from cultural diversity, energy and foreign policy, are concentrated largely in the hands of the member states. Yet the structural problems faced in these areas impact directly upon Europe's economic future and vice versa. The political integration needed if the euro is to survive and develop further cannot stop at the boundaries of the economy. At least a measure of greater integration has to take place at some point in these other domains too. Intensifying globalisation stands behind the complicated balance of opportunity and risk we must cope with today. Growing global interdependence should be understood not as a simple process of coming together but as a contradictory and complex set of practices, affecting personal and even intimate life just as much as the large-scale institutions. Flexibility, innovation and everyday creativity should no longer be seen as the antithesis of security, but is quite often the condition of it. This is a time, therefore, at which policies and strategies across the European states should be unpacked and examined critically across the board. It is just such a task that I have sought to undertake.

Conclusion

Joschka Fischer, a very well-known pro-European figure, once asked: 'How can one prevent the EU from becoming utterly untransparent, compromises from being stranger and more incomprehensible, and the citizen's acceptance of the EU from eventually hitting rock bottom?'[1] A jaundiced observer might say that all those things are actually happening in the Union at the moment. EU2 takes its decisions behind closed doors and with little or no public involvement until after the event. The only mode of direct participation the public seemingly has is in protest demonstrations on the streets. No one in power any longer takes much notice. 'Strange-seeming compromises' are made to bail out member states and banks, the result of haggling that goes on far into the night.

The very trends creating a new-found interdependence in Europe – the EU as a community of fate – are the self-same ones creating jagged fractures. Germany, as one leading newspaper put it, is 'leading but not loved'. The same paper noted that placards carrying images of Chancellor Merkel adorned with a Hitler moustache were being held aloft by protesters in streets in Spain and Italy through to Greece and Cyprus. The online edition of the Spanish newspaper *El Pais* featured a column comparing Mrs Merkel's policies to those of Hitler, although it was swiftly removed.[2] In Italy, the newspaper *Il Giornale*, owned by Silvio Berlusconi's media group, carried the headline 'Fourth Reich'. Below the headline was a picture of Angela Merkel with her hand in the air, a gesture that looked like a Nazi salute.

Anti-German feeling is widespread in some parts of eastern Europe as well. Jarosław Kaczyński, the Polish opposition leader, has played on the traditional fear of Germany and Russia. In a recent book he has written elliptically that it 'was not pure coincidence' that Mrs Merkel was elected as German chancellor. When pressed on whether he meant that the Stasi had helped to bring Merkel to power, he simply replied: 'Let's not talk about it'.[3] He also sought to stoke resentment towards the German minority in Poland. The chairman of a regional grouping of Kaczyński's party, Law and Justice, held a mass rally to protest against German influence in Lower Silesia, under the heading 'Here is Poland'.[4] Wider resentment against the EU also surfaced in many of the other member states of former eastern Europe. In January 2012, a crowd numbering about a million people congregated in Budapest, chanting 'We will not be an EU colony!', in protest against Troika involvement in the country.

We should be clear about what is at stake here. On the face of it, the advent of the euro lies behind all this turmoil, doubt and hostility. This is true on a concrete level. The EU will stand or fall depending upon whether the euro crisis can be effectively dealt with.[5] However, as I have argued in this book, what the introduction of the euro has done is to force the EU to come to terms with its own history – with structural inadequacies that have in the past essentially been held together with sticking plaster. Getting Germany to agree to give up the D-Mark, against the wishes of most of the country's population, was supposed to weaken the German economy in relative terms and bind an expanded Germany into the Union. It has worked more than would appear on the surface. For all the talk of the coming of a 'German Europe', Germany is actually heavily dependent on its fellow eurozone members. Germany is forced to be European not only because 'Never again' is taken very seriously, but because the country is intrinsically bound into the euro. Its success has been brought about in some part because of its membership of the single currency. The central difficulty in Europe is not German dominance as such, but the incapacities of EU1, both in terms of lack of democratic involvement and in terms of the absence of effective leadership.

It is in Germany's interest for economic mutuality to happen. It is in Germany's interest to escape the straitjacket of leadership of Europe through EU2. In some ways at the moment the country is in fact getting the worst of both worlds – expected to contribute with largesse to bailing out other member states, while at the same time becoming unpopular, even reviled, as a result. 'German Europe' is not a situation that will remain for the indefinite future, as so many now fear. It is necessarily temporary and it is intrinsically unstable. That is why a federal solution, backed by greater legitimacy and leadership capacity on an EU level, is the only feasible way forward. As I have tried to show, many other implications follow.

The only way forward: but are there ways backwards? Would it really be catastrophic if the euro collapsed? There have been predictions of the disintegration of the euro ever since the crisis came into being. In May 2012, for example, the economist Paul Krugman wrote a piece tagged '*Eurodämmerung*'. 'Some of us have been talking it over', he wrote, 'and here's what the end game looks like.' He then presented a list of events in sequence:

1   Greece exits the euro, 'very possibly next month'.
2   Depositors in Spanish and Italian banks try to move their money to Germany, in large amounts.
3a Controls might be instituted to prevent deposits being taken out of the country, coupled to limits on cash withdrawals.

3b At the same time, or as an alternative, the banks are rein-
    forced with very large amounts of money supplied by the
    ECB.

4a Germany accepts huge public indirect claims on Italy and
    Spain giving Spain guarantees on its debt, and at the same
    time agrees to a higher EU inflation target – or –

4b The end of the euro.

'And', Krugman added, 'we're talking about months, not years,
for this to play out.'[6]

Well, he was wrong (thus far) in prediction 1 and certainly
off in his timing. Prediction 3a has, in a certain sense, come to
pass, although so far only for a tiny part of the EU, Cyprus. It is
at least possible that it might become generalised elsewhere. 3b
has taken place, but not 4a – the source of the resentments just
discussed. Yet no one can write off the possibility that 4b might
happen, and this for two reasons. One is that the euro has been
salvaged so far mainly by fire-fighting efforts. The other is that
the crisis has roots deeper than either flaws in the construction
of the euro or the political inadequacies of the EU.

An uncontrolled collapse of the euro would do massive
damage not only to the eurozone countries, but to all EU
member states and to the world economy as a whole. The euro
was set up to produce economic interdependence, and this
outcome it certainly has achieved. Were the euro to enter meltdown, literally millions of contracts, business partnerships and
economic enterprises would have to be disaggregated almost
overnight. Countries not in the eurozone would be affected just
as immediately, and just as radically, as would be its members.
Debt would have to be cancelled or redenominated in local currencies, with huge imbalances resulting. Some countries would
have to declare bankruptcy. Banks as well as companies would
go bust, since their domestic and external liabilities would no
longer match. All the currently more successful states would be
affected as profoundly as the weaker ones precisely because, like

Figure 17 'Saving the euro'

Germany, their level of competitiveness has been partly shaped by their membership of the eurozone. The global impact would be instantaneous and could well lead to a market meltdown. The social and political consequences would be just as disturbing. Nationalists would likely rejoice, but even they might blanch at the social consequences. In 2012, a couple of days after the EU was awarded the Nobel Peace Prize, the British politician Vince Cable warned that the consequences of a sudden dissolution of the euro would be 'incalculable'.[7] 'Incalculable' is probably the right word. At the outer edge of possibility, we just don't know how extreme the consequences might be. Member states have had the opportunity to draw up contingency plans for a collapse, but these might remain wishful thinking should dissolution become a reality.

Would it be possible to roll back the euro in a controlled fashion, avoiding bank runs and the other dangers that lurk? Could one or two states just up and quit, or be forced out in a way that allowed the rest of the enterprise to continue? It has been suggested by some that, tired of supporting the rest of the eurozone, Germany might simply decide unilaterally to quit and accept the consequences. After a period of perhaps very difficult adjustment, some say, freed from the shackles of the poorer performers, the German economy would readjust and become even stronger than before. Examined more concretely, even if the will were there, such a strategy would at a minimum be highly problematic. Either a clear statement of intent would have to be made, which, because of all the knock-on implications there would be, would throw markets into disarray as soon as it happened, or the whole thing would have to be kept secret – a virtual impossibility. Moreover, the 'adjustment' the German economy would have to make would be huge. Not only would its currency appreciate steeply, but the currencies of the weaker countries would go the other way, compounding Germany's problems of competitiveness.

More feasible – and much touted – is the possibility that one or more of the smaller countries could decide to leave or be forced out by the other members. Such a happening is easy to talk about in principle, but tracing through how it might be done in practice shows how testing it would be. The most thorough exposition of such a possibility has been provided in a study by Capital Economics. Its lead author was the economist Roger Bootle.[8] It was designed to show that the exit of one or two individual states from the euro would be feasible and that such a process could be beneficial both to the country or countries involved and to the rest of the eurozone.

It is worth tracing the authors' argument in some detail just to show the problems involved. A country that quit the euro and allowed its currency to fall substantially in value would render its exports more competitive. The stronger states would gain from such an exit, they say, which it would be in their interest to support. Bootle and his colleagues argue that such an exit could be achieved without too much damage if carefully arranged.

They recognise that, historically, rather than securing greater stability, devaluations have produced chaos. Such was the case, for example, with those in Argentina from 1955 to 1970, Brazil in 1967 and Israel in 1971. However, the weak states in Europe face an uncertain future if they stay in the euro; it is a case of the lesser of two evils. How could a process of disengagement be managed? It would be advantageous to maintain secrecy as long as possible, so as to plan ahead in a sober way. There are some relevant earlier examples. For instance, in the formation of the Czech Republic and Slovakia, the decision to have separate currencies was successfully kept secret until six days before the separation (the authors do not mention the fact that, in the age of the internet, secrecy is far harder to maintain than it once was). Yet secrecy comes with disadvantages too. By definition there could be no public discussion or debate by means of which such a decision would be taken. There would be no straightforward way of establishing a cross-party consensus on the issue. If it provoked political conflict after being implemented, confidence that the measures would succeed among the public and among potential investors could be undermined and widespread social disruption could follow.

The numbers of people in the 'need to know' category would have to be small, although this would limit the level of expertise that could be drawn upon. Even so, the possibility of documents being leaked would always be there. Hence capital controls and other regulatory measures would have to be introduced fairly early on, which again would have to be put in place without public debate. Once such controls were implemented, the exit would have to be executed as soon as practicable. Because of the complicated legal concerns involved, leaving the euro would not be a run-of-the-mill devaluation of a currency. A decision to leave, leading to a heavily devalued currency, would have profound consequences for contractual obligations, public and private, denominated in euros. The economies of the eurozone countries are so interdependent that many of these stretch

across their specific boundaries. A country that reintroduced
its own currency would have to meet many of its obligations in
euros – where their value would have increased, probably dramatically, because of the slump in that of the national currency.
Hence there could be protracted struggles in the courts to settle
claims. An unknown quantity of debtors might be forced to
default upon their contracts or otherwise negotiate reductions
in their obligations.

How would an exit be organised in terms of the production of
notes and coins, especially if secrecy were to be preserved until
as close as possible to the point of exit? Some have suggested
that euro notes issued in the exiting country (distinguishable
by their serial numbers), plus coins carrying that country's
national symbols, could be used as the new national currency.
The notes could be over-stamped as the reintroduced currency.
It is unlikely such a strategy would work. The euros that were
over-stamped could well be widely regarded as ordinary euros
when circulating outside the exiting country. Moreover, notes
held privately would probably not be surrendered and would
simply disappear into the wider eurozone.

A better option would be to try to do without cash altogether
for a specified period. Most transactions would be carried on
electronically. Nearly all business dealings today take place
without physical cash anyway; payment of wages and salaries
happens in the same way. Many of the exchanges now made in
cash could be conducted by electronic means or by cheques or
other forms of IOU. Plenty of small cash transactions would
remain. A possibility here would be for these payments to continue to be paid in euros. The conversion rate adopted at the exit
inside the country, Bootle and his colleagues propose, should be
1 for 1. The common currency could still be used for a while
in such small transactions, even while its value fell on foreign
exchanges. The obvious difficulty would be that people could be
reluctant to spend euros in such a way because their value would
be substantially higher than that of the national currency. Or it

could happen that the sellers of services would accept a different price for euros than for money supplied in the national currency by electronic means. At the date of the introduction of the new national notes and coins, the euro would revert to being treated as a foreign currency.[9]

How could the flight of capital and a potential breakdown of the banking system be avoided? There would be clear difficulties of timing and the need to maintain secrecy here, since people would otherwise withdraw euros and stack them up as much as they could. The announcement of departure would have to be on a day when most banks were closed, or a bank holiday declared. Almost certainly it would be necessary to have draconian capital controls at that point, such as a ban upon acquiring new foreign assets or the holding of external bank accounts. These would in addition include a whole range of orthodox market transactions, such as the buying and selling of most forms of financial instruments. It would also be necessary to manage the wider consequences of a country's exit for the remaining members of the eurozone. These could be profound. In the worst-case scenario, even the departure of a small country could stimulate a loss of market confidence that could spread through the entire eurozone and thence to the world economy as a whole. Hence the IMF, the ECB, the World Bank and other major financial institutions would have to figure centrally in the process.

The exit of even a small country from the eurozone is thus far from the easy option that is sometimes spoken of. Most EU institutions and states have no doubt by now made 'in principle' preparations for such an eventuality – or one should certainly hope that they have. Hence there is at least a chance that an exit of one or two smaller states could be handled without significantly damaging the whole edifice. What would happen if a larger state were to choose to leave or be forced out – let's say Spain or Italy? All the problems just noted would exist, but on a larger and more dangerous scale. A study published by the

Bertelsmann Foundation offered a detailed analysis of the issue. A combined exit by Greece and Portugal would be very costly, in terms of rises in unemployment and declining demand, both inside the countries affected and in the wider eurozone. Were Spain to join them, the costs would rise in a precipitous way and by this time would affect other major economies of the world. Loss of growth in the US is calculated as the equivalent of €1.2 trillion over the period up to 2020. If Italy were then to leave, the situation could potentially run out of control, possibly sparking a further deep world economic crisis. According to the study, as a consequence, Germany would lose €1.7 trillion over the period, the US €2.8 trillion and China €1.9 trillion.[10]

It is important to remember that the creation of the euro was not only driven by political ambition. There had been a long history of monetary instability in Europe. In the early post-war period currencies were not convertible. Trade was made possible only by specific agreements between countries, and after a short while the system became unworkable.[11] With the dissolution of Bretton Woods in the early 1970s, currencies were allowed to float against one another and against the dollar. The new situation led to considerable volatilities. One of the best studies of its evolution refers to the 'unloved dollar standard'.[12] Until very recently, American monetary policy remained firmly inward looking, in spite of its repercussions for the rest of the world. It was in the interests of the European states to seek to limit its damaging effects – resulting in the creation of the European Monetary System. The EMS was essentially a currency basket, with bilateral exchange rates allowed to fluctuate within margins set for the states involved, depending on their varying economic circumstances. It was supposed to produce a system in which member states were all more or less equal in terms of their economic potential. Germany in fact emerged as the dominant influence. Such an outcome in turn reduced the competitiveness of some other EU member nations because of high interest rates.

Currency devaluations followed in Italy and Spain. The British pound and the Italian lira were removed from the Exchange Rate Mechanism, the former in a dramatic set of events labelled 'Black Wednesday'. The French currency also came under intense pressure in the so-called battle of the franc, which was in the end protected by active intervention on the part of the Bundesbank. The underlying pressures within the EMS were not quelled. The Spanish peseta was devalued along with the Portuguese escudo. The EMS was reformed, allowing wider ranges of fluctuation in the currencies, but the problems did not go away, and the French franc also had to be devalued. The divergence between the currencies and the inadequate remedies available to control it meant that they were too high against the dominant global currency, the US dollar. Even through the recent years of struggle, the euro has provided a successful counterbalance to the American currency in world markets.

The intellectual framework of economic theory which stood behind wholesale deregulation stands more or less in ruins. Given that the euro survives in good shape, the EU should be a key player in reconstruction, along with the US and particularly China. It is in the interests of creditor countries such as China at this point to allow their currencies to appreciate, as a condition of injecting more stability into the world financial order. Not only would debt be wound down to more manageable levels, but the Chinese could turn to the next stage of their development, which has to be the stimulating of domestic demand. After all, the Chinese leadership has been telling both the Americans and the Europeans for some while that the days are gone when they could just borrow their way out of the difficulties into which they get themselves. Time will tell how far a possibility is feasible on the ground, but it is hard to see how otherwise the current world imbalances can be addressed.

'Turbulent and mighty continent' – hopefully the unrest now seen again across Europe will remain superficial compared with the tensions and conflicts that have marked its past. The Union could still founder, even disintegrate, the result of a chain reaction of circumstances that member states were unable to control. The transition that needs to be made to a more unified and democratic system might prove to be politically impossible. Yet a more integrated Union could become a power of world standing. It is an outcome which pro-Europeans at this point should actively struggle to achieve. There is the chance for the EU not only to advance but to correct some of its historic limitations and contradictions. 'Therefore I say unto you: let Europe arise!' – across a gulf of some seventy years Churchill's words can still inspire.

Notes

Introduction

1 Valentina Pop, quoting Jean-Claude Juncker (now the President of the European Commission): 'Europe still has "sleeping war demons"', *EU Observer*, 11 March 2013.

2 Ian Traynor: 'Crisis for Europe as trust hits record low', *The Guardian, Europa*, 24 April 2013. Available online.

3 Ulrich Beck: *German Europe*. Cambridge: Polity, 2013. The current German leadership recognises these necessities. Wolfgang Schäuble, the country's finance minister, has said forthrightly that 'the Germans are the last people who would want to put up with a German Europe.' 'We want', he added, 'to put Germany at the service of the European community's economic recovery – without weakening Germany itself.' Wolfgang Schäuble: 'We Germans don't want a German Europe', *The Guardian*, 19 July 2013. Available online.

4 Thomas Hale, David Held and Kevin Young: *Gridlock: Why Global Cooperation is Failing when We Need it Most*. Cambridge: Polity, 2012.

Chapter 1 The EU as Community of Fate

1 'Beppe Grillo warns that Italy will be "dropped like a hot potato"', *The Telegraph*, 13 March 2013. Available online. The movement subsequently became fraught with internal divisions and lost most of its influence.

2 Nikolaus Blome and Dirk Hoeren: 'Merkozy – sieht so das neue Europa aus?', *Bild*, 1 December 2011. Available online.

3 Gavin Hewitt: *The Lost Continent*. London: Hodder & Stoughton, 2013, p. 261. This book is a very useful narrative account of the struggles of the European leaders to cope with the threat to the euro. For an analysis set against the broad sweep of European history, see Brendan Simms: *Europe: The Struggle for Supremacy*. London: Allen Lane, 2013, chapter 8 and Conclusion.

4 Jeanna Smialek: 'IMF chief Lagarde calls Merkel "unchallenged leader" in Germany', 10 April 2013, Bloomberg.com.

5 Jack Ewing and James Kanter: 'A *Troika* for Europe faces own crisis of confidence', *International Herald Tribune*, 10 June 2013.

6 Peter Spiegel and Kerin Hope: 'EU's Olli Rehn lashes out at IMF criticism of Greek bailout', *Financial Times*, 7 June 2013. Available online.

7 Alessandro Leipold: 'Inching forward in testing times', Lisbon Council Economic Intelligence, 1 July 2013. Available online.

8 Aimee Donnellan and Mette Fraende: 'Bankers demand faster action on Europe banking union', Reuters, 23 May 2013. Available online.

9 Leipold: 'Inching forward in testing times', pp. 2–3.

10 Sid Verma: 'Germany's rejection of a pan-European deposit guarantee scheme is no disaster', 13 April 2013, Euromoney.com.

11 In July 2013, Mr Draghi took a further step. For the first time, the ECB offered 'forward guidance' on interest rates, pledging to keep interest rates low, transgressing one of its established limits and bringing it closer to the practice of the Federal Reserve. There was an immediate and positive market response.

12 See Iain Begg: *Fiscal Union for the Euro Area: An Overdue and Necessary Scenario?*. Gütersloh: Bertelsmann Stiftung, 2011. Available online.

13 All quotes from George Soros: 'Germany's choice', www.project-syndicate.org: originally given as CFS Presidential Lecture, House of Finance, Frankfurt, 10 April 2013.

14 Hans-Werner Sinn: 'George Soros is playing with fire', *The Guardian*, 24 April 2013. For Soros's reply, see 'Eurobonds or exit: the choice is Germany's', Guardian Economic Blog, 30 April 2013.

15 Alan Crawford and Tony Czuczka: *Angela Merkel: A Chancellorship Forged in Crisis*. Chichester: Wiley, 2013.

16 Radoslaw Sikorski: 'I fear Germany's power less than her inactivity', *Financial Times*, 28 November 2011.

17 Joseph Stiglitz: 'Saving a broken euro', *Queries*, summer 2014: 26-7. Available online.

18 Glienicker Group: 'Towards a euro union', *Breugel*, 13 January 2014. Available online.

19 Luuk van Middelaar: *The Passage to Europe: How a Continent Became a Union*. London: Yale University Press, 2013, p. x.

20 'Federal Europe will be "a reality in a few years", says José Manuel Barroso', WordPress.com, 8 May 2013, p. 2.

21 Geoffrey de Q. Walker: 'Rediscovering the advantages of federalism', Parliament of Australia, March 1999. Available online.

22 Anand Menon and John Peet: *Beyond the European Parliament: Rethinking the EU's Democratic Legitimacy*. London: Centre for European Reform, December 2010. Available online.

23 David Brunnstrom: 'EU says it has solved the Kissinger question', Reuters, 20 November 2009. Available online.

24 Iain Martin: 'Herman Van Rompuy's greatest hits', *Wall Street Journal*, 17 November 2009. Available online.

25 Vanessa Gera: 'Kissinger says calling Europe quote not likely his', *The Big Story*, 27 June 2012. Available online.

26 For an interesting and important discussion, set in a wide global context, see Nicolas Berggruen and Nathan Gardels: *Intelligent Governance for the 21st Century: A Middle Way between West and East*. Cambridge: Polity, 2013.

27 David Marsh: *Europe's Deadlock*. New Haven, CT: Yale University Press, 2013.

28 Eurobarometer: 'The European elections made a difference', Brussels: European Commission, 25 July 2014.

29 Pew Research Global Attitudes Project: 'The new sick man of Europe: the European Union', 13 May 2013. Available online.

30 Jürgen Habermas: 'Democracy, solidarity and the European crisis', lecture given in Leuven, 26 April 2013. Available online.

31 See Mary Kaldor and Sabine Selchow: 'The "bubbling up" of subterranean politics in Europe', *Journal of Civil Society* 9(1): 78–99.

32 See Michael Bruter and Sarah Harrison: *How European Do You Feel? The Psychology of European Identity*. London School of Economics, 2012. Available online.

33 Valeriu Nicolae: 'A sick European civil society – Brussels', 18 February 2013, Wordpress.com.

34 Philip Oltermann: 'Something in common: should English be the official language of the EU?', *The Guardian*, 24 April 2013.

35 John Keane: *The Life and Death of Democracy*. London: Simon & Schuster, 2009. Keane dates his notion of monitory democracy from further back than I would do.

36 'Rampant corruption is aggravating the EU crisis', 6 June 2012, p. 1, EUobserver.com.
37 Bernard Connolly: *The Rotten Heart of Europe*. London: Faber & Faber, 1995. See also the new edition of 2012. This book remains a must-read.
38 Winston Churchill: Cabinet Memorandum 29, November 1953. Available online.
39 Jonas Parello-Plesner: 'Denmark caught between "ins" and "outs"', European Council on Foreign Relations, 24 October 2012, p. 1.
40 For an excellent and balanced discussion, see David Charter: *Au Revoir, Europe: What if Britain Left the EU?*. London: Biteback, 2012.

Chapter 2 Austerity and After

1 Mark Blyth: *Austerity: The History of a Dangerous Idea*. Oxford: Oxford University Press, 2013.
2 Holger Schmieding and Christian Schulz: *The 2012 Euro Plus Monitor: The Rocky Road to Balanced Growth*. Brussels: Lisbon Council and Berenberg Bank, 2012. Available online. All quotations below are from this source.
3 See Holger Schmieding and Christian Schulz: *Euro Plus Monitor, Spring 2013 Update*.
4 IMF: *Greece: Country Report no 13/20*, January 2013. Available online.
5 McKinsey&Company: *Greece 10 Years Ahead: Defining Greece's New Growth Model and Strategy*. Athens, March 2012. Available online.
6 Interview with George Papandreou: 'A growth strategy for Greece', Council on Foreign Relations, 20 March 2013, www.cfr.org.
7 IMF: 'Greece makes progress, but more effort needed to restore growth', IMF Survey, 5 June 2013. Available online.
8 Vassilis Paipais: 'The politics of the German war reparations to Greece', LSE Eurocrisis blogs, 8 May 2013.
9 Jorgo Chatzimarkakis: 'A new chapter in Greece's quest for reparations of the Second World War', 11 June 2013, Ekathimerini.com.
10 Helena Smith: 'Greece becomes trade battleground as foreign investors swoop', *The Guardian*, 27 May 2013.
11 Helena Smith: 'Greece: the sequel', *The Guardian*, 25 June 2013.
12 See the discussion in McKinsey&Company: *Greece 10 Years Ahead*, Section 3.
13 European Commission: *Europe 2020*. Brussels, 2010, p. 23. Available online.
14 European Commission: *Lisbon Strategy Evaluation Document*. Brussels, 2010. Available online.

15 Ray Kurzweil: *The Singularity is Near: When Humans Transcend Biology*. London: Duckworth, 2005.

16 Ann Mettler and Anthony D. Williams: *Wired for Growth and Innovation: How Digital Technologies are Reshaping Small- and Medium-Sized Businesses*. Brussels: Lisbon Council, 2012. Available online.

17 European Monitoring Centre on Change: *Portugal: ERM Comparative Analytical Report on 'Public policy and support for restructuring in SMEs'*, 14 May 2013. Available online.

18 McKinsey Global Institute: *Investing in Growth: Europe's Next Challenge*, 2012. Available online.

19 Ibid.

20 Neil Gershenfeld: 'How to make almost anything', *Foreign Affairs*, 91 (2012), p. 46.

21 Chris Anderson: *Makers: The New Industrial Revolution*. London: Random House, 2012.

22 Ibid.

23 Erik Brynjolfsson and Andrew McAfee: *Race Against the Machine*. Lexington, MA: Digital Frontier Press, 2011.

24 Metra Martech: *Positive Impact of Industrial Robots on Employment*. London, 2011. Available online.

25 Boston Consulting Group: *Made in America, Again*. Boston, 2011. Available online.

26 Boston Consulting Group: *U.S. Manufacturing Nears the Tipping Point*. Boston, 2012. Available online.

27 'Welcome home', *The Economist*, 19 January 2013, p. 11.

28 Ed Crooks: 'Steelmakers reap benefits from US shale gas revolution', FT.com, 18 June 2013.

29 Tim Leunig: 'Stop thinking of "reshoring" jobs from China', *Financial Times*, 31 October 2011.

30 Devon Swezey and Ryan McConaghy: *Manufacturing Growth: Advanced Manufacturing and the Future of the American Economy*. Breakthrough Institute, October 2011. Available online.

31 Confrontations Europe: *Manifesto for Growth and Employment: Let's Reindustrialise Europe*. October, 2012. Available online.

32 Quoted in Europa: 'Industrial revolution brings industry back to Europe', 10 November 2012, p. 1. Available online.

33 Natixis Economic Research: *Where Can We See Signs of Reindustrialisation?*, 14 February 2013. Available online.

34 Global Economic Dynamics: *Transatlantic Trade and Investment Partnership*. Gütersloh: Bertelsmann Stiftung, 2013. Available online.

35 Nicholas Shaxson: *Treasure Islands: Tax Havens and the Men who Stole the World*. London: Bodley Head, 2011, p. 15.
36 Harry Karanikas and Marina Walker Guevara: 'Taxmen have little clue of offshore companies owned by Greeks', International Consortium of Journalists, 3 April 2013. Available online.
37 Chrystia Freeland: *Plutocrats: The Rise of the New Global Super-Rich and the Fall of Everyone Else*. London: Allen Lane, 2012, p. 5.

Chapter 3 No More Social Model?

1 Murciatoday.com, 13 May 2013.
2 Quoted in Anthony Giddens: 'A social model for Europe?', in Anthony Giddens, Patrick Diamond and Roger Liddle (eds): *Global Europe, Social Europe*. Cambridge: Polity, 2006, p. 14. I draw on this article in what follows.
3 Andre Sapir et al.: *An Agenda for a Growing Europe*. Brussels: European Commission. July 2003, p. 97.
4 Paul Pierson (ed.): *The New Politics of the Welfare State*. Oxford: Oxford University Press, 2001.
5 'Northern lights', *The Economist*, 2 February 2013.
6 John D. Stephens: 'The Scandinavian welfare states', in Gøsta Esping-Andersen (ed.): *Welfare States in Transition: National Adaptations in Global Economies*. London: Sage, 1996, pp. 85–6.
7 Anthony Giddens: *The Third Way*. Cambridge: Polity, 1998, chapter 4.
8 Anthony Giddens: *Europe in the Global Age*. Cambridge: Polity, 2006.
9 T. H. Marshall: *Citizenship and the Social Class*. Cambridge: Cambridge University Press, 1950.
10 Robert Thomson, Matt Karnitschnig and Brian Blackstone: 'Interview with Mario Draghi', *Wall Street Journal*, 24 February 2012. Available online.
11 Arne Heise and Hanna Lierse: *Budget Consolidation and the European Social Model*. Berlin: Friedrich Ebert Stiftung, 2011, p. 3. Available online.
12 Ibid., p. 15.
13 Solidarity Federation: 'Corrala utopia: a direct action response to the housing crisis', 5 March 2013. Available online.
14 Ide Kearney, 'Economic challenges', in Brigid Reynolds and Seán Healy (eds): *Does the European Model have a Future?* Dublin: Social Justice Ireland, 2012, pp. 1–17.
15 Europa: *Report on Childcare Provision in the Member States*. Brussels: European Commission, 2013.

16 László Andor: 'Employment and social developments', Europa, 8 January 2013.

17 Patrick Diamond and Guy Lodge: *European Welfare States after the Crisis: Changing Public Attitudes.* London: Policy Network, 2013. Available online.

18 See Heise and Lierse: *Budget Consolidation and the European Social Model.*

19 'Northern lights', *The Economist.*

20 Annika Ahtonen: *Economic Governance: Helping European Healthcare Systems to Deliver Better Health and Wealth.* European Policy Centre, 2 May 2013. Available online.

21 'Finland hires Spanish nurses', 22 March 2012, WordPress.com.

22 Lawrence Summers: 'Foreword' to Michael Barber, Katelyn Donnelly and Saad Rizvi, *An Avalanche is Coming: Higher Education and the Revolution Ahead.* London: IPPR, March 2013, p. 1. Available online.

23 Barber et al.: *An Avalanche is Coming*, pp. 18–20.

24 World Education University, at www.theWEU.com.

25 Stephen Schimpff: *The Future of Medicine.* Washington, DC: Potomac, 2007.

26 Michel Foucault: *Discipline and Punish.* London: Penguin, 1991.

27 Graeme Wood: 'Prison without walls', *The Atlantic*, 11 August 2010.

28 Bernd Marin: *Welfare in an Idle Society?* London: Ashgate, 2013, part 2.

29 OECD: *Pensions at a Glance 2011: Retirement-Income Systems in OECD and G20 Countries.* Paris: OECD, 2011. Available online.

30 Steven Hill: 'Youth unemployment is bad but not as bad as we're told', *Financial Times*, 24 June 2012.

31 All figures from Eurostat: EU Statistics, 2012. Available online.

32 Jacob Funk Kirkegaard: 'Youth unemployment in Europe', Voxeu.org, 13 October 2012.

33 Ursula von der Leyen, Wolfgang Schäuble, Pierre Moscovici and Michel Sapin: 'How Europe's youth can recapture hope', German Federal Ministry of Finance, 28 May 2013. Available online.

Chapter 4 The Cosmopolitan Imperative

1 European Commission: *3rd Annual Report on Immigration and Asylum.* Brussels, 30 May 2012, p. 2. Available online.

2 Christopher Caldwell: 'Europe's other crisis', *New Republic*, 4 May 2013; and *Reflections on the Revolution in Europe: Immigration, Islam and the West.* London: Allen Lane, 2009.

3 Massimo Franco: 'Italy's struggle to hold back the tide', *Chatham House*, August 2014. Available online.

4 Paul Scheffer: *Immigrant Nations*. Cambridge: Polity, 2011, p. 8.

5 Robert S. Leiken: *Europe's Angry Muslims*. Oxford: Oxford University Press, 2012.

6 Scheffer: *Immigrant Nations*, pp. 1–2.

7 Eric Hobsbawm and Terence Ranger: *The Invention of Tradition*. Cambridge: Cambridge University Press, 1992.

8 'Father of Toulouse killer Mohamed Merah sues for murder', BBC New Europe, 11 June, 2012. Available online.

9 Richard Youngs: *Europe's Decline and Fall: The Struggle against Global Irrelevance*. London: Profile, 2010, p. 92.

10 Thilo Sarrazin: *Deutschland schafft sich ab*. Munich: Deutsche Verlags-Anstalt, 2010.

11 Stephen Lowman: 'German politician stirs controversy with his inflammatory views on Muslims and Jews', *Washington Post*, 30 August 2010.

12 *Bild* newspaper, 26 August 2010.

13 Thilo Sarrazin: *Europa braucht den Euro nicht*. Munich: Deutsche Verlags-Anstalt, 2012. See also 'Sarrazin strikes again: German author says Berlin is hostage to Holocaust in euro crisis', Spiegel Online, 22 May 2012.

14 Quoted in 'Sarrazin strikes again', p. 2.

15 All quotes from BBC News Online: 'Merkel says German multicultural society has failed', 17 October 2010.

16 Quotes from Charles Hawley: 'Muslims in Germany', Spiegel Online, 1 March 2012.

17 Ali Rattansi: *Multiculturalism*. Oxford: Oxford University Press, 2011, p. 87.

18 Charles Taylor: *Multiculturalism: Examining the Politics of Recognition*. Princeton, NJ: Princeton University Press, 1994, plus many later books and articles.

19 Charles Taylor: 'Why democracy needs patriotism', *Boston Review*, 19 (1994), p. 72.

20 See Rattansi: *Multiculturalism*, chapter 2.

21 Here I draw upon my discussion in 'No giving up on multiculturalism!' in my book *Over to You, Mr Brown: How Labour Can Win Again*. Cambridge: Polity, 2007.

22 Philippe Legrain: *Immigrants: Your Country Needs Them*. London: Little, Brown, 2006.

23 David Goodhart: 'Too Diverse?', *Prospect Magazine*, 20 February 2004.

24 David Goodhart: *The British Dream: Successes and Failures of Post-War Immigration*. London: Atlantic Books, 2013, p. xvi.

25 Trevor Phillips: 'Genteel xenophobia is as bad as any other kind', *The Guardian*, 16 February 2004.

26 See Will Kymlicka and Keith Banting: 'Immigration, multiculturalism and the welfare state', *Ethics and International Affairs*, 20 (2006): 281–304; and Kymlicka and Banting: *Multiculturalism and the Welfare State*. Oxford: Oxford University Press, 2006.

27 Ted Cantle: *Interculturalism: The New Era of Cohesion and Diversity*. Basingstoke: Palgrave Macmillan, 2012. See also Rattansi: *Multiculturalism*, Conclusion.

28 Cantle: *Interculturalism*, p. 5.

29 Quoted in Legrain: *Immigrants*, p. 4.

30 See the excellent discussion in Simon Fanshawe and Dhananjayan Sriskandarajah: *'You Can't Put Me in a Box': Super-Diversity and the End of Identity Politics in Britain*. London: IPPR, 2010. Available online.

31 Kerry Moore, Paul Mason and Justin Lewis: *Images of Islam in the UK*. Cardiff: Cardiff University Press, 2008. Available online.

32 Amartya Sen: *Identity and Violence*. New York: Norton, 2006, p. 75.

33 See Montserrat Guibernau: *Belonging: Solidarity and Division in Modern Society*. Cambridge: Polity, 2013.

34 Youngs: *Europe's Decline and Fall*, p. 118.

35 John Keane: *The Life and Death of Democracy*. New York: Norton, 2009.

36 Rattansi: *Multiculturalism*, p. 155.

37 Benedict Anderson: *Imagined Communities*. London: Verso, 1983.

38 Samuel Huntingdon: *Who Are We?* New York: Simon & Schuster, 2004.

39 Zhang Weiwei: *The China Wave: Rise of a Civilizational State*. Hackensack, NJ: World Century, 2012, p. 161.

40 'The China model: a debate between Francis Fukuyama and Zhang Weiwei', *New Perspectives Quarterly*, 28(4), 2011.

41 Václav Havel: 'Is there a European Identity, is there a Europe?', speech made to the European Parliament in Strasbourg on 8 March 1994. Available online. All quotes from this source.

42 Zhang Weiwei: *The China Wave*, pp. 70–1.

Chapter 5 Climate Change and Energy

1 Anthony Giddens: *The Politics of Climate Change*. Cambridge: Polity, 2011, chapter 8.

2 Sander de Bruyn et al.: *Does the Energy Intensive Industry Obtain Windfall Profits through the EU ETS?* Delft: CE Delft, 2010. Available online.

3 A. Denny Ellerman and Barbara Buchner: *Over-Allocation or Abatement?*, Report no. 141. Cambridge, MA: MIT Joint Program on the Science and Policy of Global Change, 2006.

4 Ecologic Institute: 'EU ETS – from slumping to jumping?', 25 February 2013, p. 1. Available online.

5 Carbon Trade Watch: 'It is time to scrap the ETS!', 4 February 2013. Available online.

6 Fiona Harvey: 'EU urged to revive flagging emissions trading scheme', *The Guardian*, 15 February 2013.

7 Sandbag: *Drifting toward Disaster? The ETS Adrift in Europe's Climate Efforts*, 25 June 2013. Available online.

8 Quoted in Per Meilstrup: 'The runaway summit: the background story of the Danish presidency of COP15, the UN climate change conference', *Danish Foreign Policy Yearbook 2010*, pp. 113–35. Available online.

9 Anil Ananthaswamy: 'Making waves', *New Scientist*, 219, 20 July 2013.

10 See Paul J. Crutzen and Christian Schwägerl: 'Living in the anthropocene: toward a new global ethos', *Yale Environment 360*, 24 January 2011. Available online.

11 Michael L. Rosenzweig: 'Reconciliation ecology and the future of species diversity', *Oryx*, 37(2), 2003: 194–205. See also Emma Marris: *Rambunctious Garden: Saving Nature in a Post-Wild World*. London: Bloomsbury, 2011.

12 Michael L. Rosenzweig: *Win–Win Ecology: How the Earth's Species Can Survive in the Midst of Human Enterprise*. Oxford: Oxford University Press, 2003.

13 Report of the World Commission on Environment and Development: *Our Common Future*. Oxford: Oxford University Press, 1987, p. 3.

14 United Nations General Assembly: *Rio Declaration on Environment and Development*, June 1992, Principle 15.

15 See, for example, David Vogel: *The Politics of Precaution: Regulating Health, Safety, and Environmental Risks in Europe and the United States*. Princeton, NJ: Princeton University Press, 2012; Jonathan Wiener et al. (eds): *The Reality of Precaution: Comparing Risk Regulation in the United States and Europe*. Washington, DC: RFF, 2011.

16 Cass R. Sunstein: *Laws of Fear: Beyond the Precautionary Principle*. Cambridge: Cambridge University Press, 2005.

17 See the range of studies reported by the UK Energy Research Centre – for example, Horace Herring and Steve Sorrell: *Energy Efficiency and Sustainable Consumption: The Rebound Effect*. Basingstoke: Palgrave Macmillan, 2008.

18 See the website of the Max-Planck-Institut für Meteorologie at www. mpimet.mpg.de/en.html.

19 House of Lords, European Union Sub-Committee 'D': *No Country is an Energy Island: Security Investment for the EU's Future*, HL Paper 161. London: TSO, 2013. Available online.

20 Agora Energiewende: *12 Insights on Germany's* Energiewende. February 2013. Available online.

21 Greenpeace International: *Silent Killers: Why Europe Must Replace Coal Power with Green Energy*. June 2013. Available online.

22 David Buchan: *Can Shale Gas Transform Europe's Energy Landscape?* London: Centre for European Reform, July 2013. Available online.

23 For a significant and far-reaching analysis, see Dieter Helm: *The Carbon Crunch: How We're Getting Climate Change Wrong – and How to Fix It*. New Haven, CT: Yale University Press, 2012.

24 Alex Trembath et al.: *Coal Killer: How Natural Gas Fuels the Clean Energy Revolution*. Oakland, CA: Breakthrough Institute, June 2013. Available online.

25 Marie-Martine Buckens: 'EU studies aim to reassure', *Europolitics*, 14 June 2013. Available online.

26 European Commission: 'Energy: security of energy supply', 28 May 2014.

27 Institutional Investors Group on Climate Change: *Shifting Private Capital to Low Carbon Investment*. London: IIGCC, 2013. Available online.

Chapter 6 The Search for Relevance

1 All quotes from Robert Kagan: 'Power and weakness', *Policy Review*, no. 113 (2002), pp. 1–18.

2 Quotes from Mark Leonard: 'Why Europe will run the 21st century', speech given in 2006, available online. I refer to this source, rather than Leonard's book of the same name, because it dates from a year after the book was published.

3 See Robert Cooper: *The Post-Modern State and the World Order*. London: Demos, 2000.

4 Joseph Nye: *Soft Power: The Means to Success in World Politics*. New York: Public Affairs, 2004, and many subsequent publications on the topic.

5 Robert Kagan: *Paradise and Power: America and Europe in the New World Order*. London: Atlantic, 2006, p.3.

6 Douglas Brinkley and Richard T. Griffiths (eds): *John F. Kennedy and Europe*. Baton Rouge: Lousiana State University Press, 1999.

7 Daniel S. Hamilton and Joseph P. Quinlan: *The Transatlantic Economy 2012*. Center for Transatlantic Relations, Johns Hopkins University, 2012. Available online.

8 German Marshall Fund of the United States: *A New Era for Transatlantic Trade Leadership*, February 2012. Available online.

9 Camille Grand, quoted in Steven Erlanger: 'Shrinking Europe military spending stirs concern', *New York Times*, 22 April 2013.

10 Cited in Cato Institute: *Cato Handbook for Policymakers*. Washington, DC, 2008, p. 574.

11 Dmitry Trenin: 'The end of the EU–Russia relationship as you know it', Valdai Club, 8 January 2013, p. 1. Available online.

12 Sergey Lavrov, quoted in RT: Question More, 7 April 2011.

13 Nick Witney: *Where Does CSDP Fit in EU Foreign Policy?* London: European Council on Foreign Relations, 13 February 2013, pp. 2–3. Available online.

14 Antonio Missiroli (ed.): *Enabling the Future: European Military Capabilities 2013–2025*. Paris: European Union Institute for Security Studies, 2013, p. 53. Available online.

15 Olivier de France and Nick Witney: *Europe's Strategic Cacophony*. London: European Council on Foreign Relations, April 2013, p. 1. Available online.

16 See Akbar Ahmed: *The Thistle and the Drone: How America's War on Terror Became a War on Tribal Islam*. Washington, DC: Brookings Institution Press, 2013.

17 Nicola Clark: 'European firms want a drone of their own', *International Herald Tribune*, 17 June 2013.

18 Michael Llenza: 'Print when ready, Gridley', *Armed Forces Journal*, May 2013. Available online.

19 Anthony Dworkin: *Drones and Targeted Killing: Defining a European Position*. London: European Council on Foreign Relations, 3 July 2013. Available online.

20 Christopher Patten: *East and West: The Last Governor of Hong Kong on Power, Freedom and the Future*. London: Pan Macmillan, 1998, p. 303.

21 Friends of Europe: 'Europe and China: rivals or strategic partners', policy briefing, November 2011, p. 2. Available online.

22 For an excellent and perceptive analysis, see Fatos Tarifa: *Europe Adrift on the Wine-Dark Sea*. Chapel Hill, NC: Globic Press, 2007, chapter 3.

Conclusion

1 Joschka Fischer: 'From confederacy to federation: thoughts on the finality of European integration', speech delivered at Humboldt University, Berlin, 12 May 2000, p. 5. Available online.

2 Melissa Eddy: 'Germany: leading but not loved', *International Herald Tribune*, 28 March 2013.

3 'Kaczyński campaigns with anti-German innuendo', *Gazeta Wyborcza*, 5 October 2011. Available online.

4 Elzbieta Stasik: 'Stoking anti-German sentiment in Poland', *Deutsche Welle*, 15 December 2012.

5 David Marsh: *The Euro: The Battle for the New Global Currency*. New edn, London: Yale University Press, 2011. See especially chapters 7 and 8.

6 Paul Krugman: '*Eurodämmerung*', http://krugman.blogs.nytimes.com/2012/05/13/eurodammerung-2/?_r=0.

7 John Hutchinson: 'Europe could be plunged into war if the euro collapses, says Cable', *Daily Mail*, 14 October, 2012.

8 Capital Economics: *Leaving the Euro: A Practical Guide*. London: Capital Economics, 2012. Available online. The monograph won a Wolfson Economics Prize. I draw heavily upon this precise and detailed study in the following pages.

9 Ibid., pp. 39–46.

10 'Greece's withdrawal from the eurozone could cause global economic crisis', press release, Bertelsmann Foundation, 17 October 2012. Available online.

11 Thomas Mayer: *Europe's Unfinished Currency: The Political Economics of the Euro*. London: Anthem Press, 2012, chapter 1.

12 Ronald I. McKinnon: *The Unloved Dollar Standard: From Bretton Woods to the Rise of China*. Oxford: Oxford University Press, 2013.

Index

Page numbers in *italics* refer to figures and tables.

3D printers 76, 77, 205

Afghanistan 188–9
ageing population 115–22
  and health care 108–9
  and immigration 141–2
Ahtonen, Annika 109
Amazon, UK 86
Anderson, Benedict 149
Anderson, Chris 77
Andor, László 106
anthropocene age 166–7
Arctic ice, melting of 165, 172
AROPE measure 105–6
Ashton, Catherine 33–4, 201–2
austerity
  impact of 60–3
  versus investment 13, 56, 107
  see also economic crisis; economic
     growth/recovery
Austria 105–6, 159
automated production 81

Balkans 3, 10–11, 17, 203, 206
banks
  and banking unions 22–4, 57
  consequences of eurozone collapse
    214–16
  consequences of eurozone exit 221
  financial transaction tax 86–7
  Ireland 101
Barroso, José Manuel 30, 33, 47
Berlusconi, Silvio 19, 128, 214
Beveridge, William 94–5
Bootle, Roger 218–19, 220–1
Boston Consulting Group (BCG):
    reshoring of manufacture
    79–81
Britain *see* United Kingdom (UK)
Brundtland report 167–8

Cable, Vince 217
Cameron, David 40–1, 51–2, 53
Canada 54, 138, 172, 198
Cancun Conference, UN 162–3

carbon emissions *see* climate change/
     environment
child poverty 102
child-care services 104–5
children, investment in 96–7, 104
China
     emissions/climate change 160, 161,
          162, 165, 170, 171
     energy 176, 180
     EU relations 207–8, 223
     human rights 207
     identity and democracy 150–1
     manufacturing and economy 14, 79,
          81
     solar panels, dumping of 208
Churchill, Winston 1–2, *4*, 5, 17, 32,
     33, 50, 224
citizens
     disillusionment 3–5
     and EU institutions 5, 31–2
     eurozone countries 42
     immigration concerns 129–30, 131–2
     involvement 9, 46–51
     and social welfare models 95, 98
climate change/environment 15–16,
     155
     Emissions Trading Scheme (ETS)
          156–60, 170, 181, 184–5
     Europe 2020 initiative 69
     green movement 166–7
     policy proposal 170–3
     precautionary principle 15, 167,
          168–9, 170
     sustainability, definitional difficulty of
          69–70, 167–8
     UN process 160–5, 170
     see also energy
Clinton, Hillary 161–2
coal *171*, 177–8, 179, 181, 183
Cold War/post-Cold War era 186–7,
     188, 194–7
Common European Asylum System
     (CEAS) 128–9

Common Security and Defence Policy
     (CDSP) 201, 202, 203–4
community of fate 8, 44, 213–14
     see also interdependence/integration
Connolly, Bernard 51
conservation 167
Copenhagen Conference/Accord, UN
     15, 161–2
corruption 50, 110, 151
cosmopolitan imperative 124
Council of Europe 31
Council of Ministers 31
Crimea 200–1
Cyprus 24, 84, 198, 210, 216
Czech Republic 24, 40, 159, 178, 219

de France, Olivier and Witney, Nick
     202, 203
deindustrialisation 13, 146
     and reindustrialisation *see*
          manufacturing industries
democracy 147–8
     China 151
     deficit 5–6, 31–2
     Latin America 191
     monitory 49–50
     online 47–8, 50–1
     representative 48–9, 148
     see also elections
Denmark 52, 53, 92–3
Derrida, Jacques 89–90
Desertec 182
digital technologies
     3D printers 76, 77, 205
     military 204–5
     production 72–3, 76–8
     social model (ESM) 111–15
     see also internet technologies
Dohar Conference, UN 163
Draghi, Mario 21, 24–5, 98
drone technology 204–5
Durban Conference/'Durban Platform',
     UN 163

Eastern Europe 173, 175, 182–3
economic crisis 11–12
  eurozone 2–4, 18
  impact on emissions 170
  impact on social model (ESM)
    98–102
  see also austerity
economic federalism 30
economic growth/recovery 12–13
  energy investment 181–5
  strategies 68–73
  see also manufacturing industries
economic sanctions 206–7
education
  Europe 2020 initiative 69
  internet 103–4, 111–13
  lifelong learning (Erasmus
    Programme) 46, 119, 122
  see also social model (ESM)
elections
  2014 39–40, 41
  and electorate 5, 31–2
  national 8, 39–40, 42–3
  of president of EU Commission 40–1
  of proposed European president
    33–4, 36
electricity grid 182, 185
emerging economies 55, 58, 84
Emissions Trading Scheme (ETS)
  156–60, 170, 181, 184–5
employment
  Europe 2020 initiative 69
  job creation 58, 70, 78–83
  non-economic benefits 95–6
  see also unemployment; *entries*
    beginning labour
energy
  investment 181–5
  renewable 169, 170, 176–7
  traditional sources and transitional
    technologies 177–81
  trilemma 173–7
English language 47

Erasmus Programme (and lifelong
    learning) 46, 119, 122
EU1 6–7, 21, 31, 32, 35, 194
EU2 6–9, 18–21, 24–5, 57, 58, 72, 122,
    194, 201–2, 213
EU3 30
Euratom Treaty 175
Euro Plus Monitor 60–1
euro/eurozone 18–20, *23*, 27–30
  benefits of 8–9, 223
  consequences of collapse 214–16
  consequences of exiting 218–22
  and federalism 35, 36–7, 37–8
  and Fiscal Compact 24–6, 53
  and Germany 25–9, 37, 57, 61,
    135–6, 214–15, 216, 218
  and global economic crisis 2–4, 18
  history of monetary instability
    222–3
  impact of austerity 60–3
  public opinion surveys 42
  and UK 51–3
  see also European Central Bank
    (ECB); *specific countries*
eurobonds 26–7, 28–9, 30
Europe 2020 initiative 68–73, 74, 75–6
European Central Bank (ECB) 22–5,
    26, 98
  leadership 6–7, 18, 19, 21
European Citizens' Initiative 48
European Commission 31–2
  citizen involvement projects 46–7, 48
  election of Juncker as president 40–1
  Emissions Trading Scheme (ETS)
    157, 158, 159
  energy issues 180, 182, 183, 184
  EU governance 5–6
  Eurobarometer 3–4
  Europe 2020 initiative 68–73, 74,
    75–6
  financial transaction tax 87
  former president (Barroso) 30, 33, 47
  role 31–2, 34–5

European Community, founding and
    expansion of 187
European Council 5, 6, 31, 34–5,
    194–5, 203
European Environment Agency 172
European Investment Bank (EIB) 122,
    184
European Monetary System (EMS)
    222–3
European Parliament 5, 32, 34–5, 159
European president, proposed election
    of 33–4, 36
European Rapid Reaction Force 194–5
European Security Treaty 198, 200
European Stability Mechanism 24
'European values'/Eurocentricism
    147–54
European Year of the Citizens 47
European Year of Volunteering (EYV)
    46
Eurosceptics 9–10, 30, 35, 44–5
    Germany 19
    and pro-Europeans 45
    UK 52, 55

federalism 17, 30–2
    and EU enlargement 208–9
    Eurosceptic concerns 9–10
    leadership issue 20–2, 32–6
    restructuring 32–8
    see also interdependence/integration
financial transaction tax 86–7
Finland 92–3, 110–11, 175
Fiscal Compact 24–6, 53
Fischer, Joschka 213
foreign policy and security issues 201–4
    Cold War and after 186–7, 188,
        194–7
    High Representative/Vice President
        (HVRP) and Rest of the World
        (ROTW) 202, 206–12
    Russia 197–201
    US 187–93

Foucault, Michel 114–15
France
    economy 61, 63, 75
    energy 174, 175, 178–9
    and Germany 6–7, 20–2, 37–8, 45,
        121–2
    Islam
        'headscarf wars' 139–40, 143–4
        Mohammed Merah shooting incident
            133–4, 139
    and Netherlands, comparative
        immigration policies 137–8
    security 195, 203, 205
    Mali 194
    Syria 200
    and transatlantic partnership 192, 193
    and Turkey's EU accession 210
fraud: Emissions Trading Scheme
    (ETS) 159
'Friends of the Earth' 166
Fukushima nuclear power plant 174–5
Fukuyama, Francis 151

gas
    Russia 182–3, 199
    Nord Stream pipeline 183, 197
    shale 178–81, 185
Gellner, Ernest 186
geo-engineering 172–3
Germany
    austerity programme 99
    and China 208
    dominance of 6–7, 9, 18–19, 20–2,
        213–15
    energy 174–5, 178
    Nord Stream gas pipeline 183, 197
    renewable 176–7, 185
    euro/eurozone 25–9, 37, 57, 61,
        135–6, 214–15, 216, 218
    and France 6–7, 20–2, 37–8, 45,
        121–2
    and Greece, relations between 19,
        65–6, 135

immigration 134–6, 135
Turkish 'guest workers' 125–6, 135
poverty studies 103
public opinion surveys 42
security issues 203, 205
Libya 200
and Tesla electric car factory, US
77–8
youth employment schemes 121–2
see also Merkel, Angela
global/multinational companies 85–8
globalisation 13–14, 38, 212
and migration 124–32
Goodhart, David 140–1
Gorbachev, Mikhail 187
Gore, Al 156
Grand, Camille 195
Greece
and China 151
economy 63–8
bailouts/debt 22, 26, 65
corruption 50
eurozone comparison 61–3, 75
privatisation 66
tax evasion 64, 65, 85
energy 178
infrastructure investment 184
and Germany, relations between 19,
65–6, 135
health system 110
origins of democracy 147, 148
tranformation 66–7
unemployment 64, 89
green movement 166–7
greenhouse gas emissions *see* climate
change; energy
Grillo, Beppe 19
growth *see* economic growth/recovery

Habermas, Jürgen 43, 89–90
Hatzidakis, Kostis 66
Havel, Václav 151–3
health care 108–9

Finland 110–11
and internet 109, 110, 113–14
Sweden 107
High Representative/Vice President
(HVRP) and Rest of the World
(ROTW) 202, 206–12
Hollande, François 6–7, 21, 122
human rights, China 207
Huntington, Samuel 149

identity, national and European
149–54
IEA *see* International Energy Agency
IMF *see* International Monetary Fund
Immelt, Jeff 80
immigration 123–4
anxieties 59, 92, 134–8
Common European Asylum System
(CEAS) 128–9
cosmopolitan imperative 124
and 'European values' 147–54
and globalisation 124–32
illegal 126–7
and interculturalism 15, 142–7, 149
and solidarity 140–2
UK *see under* United Kingdom (UK)
and untraditional tradition 132–4
see also multiculturalism
'inclusive growth' 70, 87
income growth 87
inequalities *see* poverty/inequalities
Institute for Security Studies 202
interculturalism 15, 142–7, 149
interdependence/integration
and mutuality 9, 25–6, 27–9, 57
opportunities and risks 13–14, 212
populist surge 38–45
progress 22–32
public involvement 46–51
UK and Europe 51–5
see also federalism
Intergovernmental Panel on Climate
Change (IPCC) 160–1

international anti-tax avoidance/evasion strategies 85–8
International Consortium of Investigative Journalists 85
International Energy Agency (IEA) 165
International Monetary Fund (IMF) 2, 6–7, 18, 19, 22, 63, 64
international relations 16–17
internet technologies 13
    and democracy 47–8, 50–1
    educational applications 103–4, 111–13
    and health care 109, 110, 113–14
    and migration 124–5, 131, 142–3, 147
    and single market 70, 74
    see also digital technologies
investment 74–6
    austerity versus 13, 56, 107
    in children 96–7, 104
    in energy 181–5
    in Greece 65–6, 68, 184
    social investment state 14–15, 94–8, 109
Iraq War 189
Ireland 4, 61–3, 75, 101, 102
Islamic immigrants 133–4, 134–5, 135, 139–40, 144–6, 148
Islamic women 133, 139–40, 143–4, 145
Issing, Otmar 26
Italy 19, 87, 214
    immigration by sea 127–8, 129

Japan
    Fukushima nuclear power plant 174–5
    investment 75
job creation 58, 70, 78–83
Juncker, J.-C. 40, 41

Kaczyński, Jaroslaw 214
Kagan, Robert 187–9, 190–2
Keane, John 147–8

Kennedy, John F. 192
Kissinger, Henry 33–4
Kosovo 203, 206
Krugman, Paul 215–16
Kymlicka, Will and Banting, Keith 141, 142
Kyoto Protocol 158, 161, 163, 190

labour flexibility/'flexicurity' 93–4, 95, 103
labour markets
    entry and exit of women 104–5, 117–18
    EU-wide 110
    older people 119
    reforms 93, 98–9
    and 'welfare dependency' 95
labour retraining schemes 103–4, 119
Lagarde, Christine 21–2
language, English 47
Latin America 191
Lavrov, Sergey 199
leadership 20–2, 32–6
Leonard, Mark 187–9, 190, 191
Li Keqiang 208
Libya 194, 199
lifelong learning (Erasmus Programme) 46, 119, 122
Lisbon Agenda 61, 68–9, 70–2, 93, 190, 195, 201–2
Lisbon Council 60–1, 64, 66
Lisbon Treaty 33, 40, 173–4, 206
Llenza, Michael 205
Luxembourg 61, 86

McLuhan, Marshall 48–9
manufacturing industries 58–9
    digital production 72–3, 73–4, 76–8
    reshoring 78–83
    and service industries, transformation of 73–6
Marin, Bernd 116–17
Medvedev, Dmitry 198, 199, 200

Merah, Mohammed 133–4, 139
Merkel, Angela
  China 208
  eurobonds 27
  Europe-wide training scheme 122
  financial integration 25
  Hitler comparison 213–14
  multiculturalism 136, 137
  as 'president' 7, 18–19, 21–2, 34, 208
  Russia 197
  and Nicolas Sarkozi 20–1
Mettler, Ann and Williams, Anthony
      73, 74, 75–6
Middelaar, Luuk van 30
Middle East
  energy resources 173, 180, 182
  instability 11, 17, 153–4, 197, 205
  Islamic fundamentalism 133–4
  migration 127, 128
  origins of democracy 148
military power see foreign policy and
      security issues; NATO
monitory democracy 49–50
'Monnet method' of governance 5–6, 7
Monti, Mario 19
Moroccan migrants 127, 130, 132, 139
multiculturalism 15, 138–40
  Dutch and French immigration
      policies 137–8
  failure of 15, 135, 136, 137
  and interculturalism 15, 142–7, 149
multinational/global companies 85–8
Muslim see entries beginning Islamic
mutuality 9, 25–6, 27–9, 57

national and European identity 149–54
national parliaments 32
national sovereignty see sovereignty/
      sovereignty+
NATO 188–9, 203
  and Canada 54
  and France 192, 194
  and Russia 17, 198, 199–200

  and US 16, 36, 188–9, 192, 194,
      195–7
Netherlands 19, 61, 105–6
  energy 176
  immigration 130, 132
  and France, comparative policies
      137–8
Nkoana-Mashabane, Maite 163
Nord Stream gas pipeline 183, 197
Nordic countries 92–3, 107, 116, 119
North Africa 127, 128, 134, 180, 182,
      197, 205
North-South division 90, 102, 117, 121
Norway 175–6
nuclear power 174–6, 185
Nye, Joseph 191–2

Obama, Barack 18, 161–2, 192–3
OECD 86, 117
oil 173, 180, 183, 197, 199
opportunities and risks 13–14, 168,
      181–2, 212

Papandreous, George 64
paper Europe 7, 16, 32, 59–60, 201–2
pensions/retirement 115, 116–19
Pew Research Center/Foundation 42,
      193
Poland 178, 179, 187, 214
populism/populist parties 19, 38–40,
      42–5
Portugal 4, 61–3, 73, 75, 82
positive welfare 94, 118
poverty/inequalities 102–6
  Europe 2020 initiative 69
  'inclusive growth' 70, 87
precautionary principle 15, 167, 168–9,
      170
prisons 114–15
privacy 48–9
public see citizens
public health 109
Putin, Vladimir 150, 197, 199, 200

Rasmussen, Anders Fogh 198
'reconciliation ecology' 167
referendums 43
    UK 53–4
Rehn, Olli 22
reindustrialisation *see* manufacturing
        industries
renewable energy 169, 170, 176–7, 185
representative democracy 48–9, 148
research and development: *Europe 2020*
    initiative 69
reshoring of manufacturing 78–83
retirement/pensions 115, 116–19
Rio 'Earth Summit', UN 168
risk management, welfare state as 95
risks and opportunities 13–14, 168,
    181–2, 212
Rompuy, Herman Van 29, 34
Rosenzweig, Michael 167
Russia 197–201
    and Crimea 200–1
    and Eastern Europe 173, 182–3
    impact of climate change 172
    national identity 150
    and Soviet Union 186–7
    and Ukraine 183, 197, 200–1

Sarkozy, Nicolas 19, 20–1
Sarrazin, Thilo 134–7, 140–1
Scheffer, Paul 129–30, 132
Schengen Agreement 129
Schröder, Gerhard 57
second-generation immigrants 125,
    131, 136–7
secrecy jurisdictions *see* tax havens/
        evasion
security issues *see* foreign policy and
        security issues; NATO
Sen, Amartya 146
service and manufacturing industries,
    transformation of 73–6
shale gas 178–81, 185
Sikorski, Radoslaw 27–9

Singh, Fauja 118
single market 70, 74
Sinn, Hans-Werner 26
Sirkin, Harold 79
small and medium-sized enterprises
        (SMEs) 73, 76–8
    'youth guarantee' 121–2
'smart growth' 69–70
social investment state 14–15, 94–8,
        109
social media 48
social model (ESM) 14–15, 89–90
    consequences of financial crisis
        98–102
    cost-cutting and reform 106–11
    digital technology 111–15
    golden age of welfare state 90–4
    and immigration 141–2
    inequalities 102–6
    social investment state 14–15, 94–8,
        109
solar energy *see* renewable energy
solidarity
    EU 211
    and migration 140–2
Soros, George 26–7
Southern Ocean, warming of 165
sovereignty/sovereignty+ 10, 45, 202,
        211
Soviet Union 186–7
Spain 3–4, 61–3, 75
    austerity policies and protests 89,
        99–101
    early democracy 148
    health-care workers, Finland
        110–11
    income growth 87
    reindustrialisation 82
    unemployment 100, 101–2
Stability and Growth Pact 24–5
Stiglitz, J. 29
'strategic cacophony' 202–3
subsidiarity 35–6

surveillance 114–15
  drone technology 204–5
sustainability, definitional difficulty of
      69–70, 167–8
Sweden 52, 53, 61, 92–3, 107
Syria 199–200

Tajani, Antonio 82
tax
  carbon 156
  financial transaction 86–7
  and welfare systems 96, 97, 141
tax havens/evasion 59, 83–8
  Greece 64, 65, 85
Tax Justice Network 84
Taylor, Charles 138–9
teenage pregnancy 104
Tesla electric car factory, US 77–8
thorium 175–6
Tobin, James 87
tolerance 148–9
transnational/global companies 85–8
transparency
  promotion of 50–1
  rule of 48–9
Transparency International (TI) 50
Turkey, EU accession 209–10
Turkish 'guest workers' 125–6, 130,
      136

Ukraine
  EU membership 209
  and Russia 183, 197, 200–1
unemployment 100, 101–2, 105–6, 117
  benefits 95
  and homelessness 89
  youth 119–22
  see also employment; entries beginning
      labour
United Kingdom (UK) 51–5
  active citizenship programmes 46
  Amazon 86
  economy 63, 75

emissions 172
  energy 176, 178, 179
  Fiscal Compact 24
  immigration 103, 115–16, 140–1
  London bombings (2005) 144,
      145
  immigration studies 103
  income growth 87
  pension system 118
  post-imperialism 38
  reindustrialisation 82
  scrutiny of institutions 49–50
  security 195, 203, 205
  Syria 200
United Nations (UN)
  climate change/environment 160–5,
      170
  Libya 199–200
  Security Council 54
  Syria 199–200
United States (US)
  banks 23–4
  and Canada 54
  emissions/climate change 15–16, 156,
      161–2, 163, 165, 170
  energy 80–1, 178, 179–80
  policy 173
  and EU 187–93
  Cold War/post-Cold War relations
      186, 188, 194–7
  eurozone crisis 25
  free trade agreement 59, 83, 192–3
  UK relations 54–5
  youth unemployment 120
  European migration to 125
  income growth 87
  investment 75
  labour re-training schemes 103–4
  Marshall Plan 56–7
  national identity 149–50
  and NATO 16, 36, 188–9, 192, 194,
      195–7
  new military technology 204–5

United States (US) (*cont.*)
  Pew Research Center/Foundation 42,
    193
  reshoring of manufacturing 79–81, 82
  Syria 200
  tax legislation 84–5

volunteering 46

welfare *see* social model (ESM)
Wen Jiabao 207
Wilders, Geert 19
wind turbines *see* renewable energy

Witney, Nick 201
  de France, Olivier and 202, 203
women
  Islamic 133, 139–40, 144, *145*
  labour market 104–5, 117–18
World Trade Organisation 190

Youngs, Richard 134
youth unemployment 119–22
'youthing', ageing population and
    115–22

Zhang Weiwei 150–1, 154